LABAN'S EFFORTS *IN*

LABAN'S EFFORTS *IN ACTION*

A MOVEMENT HANDBOOK FOR ACTORS WITH ONLINE VIDEO RESOURCES

Vanessa Ewan with
Kate Sagovsky

methuen | drama
LONDON • NEW YORK • OXFORD • NEW DELHI • SYDNEY

METHUEN DRAMA
Bloomsbury Publishing Plc
50 Bedford Square, London, WC1B 3DP, UK
1385 Broadway, New York, NY 10018, USA

BLOOMSBURY, METHUEN DRAMA and the Methuen Drama logo are trademarks of
Bloomsbury Publishing Plc

First published in Great Britain 2019

For legal purposes the Acknowledgements on pp. xv–xvi constitute an extension of
this copyright page.

Cover design: Louise Dugdale with Pavel Doušek and Todd Padwick
Cover image © Pavel Doušek (actor: Nina Fog)

A catalogue record for this book is available from the British Library.

Library of Congress Cataloging-in-Publication Data
Names: Ewan, Vanessa, 1960- author. | Sagovsky, Kate, author.
Title: Laban's efforts in action : a movement handbook for actors with online
video resources / Vanessa Ewan ; with Kate Sagovsky.
Description: London, UK : Methuen Drama, [2018] | Includes bibliographical
references and index.
Identifiers: LCCN 2018004282| ISBN 9781472528162 (hb) | ISBN 9781472533241
(pb) | ISBN 9781472532428 (ePDF) | ISBN 9781472524522 (eBook)
Subjects: LCSH: Movement (Acting)
Classification: LCC PN2071.M6 E95 2018 | DDC 792.02/8—dc23
LC record available at https://lccn.loc.gov/2018004282

ISBN: HB: 978-1-4725-2816-2
        PB: 978-1-4725-3324-1
        ePDF: 978-1-4725-3242-8
        eBook: 978-1-4725-2452-2

Typeset by RefineCatch Limited, Bungay, Suffolk

To find out more about our authors and books visit www.bloomsbury.com
and sign up for our newsletters.

For all actors

CONTENTS

Contents

LIST OF ILLUSTRATIONS AND TABLES

Illustrations

List of Illustrations and Tables

Tables

FOREWORD

Vanessa Ewan was put on this earth to teach. She is here to pass on wisdom. She has delivered, and continues to deliver, knowledge, skills and awareness to a generation of actors and theatre-makers. Yet her abundance of gifts is not limited to the performing arts. She can teach humanity how to live in, love in and explore these miraculous bodies of ours.

Vanessa is one of those teachers that changes people's lives. She reveals us to ourselves, to our common humanity, to our own profound uniqueness. And she performs this magic trick with two feet firmly planted on the earth.

In addition to specializing in the study of human physical behaviour, Vanessa is also an expert on the behaviour of the human psyche and emotions, and how these separate parts of ourselves are actually one whole. And it is here where the work becomes beyond exhilarating – a psychological key can inform a physical gesture, or rhythm, which can then go on to create a specific emotion or conjure personal memories. The endless combinations of psyche, emotion and movement provide a playground that is pure horizon. For a life in the arts, and life generally, you need that vastness of endless possibility. Vanessa's work offers us this playground. It is a rich alchemy.

This holistic approach to the complicated work of portraying characters on stage or screen continues to inspire me as I wander deeper and deeper into my own relationship with acting and storytelling. One of the genius aspects of Vanessa and the practices she has to offer is that she is interested in the uniqueness of the individual performer – in the human being bringing all of his or her own gifts and personal genius to the work at hand. To the joy of creating.

I've had the privilege to work with Vanessa for three years at drama school and then beyond into my professional life. She is a true mentor and she is also a great friend, who I feel lucky to know.

Her work with animal study is beyond profound. Finding ourselves in nature, in our oldest ancestors, can be the entire key to the character we are attempting to bring to life. And her work with Laban and the Efforts, as you will find in this inspired book, provides performers with an incredibly fertile foundation from which to create. She has found an astoundingly practical way of applying Laban's work to the quest of being a fully embodied actor. You will find tools in this book that will open door after door to your own creativity and awaken you to the endless possibility of what you can create on stage or on screen. (In fact, even on radio!)

Vanessa has been put here to inspire us. To help us realize the radical work of living here in our bodies. Fully present. And to explore and know our potentials as the divine creatures we are.

I hope every actor and storyteller and any person who is fascinated by having a body, and how best to know it intimately, reads this wonderful, inspiring book.

Thank you Vanessa for being our teacher.

Andrew Garfield, 2018

PREFACE

The need to create this book has been on my mind, in my heart and at the very core of my being for a long time. Now the book exists because in Kate Sagovsky I found someone who took it to her heart with equal force.

I have spent my adult life working with generations of extraordinary actors developing a practice which has come to be called 'Actor Movement'. Part of this practice allows the actor to benefit from all that Laban's Efforts have to offer. The Efforts must be celebrated: sharing my process and philosophy is a way to do that.

I have been very fortunate in my collaborators. Debbie Green, with whom I co-wrote *Actor Movement: Expression of the Physical Being*, first gave me courage to turn my process into words. This was an inspiring journey. My evolved understanding and appreciation of Laban stems directly from work in the studio. Sue Mythen, a former student at Central, volunteered to observe my studio sessions on Laban and notate the exercises precisely. I keep a bound edition of these notes, because I consider them to be a work of art. When Sue moved back home, I carried on alone until Kate Sagovsky, another Central alumna, said, 'if you need any help with writing …'.

What followed, as Kate grappled with everything my work is trying to do, was all that true collaboration can bring. Thanks to Kate's rare combination of careful scholarship and movement sensibility, I could trust that this practice and philosophy would not be lost or distorted during our writing process. Bringing great eloquence, a sharp editorial eye and flashes of poetic brilliance, her involvement has been passionate, rigorous and all-encompassing throughout the long and demanding task of bringing the book to completion: writing, filming, editing, rewriting. She was also instrumental in drafting material on Laban's life and undertaking further contextualising research. The book exists in the way it does because Kate dared to venture wholeheartedly on the journey to write it with me; this book would not be this book without her.

Vanessa Ewan, 2018

ACKNOWLEDGEMENTS

Audio Resources
Edited by: Dominic Kennedy
Supported by: Ken Mizutani
With thanks to The Royal Central School of Speech and Drama

Diagrams and Tables
Diagrams by: Mikala Grante with Tom Napper and Todd Padwick
Tables by: Todd Padwick

Photographs
With: Nathan Armarkwei | Debbie Brannan | Tanya Cubric | Jack Finch | Nina Fog | Leonor Lemee | Daisy Marsden | Sinead O'Keeffe | Maeve O'Sullivan | Edith Poor | Joseph Sentance | Joe Wild | Richard Wing
Photography by: Pavel Doušek
With thanks to Falling Space [www.fallingspace.com] | The Royal Central School of Speech and Drama | Image of Rudolf Laban (*Figure 0.1*) sourced from the Dance Notation Bureau

Video Resources
With: Joe Alwyn | Nathan Armarkwei | Debbie Brannan | Tanya Cubric | Sharlit Deyzac | Elena Themis Eikosipentarchou | Christa Engelbrecht | Jane Fallowfield | Jack Finch | Nina Fog | Taylor Frost | Leonor Lemee | Daisy Marsden | Sinead O'Keeffe | Maeve O'Sullivan | Victoria Pengilley | Kathryn Perkins | Declan Perring | Edith Poor | Imogen Sage | Joseph Sentance | Pernille Thisted | Reice Weathers | Joe Wild | Richard Wing
Filmed by: Bruce Melhuish with Peter Elliott and Matt Mead
Edited by: Bruce Melhuish
Supported by: Ken Mizutani and Roberto Puzoni
With thanks to Falling Space [www.fallingspace.com] | The Royal Central School of Speech and Drama

Contributors
Sarah Calver for her consistently good-natured practical support | Sam Dixon for his invaluable editorial work, sound advice, and for being a lifeline at the end of a phone | Peter Elliott for his insightful responses to the work as it progressed and his creative input during filming | Debbie Green for her unconditional support, solid advice and for

Acknowledgements

letting elements of Ewan's work from *Actor Movement* be woven into this book | Ken Mizutani for his consistent and creative response throughout the extended process of making the audios and videos | Sue Mythen for her observational notes of the work in the studio when the book was first conceived | Debbie Brennan, Nina Fog, Sinead O'Keeffe and Joseph Sentance for bringing their warmth, skill and the creativity of their acting sensibility to the project, and testing out the work from the page | Nicholas Sagovsky for making time and space to bring his invaluable and much needed editorial skills to the text | Thor Sigurdsson for his enthusiastic work on figuring out all the permutations of a Basic Effort Weave | Lettie Ransley for her characteristically intelligent and sensitive advice on book proposals and contracts | Joe Wild for his dedicated help in organizing and filming a key workshop, and for his unique collaborative support throughout the writing process | All who acted as readers and contributed their thoughts on the work. Particularly, Sue Mythen, Debbie Seymour and Jess Tucker Boyd | Also Natasha Martina, Peter McAllister, Jean Newlove, Lindsay Royan, Ayse Tashkiran and Claudette Williams. | Thank you to those that tested out some of the practicals: Antonio Chuaqui-Concha, Tina Damborg, Ioli Filippakopoulou, Alejandra Guarin, Sacha Plaige, Alexander Walsh and Sam Wightman.

Additional Support

Mary Braid | Ian Brener | Rebecca Brewer | Geoffrey Colman | Grace Cowley | Freddie Crossley | Maria Delgado | Jane Dickson | Tim Doldissen | Gavin Dwight Turnbull and Nick Johnson at ARK Coworking | Harry Elliott | Phoebe Elliott | Rowena Riden-Ellwood | Sebastian Harries | Linnea Huld | Inside Park | Daniel James at Le Santé Writers' Retreat | Peter Kormuth at KHP Coffee House | Tim Laing | Struan Leslie | Pál Lukács | Nick Moseley | Ashley Mcfaul-Erwin | Danielle Meehan | Carolina Ortega | Dennis Prinz, Eva Jost and all at Enklave | Fiona Ryan | Alex Sagovsky | Kate Hannah Sagovsky | Ruth Sagovsky | Nicole Scott | Pablo Seguí Sánchez | Nathan Solbrandt | Cristian Solimeno | Matthew Sonley | Archie Sinclair | Simon Vause | Joe Webster | Simon Willows and all at Tent.

INTRODUCTION

Skilled physical expression is essential for the actor. It is physical expression which communicates meaning to the audience and provokes a gut response from them. If the actor does not make articulate choices about their movement, then the observer is likely to feel dissociated. The observer may not be able to articulate exactly what they are experiencing but nonetheless they will know that the actor is not offering them something meaningful. The actor who works with physical expression can embody the conflict of the human condition. They can give the audience an experience of their own humanity which is, arguably, the aim of all theatre.

Any unexamined movement responses will always just be an expression of you, the actor, rather than the character. Awareness of your movement enables you to transform: to make deliberate physical choices and to communicate specific meaning. This is a lifelong process of practice and discovery. It is an art cultivated over time by examining what to develop within yourself; what to question, fine-tune or decide to leave alone.

The words are not the whole event and yet so often they are treated as such. Often, the actor is working with text but has ignored the story of their body that speaks the words. Articulate movement supports, honours and enhances the text; it can also speak on its own terms. Physical expression – the language humans didn't invent – is just as exciting as anything we articulate with words. It is the cornerstone of interaction and communication; the root of meaning. When an actor understands this, and learns how to speak with their body, they are using the language of movement. Suddenly, even the most simple everyday actions speak eloquently: a hand brushing another hand, or turning the page of a book, takes on all meaning. They are telling the story of life, which is contained in every story, every action.

This book outlines practical process for exploring a key part of Laban's work: the 'Efforts of Action Drive', which allow the actor to understand their own movement and that of others. It is simple to grasp, yet sophisticated in application and results. There is no end to the ways in which it can be applied. Understanding effort enables the actor to expand beyond their limits and discover ways of expressing meaning that they did not dream existed. They learn the key to transformation – how to fully and articulately embody different ways of being. It would benefit all actors to study and master the eight Efforts of Action Drive. They are indispensable and should be available for all. This was the driving force for writing this book.

You are an important element of this book. The actor is playful, open-hearted and receptive. You are always present, and what you think, feel and believe manifests in how you move. Trust in your own movement expression because you already contain a wealth of knowledge from your ongoing existence as a human being. This process will allow you to unlock it.

LABAN AND HIS WORK

Rudolf Laban (1879–1958) was a master of movement.[1] Nowadays his name is probably most widely known in connection with 'Labanotation' – a system he invented for analysing and recording movement in written form. Yet this is only one part of the substantial body of work he produced in his lifetime. He was a prolific choreographer, a lifelong educator and a specialist movement researcher. His work changed the perception of movement in all performance and inspired a whole new type of movement practice.

Figure 0.1 Rudolf Laban.

---

[1] For 'A Brief Chronology of Major Events in Laban's Life' see Hodgson, *Mastering Movement*, p. xi.

Early Years

Laban had little formal education and no official training in acting, ballet or other dance forms. It was other experiences gained throughout his youth which informed his later work. His artistic training began in childhood when he studied with a painter. Laban describes how it was this apprenticeship which taught him 'both to observe and to perceive'.[2] He also spent large amounts of time in nature, which fed his imagination and visceral sensibilities: he recalls how 'when as a child I roamed about in the mountains, woods and meadows I always felt as if I received answers to questions which I could ask nobody but the earth'.[3] He travelled extensively due to his father's career as a prominent military governor for Bosnia-Herzegovina. His fascination with movement was fed by witnessing the whirling of the Sufi Dervishes, and by parades, battle manoeuvres and other military forms.

Despite his lack of dance training, a choreographic instinct was already emerging. As a young man growing up in Bohemia, he created a series of *tableaux-vivants*[4] for a visit of the provincial ruler in his local town. During his time at a military academy, he put together a festival performance drawing on all the different folk dances native to the cadets' far-flung homes. Ultimately, an interest in the physical skills of the army did not become a love of the military itself. Age twenty, after a short, unhappy time as a cadet at an officers' training academy in Vienna, he left to pursue life as a jobbing artist.

Reinventing Dance

Laban's career in Germany from 1910 through into the 1920s and 1930s revolved around dance. However, an underlying interest in all forms of movement meant that his work was not constrained by traditionally recognized boundaries, and took him far beyond established dance forms. His ongoing research had a deeply practical basis. He was constantly engaging with movement through the creation of performances and through teaching – and he wrote about his discoveries as he worked. Much of what Laban originated has now become recognized practice in the contemporary dance world, but at the time both his way of working and the performances he produced were radically new.

Laban believed that all human expression is movement. This was a major shift in thinking. Early on, during the 1910s, he developed a concept he articulated as *Tanz Ton Wort* (Dance Sound Word). This recognized the interrelationships between these different elements and encouraged performance that had the potential to include all three. Laban worked from an understanding that each of these three elements is simply

---

[2] Laban, *A Life for Dance*, p. 10.
[3] Laban, *A Life for Dance*, p. 16.
[4] 'Living pictures': sequences of still images formed by groups of people with movement transitions between each held pose.

a different expression of a movement impulse and has equal status. So movement no longer had to be set to music. It could be done in silence because it was newly understood to have its own inherent meaning and structure. Movement in the 'free dance' did not have to follow or respond to music, but could speak on its own terms.

Laban's understanding that all physical expression is valued movement meant that he had as much interest in everyday, gestural movement as in classically recognized dance steps. His work with performers was also influenced by an interest in people's individual movement patterns. He recognized each person's unique expressive potential and used that as a starting point for creation, rather than attempting to make performers fit the same mould. It is these innovations which mean Laban is widely recognized as the founding father of what is now referred to as *Tanztheater* (dance theatre). They arose from a focus on expressive movement in the broadest sense, which is why Laban's work is of use to actors although it originated in the world of dance.

'Fest': Celebration of Life

Laban worked to cultivate a change in movement culture throughout the population. He believed that to move is a natural instinct for all people; that everyone has 'the right of bodily sense'.[5] He encouraged ordinary people to experience the movement of their bodies. This led him to found schools which spread his practice and to develop many projects which could be identified under the umbrella term 'community dance'. The idea of *fest* (celebration of life through community gathering) was central to his vision. Laban believed that 'people must be educated in celebration. They must learn to see beauty, to understand and enjoy'.[6] He actively cultivated opportunities for communal celebration. In 1913, he established a summer school in Ascona that brought people together to live in community and participate in study, research and festival performances. He also developed the idea of the 'movement-choir': bringing together groups of people who wished to engage in the 'shared experience of the joy of moving'.[7] The idea spread and movement-choirs sprung up in different towns across Germany.

Laban regularly worked on large-scale pageants and festivities where people from the community would take part in one-off mass performance events. The scale of these events gradually increased. The *Festzug des Handwerkes und der Gewerbe* (Pageant of Craftsmanship and Trade) which Laban directed in Vienna involved 20,000 participants drawn from movement-choirs and from ordinary working people. Laban wrote that life as celebration has an 'extraordinary attraction' to performers who want to

---

[5] From *The World of the Dancer* by Laban, as quoted by McCaw, *The Laban Sourcebook*, p. 66.
[6] From *The World of the Dancer* by Laban, as quoted by McCaw, *The Laban Sourcebook*, p. 54.
[7] Laban, *A Life for Dance*, p. 157.

'fathom the meaning of existence'.[8] It was his belief that all bodies are expressive, and through actively engaging in expressive movement every human being can perceive more of life.

Research and Collaboration

Laban constantly refined his movement theory throughout his varied working life and wrote extensively outlining the development of his thought. Over a period of fifteen years he published the following books: *The World of the Dancer* (1920);[9] *Children's Gymnastics and Dance* (1926);[10] *Gymnastics and Dance* (1926);[11] *Choreography* (1926);[12] and *A Life for Dance* (1935).[13] In 1928, he also founded the journal *Schrifttanz* (Dance-writing) dedicated to articles about dance notation.

This prolific output would not have been possible without support. Laban had many collaborators – often women – who worked tirelessly to help develop research ideas and prepare manuscripts, to teach at and run his schools, and to organize performances. Laban was married twice, first to Martha Fricke and then to Maja Lederer. He also had a number of long-term partners in both life and work. His essential collaborators throughout this period in Germany included Mary Wigman, Dussia Bereska and Suzanne Perrottet, all of whom were remarkable people and artists in their own right.[14]

Work Disrupted

Laban became increasingly established as a leading figure both in the German dance world and internationally. In 1923 his company took over the old zoo buildings in Hamburg and opened a theatre; in 1924 they began to tour internationally; and in 1930 he was appointed as ballet-master at the Berlin State Opera.

Yet, as Laban's status grew, the political landscape was also changing. The flourishing of Laban's work coincided with the rise to power of Adolf Hitler and his Nazi regime. For a while Laban continued his work unaffected by these developments and made no open stand against the Nazis. In fact, in 1934 he accepted a position as Director of the *Deutsche Tanzbuhne* (German Dance Bureau) and by 1936 he had begun work both directing a large-scale performance and running an international dance

---

[8] From *The World of the Dancer* by Laban, as quoted by McCaw, *The Laban Sourcebook*, p. 56.
[9] Published under the German title: *Die Welt des Tanzers*.
[10] Published under the German title: *Kindes Gymnastik und Tanz*.
[11] Published under the German title: *Gymnastik und Tanz*.
[12] Published under the German title: *Choreographie*.
[13] Published under the German title: *Ein Leben fur den Tanz*.
[14] To learn more about Laban's key collaborators during his lifetime, see Hodgson, *Mastering Movement*, Chapter 7, pp. 79–111.

competition as part of the Berlin Olympic Games. Perhaps through political naiveté or perhaps concerned about losing status, Laban cooperated with the Nazis (though he never joined the party or identified as a Fascist). He did not, however, remain in favour for long.

When Goebbels saw the dress rehearsal of Laban's celebration for the opening of the Olympic stadium, he vetoed its performance. Laban was later interrogated and placed under house arrest. His work was banned by Hitler, and all his artistic activities ceased. By the time he left Germany soon after this in 1937, he had lost everything he had worked so hard to build.

Laban left for Paris and then made his way to the UK where he remained for the rest of his life. He was given sanctuary at Dartington Hall by his former student and colleague Kurt Jooss, whose company had moved there at the invitation of Dorothy and Leonard Elmhurst. Here, at the age of fifty-eight, he began to rebuild his life. At first, he spent time secluded from others working on his theories of Space Harmony and developing the manuscript of *Choreutics* (although it was not actually published until after his death in 1966). Slowly, he recovered but from this time onwards he no longer actively engaged in the choreography of dance. Instead, during the Second World War and in the years afterwards he turned to a broader investigation of the role of movement in both industry and education.

A Change in Direction

Once again Laban's work in the UK was supported and championed by a community of collaborators old and new. He worked with industrialist Frederick Lawrence to examine the application of his theories to efficiency and wellbeing in the workforce. This resulted in the publication of *Effort* (1947). Lisa Ullmann also became an important long-term collaborator. She helped Laban find new avenues for his work as the war forced him to move to Wales and then to Manchester. Through Ullmann's determined promotion of Laban's theories, they were adopted as the basis for 'Modern Dance' lessons taught in mainstream schools and colleges across the UK. This resulted in the need for a new publication: *Modern Educational Dance* (1948). Laban diversified further and also initiated research in the realm of healthcare and psychotherapy.

Yet, despite such varied interests, it seems that the art of movement in performance remained Laban's chief love and in 1950 he published *Mastery of Movement on the Stage*, a seminal text exploring how a deep understanding of movement is essential for all performance. In it, Laban uses the terms 'dance' and 'movement' almost interchangeably. It is through this book that we can best understand how the work of a self-professed 'dance master' is, in fact, the work of someone who had mastered not only dance but a profound understanding of the essence of movement itself. This is why his work came to be applied in so many different fields; and it is why his work is inspiring for the actor whose art relies on physical expression of the human condition.

Development of Laban's Work

Laban did not work alone. Many of his large community of collaborators, partners, pupils and acolytes went on to apply Laban's work in all kinds of contexts, thereby deepening and furthering it.[15] Laban himself set the precedent for applying movement work in a range of fields, including performance, industrial efficiency, education and healthcare.

This was possible because Laban never set out to fix his work in an all-encompassing manual or system. In conversation with Kurt Jooss, Laban said that 'he did not want a system because firstly there would have to be too many exceptions and exemptions, and secondly his theory was still evolving, always changing'.[16] His body of work grew and developed over time. Consequently, it is not without its internal conflicts and contradictions, and his writings are complex and wide-ranging. As a result, interpretation of his work varies from practitioner to practitioner according to when they encountered Laban and what they understood of his teaching from their own point of view; or from whom they learnt Laban's work if not from Laban himself.

How a practitioner interprets Laban depends on which parts of his work they choose to place particular emphasis, and in what context they apply it. What could be viewed as a confusing lack of clarity in fact allows creative space for interpretation. There is no one orthodoxy. Instead, each practitioner finds their own way to understand and draw on Laban's work; and every new generation can find a sense of ownership over the parts of Laban's work that are most relevant to them. It seems fitting that a body of work about the ephemeral art of movement remains unfixed. Laban said that he was 'thinking about life and life is never exact. Life is free'.[17] His legacy remains a living entity in continual development.

LABAN'S WORK ON EFFORT

Laban divided his movement research into two key areas: the study of movement form (*Choreutics*) and the study of movement quality (*Eukinetics*).[18] One interrogates the

---

[15] It would be impossible to trace the whole lineage of Laban's legacy or what each of his original students and collaborators, or their students in turn, have achieved. Some of these first and second-generation followers have focused on education (Marion North; Lisa Ullmann); some on movement rehabilitation and physical therapy (Irmgard Bartenieff; Betty Meredith-Jones); some on psychoanalysis (Judith Kestenberg); some on further research into Laban's work and life (John Hodgson; Dick McCaw; Valerie Preston-Dunlop; Samuel Thornton); some on industry and business (Warren Lamb; Frederick Lawrence); some on dance choreography (William Forsythe; Kurt Joos) or Labanotation (Ann Hutchinson Guest; Albrecht Knust); and some on theatre (Philip Hedley; Joan Littlewood; Yat Malgrem; Jean Newlove; Geraldine Stephenson). This is by no means an exhaustive list. However, these names are included because using them for an online search may prove useful. It will bring up information regarding each practitioner and their research/writings, which will unlock further enquiry into any of these specific fields and applications.
[16] As reported by Hodgson in Hodgson, *Mastering Movement*, p. 115.
[17] As reported by Hodgson in Hodgson, *Mastering Movement*, p. 115.
[18] Exactly what these terms meant shifted over time. Laban sometimes referred to *Eukinetics* as being one part of *Choreutics*. However, they now tend to be separated in this way, whilst the field of study that encompasses

outer manifestation of movement, the other focuses on the inner forces which dictate how the movement is done. Laban later called *Eukinetics* (i.e. the study of movement quality) a study of 'Effort'. In reality, the two fields of study cannot ever be wholly separated: all movements have both form and quality.

It is useful for the actor to focus on Effort because it is the Effort Quality with which we move that rules our physical expression. The type of Effort that drives a given action dictates *how* that action is carried out. This, in turn, expresses something of who we are and what we are thinking and feeling. How we carry out action – how we *act* – defines us to ourselves and others. One person will walk, talk or pick up a cup very differently from another. So, for the actor, consciously choosing ways of carrying out action is a vital part of expressing character. By changing the way you express action, you are able to transform your way of being in the world into that of others.

What are Laban's 'Efforts'?

An Effort can be understood as a way of identifying the 'quality' of our movement during action: the sensation or feel that our movement has both for ourselves and others. During action there are eight types of Effort that emerge. Laban called them the Efforts of Action Drive. In other words, they are the key types of Effort that are expressed when we are motivated to act.[19] Laban named these Effort Qualities: Floating, Dabbing, Wringing, Thrusting, Pressing, Flicking, Slashing, and Gliding.[20]

Laban identified these Efforts by breaking down movement into what he called the Motion Factors of Weight, Time, and Space.[21] These three factors combine in different ways to create each of the eight Efforts.

He observed that one or more of these eight qualities of Effort is present in all action and so they 'form the substance of man's movements'.[22] They are sometimes referred to as the 'Basic Efforts', or simply 'The Efforts'. Whenever the term The Efforts is used in this book, it is referring to these eight Efforts of Action Drive.

The way we think about colour can help us to understand what is meant by Effort 'quality'. Different Efforts give movement a specific quality, just as colour gives light a specific quality. We identify seven colours (those that make up the rainbow) which can all combine to make up an eighth colour, white light.

---

both *Choreutics* and *Eukinetics* is referred to as 'Choreology' or 'Choreological Studies'. Whatever these areas of research are labelled, when they are studied together as a whole what they give is: 'a kind of grammar and syntax of the language of movement, dealing not only with the outer form of movement but also with its mental and emotional content' (Laban, *Choreutics*, p. viii).

[19] Laban also identified other possible Drives. For more information, see 'Other Drives and the Incomplete Efforts', p. 269.

[20] Sometimes 'Thrusting' is referred to as 'Punching'. For more detail, see 'Use of Thrusting', p. 266.

[21] Flow is the fourth Motion Factor but it is not consciously worked on as part of the Efforts of Action Drive.

[22] Laban, *The Mastery of Movement*, p. 127.

Just as colours can be separated out or placed together in combination, so too can the Efforts. The actor can work with one or more Efforts at a time. Painters know how to work with combinations of colour to form a million different shades; weavers know how to bring together threads of various colours to create different effects. The actor who can work with all eight Efforts – and different combinations of the Efforts – can communicate physically with the same expressive skill that a master painter brings to their canvas.

APPROACHING THE EFFORTS

Identifying Universal Truths

Laban did not invent new ways of moving. Rather, he identified pre-existing patterns of movement. We all have an innate knowledge of the movement structures he identified because we live them every day: there is an accumulation of experiential knowledge that is stored in our bodies, and which has been gained simply from existing as a human being on the planet.

Our physical interactions with each other and the world around us are governed by universal laws. We are all, for example, subject to the law of gravity and this dictates the way in which we physically inhabit the world. Likewise, we all know that if you apply enough pressure, something will crack. We understand this to be true both mechanically (applying pressure to a nut cracks the shell) and metaphorically (applying 'pressure' through emotional or physical violence will make someone 'crack').

There are also universally understood laws of behaviour or physical expression that tend to be less consciously identified or articulated. For example, how near or far from us someone stands conveys meaning; as does their choice of Gesture and facial expression; the speed and size of their movements, and so on.[23] The way in which we are governed by these laws of behaviour might be referred to as 'instinct' because we understand them in a way that normally bypasses conscious thought.

Sometimes identification of this kind of non-verbal behaviour and its meaning is referred to as 'body language'. Yet this can be a restrictive term. Often the study of 'body language' focuses on small details of behaviour (outcomes) rather than identifying the more fundamental laws of physical expression which result in the observed behaviour (causes).

Laban identifies universal patterns of movement which govern – and are manifested in – the space around and between us, as well as the emotional and imaginative space

---

[23] As with all laws there are, of course, exceptions. How we are governed by laws of physical expression can be affected by context. However, there are identifiable truths which are, broadly speaking, universal. So, for example, how one understands proximity will be affected by cultural background, but all human beings read meaning into proximity and have some variation of Personal Space.

inside and beyond us. Laban's terminology can also be used to observe not just human movement but all movement everywhere in the world.

Working with Language

We experience the world as physical beings. This is reflected in our language: without even realizing it, much of our day-to-day language has a strong basis in physicality. The sensation of embodied experience is captured through use of metaphor (e.g. 'she broke my heart in two'; 'put your best foot forward'; 'he grasped what I meant').[24] So the actor already has an inbuilt ability to transform embodied experience into language, and vice versa.

For the actor, language provides a link between a physical experience and an intellectual understanding of it. By breaking something down and naming its constituent parts, you have the ability to think and speak about it. This lets you analyse it, and so understand it better. You are also then able to pinpoint and alter one or more of its components as you desire.

The use of Laban's words enables you to make your unconscious bodily experience conscious, and then to make choices about it according to what you want to express. In this way, Laban gives us a terminology with which we can access what he refers to as our 'movement-thinking' – that is, 'the gathering of impressions of happenings in one's own mind' for which we tend to have little or no vocabulary.[25] This allows us a new, articulate way of accessing our inner experiential world.

Choosing Movement Terminology

Laban felt the limitation of language. He was aware that no movement terminology is perfect: sometimes there is simply a shortage of relevant words in a given language, and often many words are needed to adequately describe just one movement. Laban himself repeatedly acknowledges that 'what one experiences in movement can never be expressed in words'.[26]

Nonetheless, he aimed to use words that were a perfect linguistic match for each movement component he identified and constantly sought the most appropriate terminology. This meant that his choice and use of words shifted throughout the development of his work, and that the same or similar concepts are sometimes referred to by different terms.

This differing terminology can sometimes seem confusing as you read Laban's works. However, it is actually a gift. It means that there are a range of words available, and you

---

[24] For more about how metaphors structure our interaction with the world, see Lakoff and Johnson, *Metaphors We Live By*.

[25] Laban, *The Mastery of Movement*, p. 9.

[26] Laban, *A Life for Dance*, p. 35.

can choose the ones that work best for you. The bespoke version of Laban's terminology used in this book has developed over time through practical work in the studio. It is a specific use of language which best facilitates the actor: the chosen terms are instantly graspable and so provide the actor with simple access to bodily experience.[27] The words aim to provide an instant inspiration to movement.

It is impossible wholly to avoid minor clashes and discrepancies with our existing cultural understanding and usage of words. So if there are terms that feel confusing, or do not instantly resonate with you, don't spend too long thinking about it – instead puzzle it out in your body as you move. Use the words to help you, whilst always remaining in the mindset of an actor.

Fundamental and Expressive Movement

Actor Movement can be broken down into two key areas of interlinking work: Fundamental and Expressive. Fundamental work involves examining and training movement mechanisms, and thereby developing your body's capacity to meet the demands of any given job. Expressive work involves discovering ways of making physical choices that communicate meaning. Performing classical text in a large-scale space, for example, has inherent demands such as a high level of physical stamina and a supported voice. For these you need Fundamental movement work. Expressive movement work would then be used to discover and refine a character and create the world of the play. All Expressive movement is supported by work on Fundamentals; and you cannot work on Fundamentals without being Expressive. When something is referred to as Fundamental or Expressive movement, this is simply identifying the primary focus of any given exercise, exploration or process. [28]

This book is largely focused on Expressive movement. Learning to embody the Efforts is Expressive: it is learning to express the human condition through transformation of your own physicality. It enables you to create a huge range of different characters. The book also includes some necessary Fundamental work to make this Expressive movement process possible. To succeed, the actor must engage with both.

The Efforts and Acting Systems

No actor should be afraid to use the Efforts in conjunction with other approaches. Working with the Efforts in this way does not replace the acting processes and systems that you or your director use. They can be used in partnership.[29]

---

[27] For more detail regarding specific word choices and possible alternative options, see Appendix B: A Note on Word Choices, p. 264.

[28] More on Actor Movement can be found in Ewan and Green, *Actor Movement*, pp. 10–11, 90–92.

[29] The only exception to this is acting techniques which already work with application of the Efforts, such as that of Yat Malgrem.

Stanislavsky-influenced approaches, for example, tend to focus on the who, what, when, where and why of a text, but can be neglectful of the how. Many actors have had the experience of sitting at a table to do an extensive amount of research work into a text, but then being somehow unable to translate this into action when they get up on their feet. It is vital for the actor to inform the creation of a role by mining the text for information.[30] Yet ultimately they also have to know how to translate this knowledge into physical action. This is where the Efforts come in: they enable the actor to make movement choices in response to the given circumstances (discovered context).

An understanding of the Effort Quality being expressed by the character can help the actor with selecting character-specific actions and particularly with how to carry those actions out. This means you can also use the Efforts to inform your own individual response to a rehearsal process in a situation when the director works with you in selecting 'actions' (transitive verbs).[31] The Efforts are always there for the actor to work with during any process; they are an inherent part of all life.

ABOUT THIS BOOK

Laban for the Actor

Laban's writings contain key insights for the actor, but it can be daunting to try and find them given the extent and complexity of his writing. Within his books, Laban himself gives some practical guidance, but it is often written for the dancer, observer or analyst (even when it states that it is for the 'actor'). So the actor can be left confused and unsure how to convert Laban's insights into a scheme of practical work.

This book aims to help the actor in this task. It offers a working process through which they can explore and apply Laban's Efforts for themselves. This process has evolved over more than thirty years of work with actors in the studio, in which Laban's Efforts are approached through experimentation and play. As such, it presents a particular view of Laban's work with the actor at the centre of the process. Laban's original understanding of the Efforts is developed through this practical process and philosophy. Such prolonged focus on one section of Laban's work has allowed the richness of this part of his research to unfold. This book celebrates the Efforts and all that they can give to the actor.

The practical process outlined in this book deliberately selects parts of Laban's work which are most useful for the actor and therefore focuses on the eight Basic Efforts.[32]

---

[30] This essential process of analytical 'table-work' is discussed in Mitchell, *The Director's Craft*.

[31] Commonly referred to as 'Actioning'.

[32] We have explained details of our selection process in Appendix C: Focusing the Theory for the Actor, pp. 266–270. It also points towards more information that is not included in this book should you wish to delve deeper into other parts of Laban's work.

Analysis of movement is essential: the actor's instinct is informed through intellectual enquiry as well as physical exploration. Yet an overly complex assessment involving many detailed variables can become detrimental to the actor. An excess of information can be overwhelming, drawing the actor into an ongoing state of intellectual scrutiny that paralyses them.

The key task of the actor is to act (including thinking and feeling, which can be categorized under the umbrella of action).[33] So, when applied in this process which includes thinking and feeling as action, the eight basic Efforts of Action Drive already enable the actor to do their job. The actor can apply the eight Efforts to transform their whole self, including both their inner life and outer expression. This has a simplicity of application: there is no need for the actor in process to retain many complicated permutations of stressed and unstressed Elements. They are able to use the Basic Efforts for transformation of physical expression, while still having the capacity for the vital business of engaging with the character, the world of the play, the given circumstances, and dealing with all the other demands that arise during the technical process of rehearsing and performing. Through applying Laban's work in the bespoke process this book outlines, the actor is ultimately able to 'rely more on the feel of the movement than on a conscious analysis of it.'[34]

Laban for the Modern World

Laban was a pioneer of movement research. His innovative work remains a source of fresh inspiration. However, his writings contain occasional passages which reflect some of the racist and sexist attitudes of the era in which he lived.

At heart, what Laban articulates is a great love of humanity, and a childlike enthusiasm for the experience of life. He openly advocated 'a spiritual attitude which should concentrate on deepening the sense of mutuality and the appreciation of the personal identity of each individual.'[35] In the light of these beliefs, it seems appropriate not to disregard his valuable work, but rather to re-frame his writings and offer a process in which this is the central tenet. This ensures that no actor is alienated or excluded from use of Laban's work by outdated attitudes of a past era.

Laban for the Wider Audience

This book can be used by anyone with an interest in the actor's craft, although it is principally aimed at the actor. Practitioners who work with actors (directors, movement

---

[33] Cf. 'What is Action?', p. 29.
[34] Laban, *The Mastery of Movement*, p. 95.
[35] Laban, *A Life for Dance*, p. 84.

directors and tutors of actor training) will find this process useful. There is also much to be gained by readers whose interest is in human movement and behavioural studies, not simply those who are expert in performance-based work.

For those who are not actors but nonetheless wish to access the work, it is important to read this book through the lens of the actor. To understand the actor's mindset is to recognize their hunger to become 'other' – to take on new ways of being. How Laban's work is applied in this process is guided by this aim of transformation: the desire to identify, embody and express an infinity of ways of being in different imagined worlds. Through transformation the actor deepens their sense of their own and others' unique humanity, as well as the universal sense of what it is to be human. Through their craft they open a door for all of us to perceive, question and celebrate the human condition. They become, as it were, an ambassador for all humanity.

HOW TO USE THIS BOOK

Working Practically: The Book as 'Buddy'

This book is designed as an Actor Movement handbook that can be mined for information both in and out of the studio. Some sections require more concentrated reading, but it is first and foremost a practical handbook. Dipping in and out of the book – particularly if you use the index to find an area of interest – will provide useful insights about specific ideas or concepts. However, to gain the full embodied understanding needed for use of the Efforts as an actor, it is ideal to use the book to guide you through a practical process. Ultimately, movement can only be understood through doing it: 'one must DO movements, just as one has to hear sounds, in order to appreciate their full power and their full meaning'.[36]

Part A offers important background information and gives you all the information you need to access this process. However, you may wish to dive straight into practical work on the Efforts. In this case, you can begin with Part B and refer back to Part A as and when you need.[37] Once you have worked through the book, re-visiting it over time will deepen your understanding of the work and allow you to re-discover parts you have forgotten. This book is not meant to be kept pristine on a library shelf. Let it become your 'Buddy': an underlined, highlighted, dog-eared companion on your journey as an actor.

---

[36] Laban and Lawrence, *Effort*, p. 74.
[37] Your level of movement experience will also affect this decision. Those with less movement experience will find it helpful to start with Part A.

The Outside Eye

An Outside Eye is a designated person who is not working practically but observes the work to give feedback to the actor. The internal experience of a movement is often very different from the externally perceived 'reality'. So an Outside Eye is important for the actor. Normally the term is used to refer to a director, movement director or tutor. However, it can be another actor.

An actor can operate as their own Outside Eye by filming their work and watching it back. This allows you to compare your impressions as an observer with those you gained when inside the work, noting any gap between the two. Filming yourself must be done with awareness. Footage can give you useful pointers about the external impression of your work. Yet it is only one mirror of 'reality', and what is communicated through live performance can be flattened or distorted by the camera. Make sure you are watching footage with a specific analytical agenda. Focus solely on what you have chosen to examine and only watch the amount of footage you need to see. Don't get tempted to start watching for a generalized impression of yourself. If you find that using video footage feeds anxiety and impacts negatively on your work, use other methods of self-reflection. You might choose to work through the book with another actor (Buddy) and be each other's Outside Eye; or in a small group made up of several different partnerships. Either way, use the prompted opportunities for reflection and self-analysis to the full.

Working with a Buddy

A Buddy is another actor with whom you work through a process. They provide an Outside Eye to your work, and you to theirs. A Buddy can be a useful resource, because often it is in dialogue with others that our own experiences are most clearly revealed to us. For further guidelines on 'Buddying', refer to Appendix A.[38]

The Role of Feedback

Giving and receiving feedback is a vital part of the actor's training and ongoing practice. Reflection and analysis is central to the process of discovering and working with the Efforts. So you will be asked to engage in feedback. This might be self-reflective; or it could be with a partner (Buddy) if you are working through the book with someone else. For further guidelines on how best to engage in feedback, refer to Appendix A.[39]

---

[38] Cf. 'Buddying', p. 259.
[39] Cf. 'Feedback', p. 259.

The Structure of the Text

Each chapter introduces a new stage of learning. If you were to structure your exploration of the Efforts as a scheme of work, you could broadly equate each chapter to a new practical session.

In places, the text is divided into short, bite-size sections each of which outline a specific thought. These have a '//' symbol placed to indicate the start of each thought, so that you can easily refer back to ideas as you work.

The sections that provide guidance specific to each Effort are written using the Effort Quality to which they refer. This is so that when you refer to them during practical work, the action of reading does not draw you out of the Effort you are seeking to embody.

Following the Practical Instructions

The practical instructions use bullet points to introduce each new moment of the exploration. The key prompts are in *italics*. First, read all the instructions in advance to gain an understanding of the exploration. You can then refer back to the book as you work, just scanning the key italicized sentences, or even record them to play back to yourself as you do the exploration. If you are working with a Buddy, they can read the key italicized prompts to you as you move. The guidelines should function a little like a good recipe book: at first attend to all the specific detail but later, once you know a recipe better, you may not need to read every part of it, or you may even begin to improvise your own version of the recipe.

Pattern of Work

If you are working individually, your general pattern of work will be:

- *Read the instructions to understand the guidelines for the exploration. If necessary record the italicized prompts to replay as you move.*
- *Do your movement exploration and film it.*
- *Reflect on the experience by making a few brief written notes. Watch the footage back once.*
- *Use your self-feedback to set an Agenda for your next movement exploration.*

If you are working with a Buddy, you will follow a very similar pattern:

- *A and B read the instructions to understand the guidelines for the exploration.*

- *A moves while B observes (or B reads the italicized prompts aloud).*
- *Joint reflection during which B offers feedback to A.*
- *B helps A to set an Agenda for A's next movement exploration.*
- *A moves while B observes, etc.*

Depending on the current task, this cycle may happen a few times in a row before A and B swap roles; or it may be that they swap roles after the first period of reflection and feedback, and then continue to alternate.

Safety

Where possible, any necessary safety precautions have been highlighted. However, you must take responsibility for your own safety as you work. Always begin with a warm-up before working practically and bear in mind that this is a process of playful exploration: approach the work in an exploratory way that feels right for your body. Trust your instincts. Never do any physical activity that does not feel safe for you, and do not be afraid to stop an exploration earlier than you intended if you feel you need to. Check in with yourself regularly. If you pay careful attention to how you are within the work, this will enable you to bring the whole of your being – body and mind – safely into an integrated process of transformation.

Working with the Additional Resources

There is no one way adequately to convey movement work. This text is therefore supplemented by a range of additional resources so that as much as possible of the work can be accurately passed on by a variety of means. Within a taught class, the teacher only ever facilitates a process in which the student is able to make their own discoveries. The same is true of these resources – they should facilitate you confidently to guide yourself through this process.

Video Footage

You will find links to online footage of some practical explorations at relevant points in the text, and also as a full list on p. 284.[40] Often movement that works in live performance can appear either lifeless and dull, or overblown and hollow, on video. So this footage is in no way a monument to the 'perfect process'. Rather, it is a record of various groups of real actors who have experienced parts of this process in a range of different contexts. Some have only just encountered the Efforts in a ten-day workshop; others have worked with

---

[40] List of Video Resources, p. 284.

the Efforts for several years. In reality, the practical explorations in the studio involve a lot of noise – particularly when the actors are vocalizing the Effort ('Sounding'). For the video, the actors worked more silently to ensure the soundtrack would not be off-putting. Use the videos as a source of reference if you are unclear about details of the work, and to give you the sense of working in community with other actors. Sometimes you may find you wish to watch a video before you attempt a practical exploration; at other times you may wish to try for yourself and watch the video afterwards. Don't fall into the trap of looking to them to show you the 'right' way to do anything. Only you can unlock the discoveries the work holds for you and your body. There is only one you: your body, your experience, your humanity. Nothing beats your own practical exploration.

Audio Recordings

Instructions for two longer types of guided improvisation ('Effort Journey' and 'Effort Weave') are available online as audio recordings. They contain the type of verbal guidance that is used when leading this work for actors. The recordings are not designed to be used out of context. It is important that you work with them at the points indicated in the text and that you listen through to the end of the exploration to understand the work in full. There are also audio recordings of a group of actors embodying each Effort. These will sound very peculiar in isolation. However, if you are working alone, they can be played as a soundtrack when doing practical explorations. This will give you a sense of community so that you feel less vulnerable or exposed when you make sound as you work. You will find links to the recordings at relevant points in the text and also as a full list on p. 285.[41]

Images

A photograph freezes a moment in time. Yet, when you look at the image, your bodily response and your imagination give you a sense of what was going on before and after this moment and of the internal experience of the pictured person. So look to the photos for inspiration. No image can communicate the full power of live movement but let looking at these photographs give you a sense of possibility. These images are examples of where the movement might take you, not specific movements or positions you are supposed to do. They capture moments of the full expressive beauty and power you too will unlock in your own way as you begin working with the Efforts.

Accessibility

Whenever a word is used as a specific term, it is capitalized. This is true even in quotations where originally the term may have been printed without capitalization. This is for clarity and ease of reading.

---

[41] List of Audio Resources, p. 285.

The main aim of this book is to allow the individual actor to discover and fall in love with the Efforts, so it is deliberately addressed in the 'you' voice. Where needed, the text refers to 'the actor' (used as a gender-neutral term) or 'they' (rather than 'she' or 'he') to make clear that this book is for all actors of any gender and identity. It is the hope that this book speaks to you, whoever you are.

PART A
THE BIGGER PICTURE

CHAPTER 1
MOVEMENT AND THE ACTOR

Movement is a common word, so it is easy to assume that we all know what it means. Yet pinpointing its meaning and articulating its relationship to the actor's craft is complex. A shared understanding of some of the key concepts which underpin this work is vital for grasping its true meaning and potential. So interrogating the concepts of '**movement**', '**effort**', and '**action**' is the place to start.

WHAT IS MOVEMENT?

//Everything moves; movement is expression
Movement is 'the basic experience of existence'.[1] Who we are, how we are and what we want is all felt through the body moment by moment. As it is felt, we move and it is expressed. Movement is such a vital part of expression that it could be argued movement *is* expression. We most often think of the verbal as different to the physical. Yet all words spring from the movements of breath and body. Words are only one part of human expression, all of which depends on movement as a vehicle. Even thoughts and feelings have their own 'rhythm': a certain sensation which is physical and which we refer to as the 'movement' of our thoughts and feelings.

//The body speaks silently as clearly as it does with words
We often assume words are our most active and effective way of expressing ourselves. Yet we actually communicate far more with our bodies, and even the relationship between our physicality and our words has meaning. Sometimes our body says the same thing as our words, and sometimes it contradicts them. Sometimes we may choose not to speak using words, but our body is broadcasting what we think or feel just as clearly as if we had spoken audibly. The body is always communicating, whether we want it to or not. The body will speak and if it is not guided it will not say what the actor is trying to communicate. Just as the playwright chooses the words of the text, the actor must make deliberate choices regarding their physical expression.

//When words fail us, the body speaks
Physical expression also surpasses what we are able to say with words. When we cannot communicate our inner experience verbally, movement is 'the language in which our

---

[1] Laban, *Choreutics*, p. 6.

highest and most fundamental inspirations are expressed'.[2] When we experience deep emotion, we speak of being 'moved' – our response is in the realm of the physical. Even the word 'emotion' comes from a root meaning 'out of movement'.[3] A touch, a gesture, a look can all express what is otherwise inexpressible.

//Movement is more than identifiable physical skill-sets
Actors often have to learn particular physical skills for a production, such as period dance, stage combat, choreographed études, etc. These lead to easily identifiable sections of physical action within the performance. So an observer might well believe that learned skills like these are the main kind of physicality in acting. In fact, movement in performance is so much more than this: 'the art of movement embraces the whole range of bodily expression'.[4]

//Movement reveals and communicates who we are
How we move expresses who we are. By changing their physical expression – moving differently – the actor can become someone other. Movement expresses who someone is both in the present moment as they respond to their context and as a result of ongoing character traits: 'it can characterise momentary mood and reaction as well as constant features of personality'.[5] Movement allows the actor to convey different characters.

//Movement is the basis of the actor's craft; the basis of theatre
The art of theatre *is* the art of movement. The actor cannot act without movement. The actor is transformed not only by speaking a character's words but by creating and embodying the character's physical experience. Physical choices, manifested in movement, are how the actor communicates meaning. So 'human movement, with all its physical, emotional, and mental implications, is the common denominator of the dynamic art of the theatre'.[6]

WHAT IS ACTOR MOVEMENT?

//Actor Movement explores physical expression
The term 'Actor Movement' refers to the field of expertise which involves the study and development of movement processes specifically for actors.[7] Actor Movement cultivates an embodied understanding of the world. The actor observes and analyses their own physical expression, and then makes choices about how to shift it in order to express

---

[2] Laban and Lawrence, *Effort*, p. 73.
[3] 'Emotion' comes from the Latin *ex* meaning 'out' and *movere* meaning 'to move'.
[4] Laban, *The Mastery of Movement*, p. 4.
[5] Laban, *The Mastery of Movement*, p. 2.
[6] Laban, *The Mastery of Movement*, p. 7.
[7] 'Actor Movement' is taken to mean the theory and practice outlined in Ewan and Green, *Actor Movement: Expression of the Physical Being*.

something different. Altering their physical expression brings the potential to entirely transform their way of being to that of another person, animal, object or thing. They can thereby create the imagined world of any play.

//Actor Movement is not a style of performance
Many people assume that a focus on movement means that abstract physical expression will be performed in the end work. This is not the case. Actor Movement work uses movement in a way that is applicable to all acting. The tools, techniques and processes of Actor Movement can be applied in different ways to any style of performance. It is a mistake to confuse it with 'Physical Theatre' (i.e. the use of creative movement as an expressionist performance style for theatre).

//Actor Movement informs the actor's instinct
For an actor each part of a process starts with instinct and ends with instinct, with all the observing, analysing, experimenting, examining, reflecting and crafting in between. The actor can inform and train their actor's instinct by developing curiosity, observing the world and questioning 'why?' and 'how?' about everything. In this way, they gain the capacity to respond intuitively at every stage to all the practical and creative demands of the actor's job.

//Actor Movement draws on existing movement practices
Movement practices such as Alexander Technique, Feldenkrais, Pilates, T'ai Chi and Yoga are widely used during training for performance. Yet often they are taught in exactly the same way for training actors as they are for self-improvement or for therapy. Actor Movement draws on a wide range of movement practices but in such a way that the work is specifically adapted for the actor. Actor Movement work is designed to ensure that movement training is always directly relevant to the actor's craft.

//Actor Movement is not dance
The true actor loves all types of physical embodiment. They do not strive to be virtuosic in one physical form but able to transform into anyone or anything. Actor Movement uses many different processes to work towards this aim of transformation. Dance tends to use more narrowly defined techniques to work towards very particular physical forms. The actor may dance during a performance, but their transformed being is fully present in the dance (i.e. even when dancing they remain in character, or within the context of the world of the play). Nowadays, the definition of dance is broadening to include a wider range of movement. Yet there is still an identifiable difference in focus. It could be said that Actor Movement employs physical expression, dance emphasizes it.

//Actor Movement is invisible
Movement work is a vital part of the actor's craft even in modes which seem to lack overt 'physicality', such as naturalistic film-acting. Often, successful Actor Movement remains invisible in the final work. Much of human movement is the unconscious manifestation

of instinct. So when an actor perfectly embodies the movement of a character, the assumption is that the actor is working purely from instinct. In fact, the actor is using intuitive responses that are the result of an instinct that has been examined and trained. What appears effortless is actually the product of highly developed skills.

//Actor Movement rejects the need for a 'perfect' body
An actor needs to understand as many experiences of being human as possible. Their work is to empathise with the whole span of the human condition: they should have the potential to express the experience of bodies of all shapes, sizes, ages, abilities, genders and backgrounds. The actor cannot do their job if they remove themselves from the 'real' world and aspire to become the socially constructed mirage of the 'perfect being'. An actor's transformation is realized through the imagination. They do not have to gain or lose weight for a role, or undergo other extreme physical manipulations. An actor does not have to become an Olympic athlete to play the role of one. Rather, they can embody a way of being in the world which expresses all the power, strength and potent energy of the trained athlete, without resorting to acquiring their muscle mass. If the actor expresses a particular way of being in the world, we will believe the story being told.

WHAT IS EFFORT?

//Effort is part of all movement
Laban identified one of the main areas of his work as a study of 'Effort' (*Eukinetics*). When we speak colloquially of something being 'an effort' or 'taking effort', we tend to mean a concerted use of extra energy in order to do something. We habitually think about the amount of effort something takes (a lot of effort versus not much effort), but no movement can be without effort entirely: 'the meaning of the word effort does not only comprise the unusual and exaggerated forms of spending effort, but the very fact of the spending of energy itself. Even the most minute exertion demands some kind of effort.'[8] So effort is part of all movement: it both originates movement and is an ongoing aspect of all movements.

//There are many different types of effort
All movement uses effort not only in varying amounts but of differing kinds. It may take about the same amount of energy to lift a small pile of books as it does to lift a baby, but the way in which we lift the baby will be very different. Without thinking we suit the type of effort to the task in hand. Not only this, but how one person lifts a baby will differ from how another person lifts a baby. Each will lift the baby using effort in the way which

---

[8] Laban, *The Mastery of Movement*, p. 169.

is habitual for them. An actor can use observation of effort to identify and embody these kinds of differences.

//The type of effort dictates the movement quality
Every movement has a certain quality to it which is 'not its utilitarian or visible aspect, but its feel'.[9] The type of effort used for a movement dictates how it feels both for the mover and the observer: it changes the way we experience the movement, because it changes the quality of the movement. So we can refer to the 'Effort Quality' of a movement.

//Effort is made up of different factors
Different types of effort exist because effort 'is a compound of several Elements mixed together in an almost infinite number of combinations'.[10] Laban analysed effort and broke it down into four 'Motion Factors', which he called Weight, Time, Space, and Flow. All effort contains these four factors. The type of effort depends on how each of the four factors is being expressed. In life, we unconsciously change the component parts of the effort depending on what we are trying to do or express. The actor can learn consciously to combine them in different ways, thereby changing the type of effort being expressed.

//Effort is always expressed by the whole self
We cannot separate the workings of our mind from the movement of our body. Both intense emotions and intellectual activity leave us physically tired: 'physical exertion is also contained in an effort of the mind'.[11] As Laban explains, no-one can 'exert either his muscular power or his thinking or feeling power in clearly separated ways', so 'to make an effort involves the whole person'.[12]

//Difference in effort can be perceived through seeing, hearing and imagining
No matter what a person does, their individual use of effort is noticeably expressed through their actions. We are able to identify this difference not only by sight but also through hearing and imagination. If we hear music, we understand the Effort Quality being used by the musician to make the sounds. If we see a painting, we are able to imagine the Effort Quality that has produced the particular kind of brush strokes we are looking at. The same is true with the written word. The actor 'derives a certain inspiration from descriptions of movement that awaken his imagination'.[13] They are able to connect to the Effort Quality being described: the rhythm of the words in a script, the use of certain verbs and the stage directions all convey a particular expression of effort.

---

[9] Laban and Lawrence, *Effort*, p. 74.
[10] Laban and Lawrence, *Effort*, p. 3.
[11] Laban, *The Mastery of Movement*, p. 169.
[12] Laban, *The Mastery of Movement*, p. 169.
[13] Laban, *The Mastery of Movement*, p. 21.

//Variation in effort can be controlled both consciously and unconsciously
Normally, we do not consciously control the expression of effort. We allow our body to respond instinctively to a given context. So, although we know that we need to handle an egg more gently than a potato, we tend not to think about it consciously. We let our body adjust our effort automatically. Many of these automatic responses are variations in effort that we have learned and are now an in-built part of our bodily knowledge. A young child who accidentally breaks an egg in their hand learns that they need to adjust their effort when handling eggs. Soon, they no longer need to think about it. Yet it is also possible to adapt our use of effort consciously, and to make active choices about its expression. Someone who leans back to let a barber shave their beard with a razor will alter their Effort Quality to be as still as possible, while someone who is frightened by a spider on their arm will alter their Effort Quality to shake it off as fast as they can.

//Intuitive variation in effort can be deliberately trained
It is possible to gain insight into the effort expression of yourself and others. This can be done through observation, analysis and physical exploration in which you play with embodying variations in Effort Quality. Once you have a clear physical understanding of different Effort Qualities, you can then begin to make deliberate choices about your Effort Quality during action. This is an essential skill for the actor 'whose job it is to convey thoughts, feeling and experiences through bodily actions'.[14]

//Effort training occurs through play
Laban observes how young animals and children learn to shift and control their Effort Quality through play – by playing, they develop specific physical skills and become adept at communicating meaning. Laban concludes that 'play is the great aid to growing effort capacity and effort organization'.[15] We also call adult training of effort expression 'play', when it is explored through acting.

//Complex training of effort is unique to human beings and leads to the creation of Art
Laban believed that 'while animals' movements are instinctive, man can become conscious of his effort patterns and reshape them'.[16] This capacity to alter our effort patterns consciously is what gives us the ability to reshape ourselves. We can cultivate certain types of effort and so shift our way of being in the world. Laban calls this capacity for conscious choice 'Humane Effort' and believes that it is the reason 'man is able to control negative habits and to develop qualities and inclinations creditable to man'.[17] However, this control is hard-won. It is the ability to control effort that allows man to create art; and the struggle to control effort, and its resulting conflicts, which are portrayed.

---

[14] Laban, *The Mastery of Movement*, p. 68.
[15] Laban, *The Mastery of Movement*, p. 14.
[16] Laban, *The Mastery of Movement*, p. 68.
[17] Laban, *The Mastery of Movement*, p, 13.

WHAT IS ACTION?

//Action is 'doing'

To understand exactly why working with effort is transformative for the actor, it is necessary to define not only 'effort' but also 'action'. We might think of 'action' as meaning physical movements that are both functional and identifiable, such as the action of sawing a log in two or hitting a tennis ball.[18] Yet the broadest understanding of 'action' is that it refers to anything that we 'do'. So action can be understood as the doing of something, or, in fact, the doing of anything. Children are often taught that verbs are 'action words'. Verbs include 'to be'. Existing is in itself an action. Even if this is just one way of framing how we use language, it is a useful understanding for the actor. If everything you do (including simply 'being') is action, then the actor is engaged in embodied action at all times. The idea of 'acting' is no longer conceptual, indefinable or about performing: the actor's job is to embody ongoing action in different ways – quite literally to 'act'.

//Action is always real

You cannot pretend to do an action. The actor does not pretend to act. The actions carried out on stage really are done with the actor's material body. Imagination creates the motivation for the action and the circumstances in which it happens, but the body does do something. Sometimes the story of the action is different from the action itself: what appears to be a slap to another person's face may in fact be an actor slapping their other hand. The imagined story of the action is different to the objective reality, but nonetheless the actor has done a physical action that involves movement of the body.

//Action is always expressive

Even if an action has a functional purpose, it will still be expressive. You may wash the dishes in order to have clean dishes, but there are many other things you might simultaneously be expressing through this action. You might be washing them lovingly because to you they represent taking care of your family; or angrily because no-one else ever shares the task; or loudly so that everyone notices how virtuous you are for washing the dishes. These intentions may be conscious or unconscious. Even if you think you are simply washing the dishes, your actions will be expressing many different things. It is impossible to do an action in a wholly neutral way because 'actions are never devoid of expressive elements'.[19] So we are constantly reading the meaning in the actions of others. It is why the actor uses actions to tell a story.

//Theatre is action

Theatre is an art form in which meaning is communicated through live action embodied by the actor. So it is vital that the actor acquires the 'ability for distinct bodily action, i.e.

---

[18] That is, actions that we actively 'perform'.
[19] Laban, *The Mastery of Movement*, p. 68.

clear use of the body and its articulations both in stillness and in motion'.[20] Working with the Efforts helps the actor develop that precision and clarity. All actions both require and express effort: 'effort [...] is mirrored in the actions of the body'.[21] It is the Effort Quality of an action that communicates meaning. Ultimately, theatre is 'the visible and audible performance of effort manifested through the bodily actions'.[22]

//Thinking and feeling initiate actions; thinking and feeling are actions
What we are thinking and feeling dictates what actions we do, and how we do them. A significant part of what the actor does is channel specific thoughts and feelings by embodying them and so making them into physical action – they *act* them. An understanding of thought and feeling as action allows the actor to work with their internal world in the same way as they work with more visible physical actions. Colloquially we speak of the 'movement' of our thoughts, or of being 'moved' by emotion, because we have a visceral sense that 'all actions and reactions spring from movement within us'.[23] An actor can change the Effort Quality of the movement of their thoughts and feelings, just as they can their more externalized physical actions. Both their internal actions of thought and feeling, and the external physical actions their thoughts and feelings provoke, are expressed through the Effort Quality. The internal landscape of thoughts and feelings becomes visible through the actor's embodied expression of them as physical action. So, in the broadest understanding of 'action' as applied to the actor, both thoughts and feelings can be categorized as actions in and of themselves.

LABAN'S EFFORTS AND THE ACTOR

All expression of effort during action communicates something, and the actor can create meaning by deliberately choosing to express effort in one way or another. So being able skilfully to control effort expression is a crucial part of the actor's craft. You will learn how to do this through exploring Laban's eight Efforts: **Floating**, **Dabbing**, **Wringing**, **Thrusting**, **Pressing**, **Flicking**, **Slashing**, and **Gliding**.[24] This process enables the conscious expression of chosen Efforts. Through it, you will become able to communicate meaning with both precision and control: 'the performance becomes articulate'.[25]

---

[20] Laban, *The Mastery of Movement*, p. 50.
[21] Laban, *The Mastery of Movement*, p. 80.
[22] Laban, *The Mastery of Movement*, p. 88.
[23] Laban, *Choreutics*, p. 114.
[24] Cf. 'What are Laban's Efforts?', p. 8.
[25] Laban, *The Mastery of Movement*, p. 96.

Observation and Translation

The actor is a constant observer of the world. They engage in watching; attending with mind and body to both see and perceive. In this way, they can 'collect' impressions of people and interactions: a vital store of information to draw on when creating characters and the world of a play. They observe what they can then 'translate' into their own body to transform their way of being into that of another. They inform their imagination and then use it to create embodied action. Through ongoing **Observation** and **Translation** the actor learns more and more of what it is to be human.[26]

Observation is an essential skill that all actors should cultivate and which can be 'acquired and developed through exercise'.[27] Once the actor has embodied the Efforts, they become a key part of Observation and Translation. They become a way of seeing: a clear language to analyse what is being observed and with which to 'bank' a detailed impression for later recall. Laban calls this 'thinking in terms of effort' in order to 'mirror the Efforts of other people'.[28]

Types of Observation

It is possible to use the whole of Laban's work to undertake comprehensive movement analysis pinpointing all the intricacies of a real person's movement.[29] This is extremely useful for application in a range of contexts. However, it is important to note that this kind of observation can lean towards detailing the external (observer's) impression of the movement. In contrast, the actor as observer should not look at movement from an external standpoint but 'should try to feel it sympathetically from within'.[30]

The actor must identify the internal experience of the subject's movement so it can then be translated into their own body. In this way, they can discover the truth of somebody else's way of being in the world and how to inhabit it themselves. By using the imaginative empathy of the body when observing – looking from a 'bodily perspective'[31] – they can discover how the person's inner landscape is informing their external movement. The analyst will also draw on this type of felt observation but for the actor it is the main mode of observation.

The analyst tends to be seeking to notate every outcome of the real person's varying Efforts. The actor, however, seeks solely to identify the key Efforts of the subject so they

---

[26] For more details on the process of Observation and Translation, see Ewan and Green, *Actor Movement*, pp. 101–125.

[27] Laban, *The Mastery of Movement*, p. 95.

[28] Laban and Lawrence, *Effort*, p. 93.

[29] This kind of extensive analysis can be found in systems such as Warren Lamb's Movement Pattern Analysis (MPA) and Irmgard Bartenieff's Laban Movement Analysis (LMA).

[30] Laban, *Choreutics*, p. 90.

[31] Laban, *Choreutics*, p. 91.

are able to translate these into their own body. The actor's mode of observation is just as rigorous as that of the analyst. The actor must be able skilfully to select the essential components from the observed movement for each character/situation they are exploring. The analyst observes the detailed outcome of a person's movement 'recipe' (the finished 'dish'); the actor seeks to identify the key original ingredients, which then allows them to remix the recipe in their own body. Through translation from real-life the actor can embody 'a great variety of Efforts which are characteristic of almost all shades of human personality'.[32] This includes ways of being that are very different from the actor's own.

The Actor's Imagination

Some expressive stories are beyond the anatomical limits of the human body. Work on the Efforts demands, for example, that the actor becomes a straight line. Of course, it can be pointed out that this is impossible because we are anatomically built in such a way that we are made of curves. However, intention and imagination affect expression through the body to radically alter the story being told. If the actor becomes fully occupied in imagining being a straight line – and communicating this embodied experience – it is the actor's *experience* of being a straight line (rather than their natural

Figure 1.1 The Actor Can Be Anything (The Actor's Imagination).

---

[32] Laban and Lawrence, *Effort*, p. 5.

structural curves) that the audience will receive. It is their experience that forms the heart of the intended expressive story and therefore becomes 'real' for both the actor and the audience. So an actor's imagining is crucial: anatomically (objectively) they remain the same, but expressively (subjectively) they transform.[33] A key for any actor is to make what they do feel 'real'. Actors have to believe that they can be anything – not playing at being it; not experimenting with being it; not taking things from it; but really transforming into it. If the actor uses their imagination to transform their experience, they can express anything.

---

[33] This perspective draws on Phenomenology, as outlined by thinkers like Maurice Merleau-Ponty in works such as *Phenomenology of Perception*; or, for a shorter introduction to his thinking, see *The World of Perception*.

CHAPTER 2
UNLOCKING MOVEMENT POTENTIAL

The learning of any specific movement technique or process always takes place against a wider backdrop of other movement knowledge. The process of exploring and applying the Efforts intersects with and uses all of the movement ideas addressed in this chapter.[1] Whether or not the following ideas are familiar to you already, it is useful to review them. They will be referred to throughout the book and a clear understanding of these concepts now will help you later on.

THE BODY IN SPACE

Broadly speaking, there are two identifiable areas of Space: your **Personal Space** (the Space that immediately surrounds each person's body) and **General Space** (all other Space). To say it is 'your' Personal Space makes it sound as though you have selected it and chosen to own it. In fact, you cannot go beyond it. It can shrink and grow, or be shared with or invaded by someone else, but you cannot ever leave it. Even if you ignore it, it still goes with you and defines the Space around you. Laban identified a number of geometrical forms that can be used imaginatively to understand the inherent architecture of Personal Space.[2] Below are some of the key forms which are of most use to the actor. Exploring these forms allows the actor to discover how moving through different locations and pathways in Space creates meaning.

The Kinesphere

The Personal Space that surrounds the body can be envisaged as a sphere: Laban called this the **Kinesphere**. Its natural boundaries are defined by 'the normal reach of our limbs, when they stretch away from the body without changing Stance'.[3] It is possible to reach

---

[1] The content of this chapter draws both on other areas of Laban's work and on wider Actor Movement work.
[2] Ideas about the interrelationship of Space and movement permeate all of Laban's writings. His book *Choreutics* (1966) is an in-depth record of his practical research into Space, which can be referred to for an extremely detailed account of this work.
[3] 'Stance' here is used as Laban defines it: 'the spot where one or both legs supporting the weight of the body rest on the ground' (Laban, *The Mastery of Movement*, p. 26). So you can change how you are standing through bending, twisting, stretching and shifting weight from one foot to another without affecting the current manifestation of your Kinesphere, but not the location/orientation of both your feet.

all its zones, including those behind you, using simple combinations of stretching, bending and twisting. If you change location in Space, your Kinesphere moves with you: it 'remains constant in relation to the body'.[4]

Physicalizing the Kinesphere

You are able to visualize the Personal Space around you by marking its boundary with your hands and feet. Once you have physicalized the Kinesphere in this way, you will be able to sense it much more clearly in all other actions, including everyday actions such as standing and walking. You will consciously own and inhabit the full potential of your Personal Space.

- *Stand and imagine the Personal Space around you as a sphere (i.e. your Kinesphere).*
- *Start by reaching to the edge of your Kinesphere with your fingertips.* You are marking the Space which 'belongs' to you. You can step with one foot to lunge and reach further into Space with your hand, but the other foot stays planted in the same place.
- *Now reach to another point, and another, and so on.*
- *Imagine you are marking specific points on the sphere. Bring your attention and eye focus to the points you are marking. Feel a sense of ownership over each marked point: 'that's mine'.*
- *Imagine that at each point of contact your fingertips leave a lightly coloured dot on your Kinesphere.*
- *Remember Space is behind you, above you and below you as well as in front of you.* You will have to stay facing front and twist, bend and stretch to reach behind you: if you turn your whole self around to a different facing, your Kinesphere turns with you.
- *Make sure you are not over-reaching. Keep your breath easy and released.*
- *Start to mark points on the Kinesphere using the lower body (feet) as well as the upper body.* You can use an arm as a support so the leg can reach in Space.
- *Now use sweeping movements of your hands and feet to fill in all the surfaces of your Kinesphere around you.*
- *Imagine that you are painting the whole surface of the sphere a light colour.* You are not filling the sphere with colour but just covering the surface. Make sure you are imagining a light-coloured transparent paint through which you can still see out to the world beyond.

---

[4] Laban, *The Mastery of Movement*, p. 35.

- *Pay particular attention to the areas that are not in your immediate vision (i.e. behind you; above you; at low level).*

- *Now stand still while keeping an imaginative sense of your Kinesphere around you.*

- *Take a walk in the room retaining this clear sense of Personal Space that travels with you as you move.*

The Planes

We experience three Dimensions with our body: Height (length), Breadth (width) and Depth. The dimensions of Height, Breadth and Depth can be drawn as three lines that intersect in Space to form the **Dimensional Cross** (*Figure 2.1*). Laban described Height as an 'up–down Dimension'; Depth as a 'forward–backward Dimension'; and Breadth as a 'right–left' Dimension.[5] When placed inside the body they cross at the centre. Physicalizing just one line of the Dimensional Cross gives the experience of embodying a one-dimensional pathway. It offers the actor an essential understanding of connection to Space through these six key directions (upwards, downwards, forwards, backwards, sideways right, sideways left).[6]

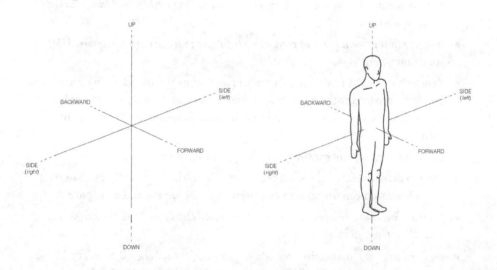

Figure 2.1 The Dimensional Cross.

---

[5] Laban, *Choreutics*, pp. 139–141.
[6] Laban created a Scale that moved through these six directions: the Dimensional Scale. For practical instructions on how to move through this Scale, visit www.labaneffortsinaction.com

However, usually the Dimensions 'are not felt in the body as lines but as Planes'.[7] Each of **the Planes** combines two out of the three dimensions (Height, Breadth, Depth). They can be referred to as the **Door**, **Wheel** and **Table** Planes and can also be drawn to show how they intersect in Space (*Figure 2.2*). Focusing on physicalizing a particular Plane allows the actor to express an experience of being two-dimensional. It offers the actor a way to discover meaning through the possible variations of the body's placement in Space (*Figure 2.3*).

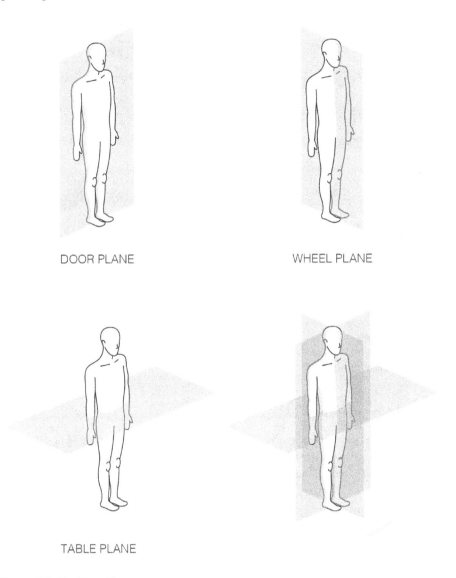

DOOR PLANE

WHEEL PLANE

TABLE PLANE

Figure 2.2 The Three Planes.

[7] Laban, *Choreutics*, p. 141.

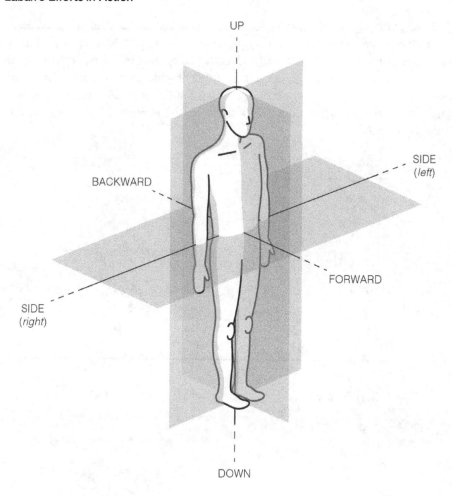

Figure 2.3 Relationship of Dimensions and Planes.

Physicalizing the Planes

- Start this exploration with the **Door Plane:** *Imagine you are standing in a rectangular Plane placed like a large door. It divides your body in half. Become aware of the separation between the Space in front of you and the Space behind you.*

- *Reach to each of the four corners of the Door Plane with your fingertips.*

- *Now, use your fingertips to imagine marking specific points along the edges of the Door Plane at high, mid and low level on either side of your body.*

- *Take a walk around the space maintaining a clear sense that your body is in the Door Plane. If it helps, use your arms to expand outwards in a broad open wing-span to give a sense of the wide, flat plane.*

- *Try the simple action of waving (greeting someone) while remaining wholly in the Door Plane.*

- Repeat this exploration but with the **Wheel Plane**: *Imagine you are standing in a rectangular Plane placed like a large wheel. It divides your body in half. Become aware of the separation between the Space to your right side and the Space to your left side.*

- *Reach to each of the four corners of the Wheel Plane with your fingertips.*

- *Now, use your fingertips to imagine marking specific points along the edges of the Wheel Plane at high, mid and low level at the front and back of your body. Use both arms.*

- *Take a walk around the space maintaining a clear sense that your body is in the Wheel Plane. If it helps, lift your arms in front and behind you to trace the form of the flat plane that extends forwards and backwards.*

- *Try the simple action of 'shooing' something in front of you away while remaining wholly in the Wheel Plane.*

- Repeat this exploration but with the **Table Plane**: *Imagine you are standing in the centre of a rectangular Plane placed like a large table. It divides your body in half. Become aware of the separation between the Space above you and the Space below you.*

- *Reach to each of the four corners of the Table Plane with your fingertips.*

- *Now, use your fingertips to imagine marking specific points on the edges of the Table Plane in front, to the sides and behind of your body.*

- *Take a walk around the space maintaining a clear sense that your body is in the Table Plane. If it helps, extend your arms out at waist height with your palms down as though smoothing a table as you walk. Imagine smoothing the same horizontal Plane with the underside of your chin as you turn your head from side to side, keeping your eyes fixed in your head as you scan the horizon.*

- *Try the simple action of reaching towards something while remaining wholly in the Table Plane.*

BASIC LOCOMOTION

Balance

Centre of Gravity

Our body is channelling and responding to gravity all the time to keep us from falling. In an upright standing position, the legs are the main weight-bearing part of the body and the **Centre of Gravity** is 'situated in the pelvis region ... above the point of support'.[8] More specifically, it is at the point where the axes of the Dimensional Cross meet, which is also the centre of the Kinesphere (cf. *Figure 2.1*).

As we move, however, the choice of muscles employed changes our relationship to gravity. Increasing or decreasing the engagement of different muscle groups gives us the ability to migrate our Centre of Gravity. When stood, for example, engaging the core muscles can draw us into an upwards verticality so we experience a sensation of 'lifting' body weight out of the pelvis and feel lighter on our feet. We can describe this as having 'raised our Centre of Gravity'. In Actor Movement we may talk about having a 'high' centre (where it feels as if more weight is carried high in the chest) or a 'low' centre (where it feels as if more weight is carried low in the pelvis).

An ability to migrate our Centre of Gravity gives us an immense sensitivity to weight placement in the body. It means we can choose between many combinations of weight-bearing body parts. This allows us to vary how we are supporting the mass of our body and retain balance in different positions.

Counter-tension

Muscular engagement that moves the body in one direction is balanced by concurrent muscular engagement creating force in the opposite direction. This employs Strength and is a form of internalized resistance referred to as **Counter-Tension** (or counter-resistance). It helps us control our movements and is a key part of maintaining balance: it enables movements in one direction to be simultaneously countered, and therefore controlled.

We instinctively employ Counter-Tension. Think of standing and reaching up to get something from a high cupboard. As your reaching hand pulls the body upwards there will be an instinctive muscular engagement that simultaneously pulls downwards through the opposite leg. This helps to maintain controlled balance in an action which shifts the Centre of Gravity away from its habitual placement, and so might otherwise cause us to fall.

Stability and Lability

'Stable' is a commonly used word, so we understand the concept of Stability. Yet the opposite of **Stability** is normally only referred to using a negative inversion. We talk about being 'stable' or 'unstable'; 'balanced' or 'unbalanced'; 'centred' or 'off-centre'. In fact, the opposite of Stability is a state in its own right called **Lability**.[9]

At any given time, one can be either **Stable** or **Labile**. Laban explains: 'The body is in its most *Labile* state of action when the Centre of Gravity ... is out of line with its normal

---

8 Laban, *The Mastery of Movement*, p. 53.
9 Laban also uses the terms 'Motility' or 'Mobility' interchangeably with 'Lability'.

support. The body is in its most *Stable* state of action when the Centre of Gravity is in vertical line above the point of support.'[10]

We tend to differentiate between the overall experience of being either Stable or Labile during a whole sequence of movements. However, in reality, 'neither pure Stability nor pure [Lability] exist.'[11] In order to retain control over our movement, we are constantly shifting between them: 'Stability and [Lability] alternate endlessly.'[12] This pattern can be observed in walking: shifting our Weight forwards takes us into Lability; placing a foot down then allows us to move through momentary Stability (preventing ourselves falling); then we shift forward again into Lability during the movement of the next step; and so on. This alternating cycle between Stability and Lability occurs constantly during all our movements without us even noticing it.

We tend to associate Stability with positive emotions (think of 'striking the right balance') and Lability with negative emotions (think of being 'knocked off course', or 'left reeling' by unexpected events). This assumption is limiting. Stability and Lability have the same potential for expression. Each can express a range of experiences (think of 'falling' in love, which places Lability in a positive light; or being too 'uptight', which places Stability in a negative light).

Figure 2.4 Left: Stability | Right: Lability.

---

[10] Laban, *The Mastery of Movement*, p. 61.
[11] Laban, *The Mastery of Movement*, p. 90.
[12] Laban, *The Mastery of Movement*, p. 94.

Discovering Lability

As we grow up we fall less. In fact, we actively work to avoid falling. This means that we have an inherent distrust of Lability and fight to remain Stable whenever possible. It is important to discover ways that you can fully enter into Lability, whilst still remaining safe.[13] This exploration involves using additional support (a wall) to counteract your instinctive fear of falling and safely discover new ways of moving. It helps you to experience Lability by finding body-positions with an altered Centre of Gravity. It will help you to learn the outer limits to which your body can go before over-balancing. It also allows you to understand what asymmetry feels like. These shapes will remain banked in your physical memory as places to which you can safely go, and when you are working on the Indirect Efforts they will emerge to surprise you.

- *Find a Labile body-shape. Make sure it is off-centre and asymmetrical. You can use something Stable to help you (if you have access to wall bars, then that is ideal; if not, use another object that is fixed to a wall).* We tend to think of the body as two pairs of mirroring body sections (i.e. two arms and two legs creating symmetrical shapes). So, to find asymmetrical body shapes it can be useful to think of the body as having four distinct sections (four limbs each potentially doing different things).

- *Now move back and forth between two Labile body-shapes.*

- *Begin by transferring from one shape to the other using a count of eight, leaving the first shape on the count of one and arriving at the second shape on the count of eight.*

- *Find different pathways between the two shapes.*

- *Now experiment with moving between the two shapes in different rhythms and at different speeds.*

- *Repeat the steps above to find two more Labile body-shapes and various ways to move between them.*

- *Now play with all the different ways you can move between the four Labile body-shapes in different orders.*

- *Add some more shapes to your growing repertoire. If you haven't already, find some at mid and low level, including on the floor.*

Inwards and Outwards

Movements tend to move either inwards towards the body, or outwards away from the body. Laban used the terms 'Gathering' and 'Scattering' to identify these 'two main action forms'. **Scattering** 'goes from the centre of the body outwards into Space' while **Gathering**

---

[13] It is necessary to enter into Lability to discover the Indirect Efforts. This can be challenging – particularly in Flicking and Slashing which are also Sudden, and so have an increased risk of falling because you move off balance abruptly. This preparation work will help equip you to explore these Efforts.

'comes from the periphery of the Kinesphere inwards towards the centre'.[14] These two action forms are particularly noticeable in the Gestures of the arms and hands, but are also present in whole-body movements. When the whole body is involved it is more common to speak of **Expansion** and **Contraction**.

- *Lying on the floor, begin to experiment with contracting and then expanding the body. Discover the two sensations of closing inwards and opening outwards.*
- *Notice how the breath naturally leads towards an alternating sense of Contraction and Expansion.*
- *Start each Contraction and Expansion in your core so that you curl inwards and widen outwards.*
- *Make sure you are using the body as one unified whole in which every body part is involved.*
- *Begin to allow the Contraction and Expansion to move you along the floor. You will need to shift your centre off-balance and find different points of contact with the ground.*
- *Discover how you can change levels.*
- *Play with different tempos and rhythms.*
- *Now find Contraction (Gathering) and Expansion (Scattering) in one area of the body at a time.*
- *Play with contracting (Gathering) and expanding (Scattering) at the same time in two different body parts (e.g. one arm Gathering, one arm Scattering; core body Gathering and arms Scattering).*

Sequential and Simultaneous

Sequential involves a continuous pathway of movement: a sequence of movements travelling from body part to body part, each following the last and triggering the next.[15] **Simultaneous** involves movement that occurs in at least two separate body parts at the same time. Laban illustrates this by explaining the movement of twisting an arm: 'when moving [Sequentially] the whole arm is only gradually involved in the twist, while in Simultaneous action the twist occurs in the whole arm at once'.[16] In other words, it is possible for a twist of the arm either to travel in sequence from the fingers, to the wrist, to the lower arm, and so on; or for all the parts of the arm to twist at the same time. The actor needs to be able to execute both of these two very different ways of moving.

---

[14] Laban, *The Mastery of Movement*, p. 83.
[15] Cf. 'Use of Sequential', p. 264.
[16] Laban, *The Mastery of Movement*, p. 58.

Video Resource

Understanding Sequential
https://vimeo.com/251493578

Video Resource

Understanding Simultaneous
https://vimeo.com/251493793

Explorations of Sequential Movement

First, take some time to discover the sensation of Sequential movement while remaining in one location.

- *Lie on the floor and visualize a pinball somewhere inside your body.*
- *Imagine moving in such a way that the pinball rolls through the interior pathways of your body.*
- *Discover how it rolls through the body bouncing off the body's inner surfaces as you move, like in a pinball machine. If you move smoothly, the ball will also travel smoothly through the body.* If the pinball is imagined with precision, it stimulates Sequential movement in the body where one part moves, then a neighbouring part, and so on in pathways around the body.
- *If your imagined pinball reaches your hand or foot, you can touch the hand or foot to somewhere else on your body to pass the ball back into the body in a different place. If it comes out of your mouth, catch it in your hand and put it back in.*
- *Be specific: if you were to freeze at any given time you should know the exact location of the pinball, and an outside observer should be able to see exactly where it is as it moves.*
- *Try changing level whilst still moving the pinball around your body. Shift between high, mid and low level.*

Now discover how to use Sequential movement to travel through the space:

- *Begin with rolling: lie fully outstretched on your back with your arms above your head. Make sure your whole body is released so you feel you are sinking into the ground.*
- *Imagine your foot is being gently pulled away from you in a diagonal across the other leg towards the direction in which you want to roll. Feel the pull across your hips and ribs. Let this lead your movement so that gradually your body turns in a Sequential roll, spiralling up through the pelvis, waist, ribs, shoulder and head.*

- *Feel your torso turning over, as you softly and gradually drop onto your front and roll sideways into the floor.*
- *Keep the movement flowing and allow the ongoing twist of the shoulder, then the waist and then the hip to keep rolling you until you arrive on your back once more.*
- *Carry on rolling so that you steadily travel through the space.*
- *Once you have tried Sequential rolling, return to lying on the floor. Use what you have learnt from the experience of rolling to find other ways of moving through the space with Sequential movement. Try returning to imagining a pinball moving through your body. As the pinball travels through the body, imagine that it is searching for something, so that it motivates movement through the space. Allow yourself to be moved by the pinball as it passes through different places in your body.*

Explorations of Simultaneous Movement[17]

First, take some time to discover the sensation of Simultaneous movement while remaining in one location:

- *Experiment with moving two body parts at the same time (e.g. your two arms; your two legs; an arm and a leg; your hand and your foot). The movement of both body parts should have equal force and duration.*
- *If you try moving two parts at the same time but it is not exact, repeat the movements until you can perform them together with precision.* When you find truly Simultaneous movement, it will feel satisfying.
- *Don't get stuck just using your arms and legs: try different body parts.*
- *Play with both symmetrical and asymmetrical pairs of body parts and movements.* You are likely to have instinctively been finding symmetrical pairs of movement (e.g. both arms doing the same move). However, simultaneous movement does not have to be symmetrical (e.g. you could move your left arm and your right arm but doing different moves; or you could move your left arm and your right leg)
- *Try moving in different rhythms.* The movements can occur in any rhythm – they can be fast or slow, long or short.
- *Now try Simultaneous movement at high, mid and low levels.*

Now discover how to use Simultaneous movement to travel through the space:

- *Experiment with ways of travelling across the space using Simultaneous movement.*
- *Try a new way of moving each time you journey through the space. This will help you build a vocabulary of Simultaneous movements that allow you to travel.*
- *Play with moving at different levels across the space; and switching levels during the journey.*

---

[17] This exploration uses corresponding movement in both body parts as a preparation for the ways in which Simultaneous movement often occurs in the full-body Efforts.

THE BODY AS ORCHESTRA

The body is often referred to as an 'instrument' of expression. In fact, it is more like an **orchestra**: it is one entity made up of many parts, all of which participate in expressing meaning. These parts relate to each other in different ways. They can work with or against each other in unison, harmony, counterpoint or discord; and they vary in relative status according to what is being expressed.

Working with the Whole Body

The Body as an Integrated Whole

Working with **the whole body** means that the actor has an awareness of every part of their body. The actor can work with the whole body on big, complex actions such as jumping, crouching, falling, etc., or on actions as simple as standing or sitting still. By working with the idea of the whole body as one integrated organism, you can experience involving every single part of yourself in physical action.

Using every part of the body for physical expression demands full commitment. In return, it offers a powerful expression of unified harmony. Everyone has areas of the body that they tend not to use expressively. There is a sense that these body parts just don't want to join in – that they are 'dead' areas. It is important to practise involving these areas in your movement so that you are capable of using your whole body as an expressive resource. You will then also be able to choose which body parts to use and which to restrict according to the character you are creating, rather than your own limitations.

- *Re-visit a simple movement exercise with which you are very familiar (e.g. a roll-down, swings, or even an action as simple as walking across the space).*

- *As you move through the action, bring your attention to all the different areas of your body. Notice which parts of the body are not joining in fully: it may feel as if they are more held (less free to move) than other parts, or that it is hard to sense their movement or to bring your attention to them in the first place.*

- *Keep your attention in these areas as you move. Work on integrating them into the movement so that they are alive and have equal presence to all the other body parts.*

Working with Body Parts

Isolating Body Parts

'**Isolations**' involve moving one part of the body separately from the rest. Practising them develops your skill to break down the body into component parts. Relating to the body as an accumulation of many parts also gives you the potential to embody various actions in different areas of the body at the same time. When one isolated part is moving, the rest of the body is alert and energized, and so supporting the action that is occurring.

- *Move just one body part while you maintain an alive stillness in the rest of the body.*
- *Work for accuracy in the movement, but remember that precision does not equate to muscular tension: keep a released sense of ease as you move.*
- *Try moving different body parts in isolation (e.g. shoulders, hips, ribs, head).*
- *Play with different tempos and rhythms.*

Working with One Body Part as the Whole

Sometimes it can be useful to wholly focus your action in **one body part**. Our perception of ourselves and other people is often affected by the parts of the body that are favoured. So being able to place more focus on selected body parts can be a useful skill. Detailed focus or attention can be brought to a body part by thinking of it as having the same structure as the whole body: a hand or a foot, for example, has its own centre and periphery, component parts, and spatial orientation.

- *Choose a body part.*
- *Play with simple actions such as sitting, walking, gesturing, etc. Imagine that all of your physical expression is channelled through your one chosen body part: you are only a hand, or a foot, etc. Other body parts will be involved in the movement but only as a result of your chosen body part's lead.*
- *Experiment with focusing on different body parts. Notice how your movements change according to your choice.*

Body Components: Bony, Muscly, Fleshy

We tend to name and work with body parts we can see such as the finger, hand, arm, etc. Yet it is possible to work with all body parts, including those which are internal (e.g. your organs). We can also identify three main **body components**: bone, muscle and flesh. Each of these components has a different role in our movement.

Just as we tend to have greater or lesser awareness of some parts of the body, we each relate to these internal body components differently. Someone may have a heightened awareness of one of these three body components either because of body-type or because of body-attitude (i.e. someone may move in a muscly way because they have a lot of muscle mass, or they may move in a muscly way because they have a keen awareness of their muscles). A heightened awareness of one component or another informs an unconscious idea of self that we perform: a person who has a high awareness of being 'bony' will move differently from someone who has a high awareness of being 'muscly' or 'fleshy'.[18]

---

[18] There is no connection between these terms and the categories of fixed body type 'Ectomorph', 'Endomorph', and 'Mesomorph' which are used in some fitness approaches.

These are also colloquial words that other people use to define someone's appearance. A person, for example, who has a lot of muscle might be called 'muscly'. Yet everyone is made up of all three of these body components. So, in fact, we all have the capacity to tell the story of being 'muscly', 'bony' or 'fleshy'. The actor can transform their expression – and the perception of others – by moving from an altered awareness of any of these body components.

- *Re-visit a simple movement exercise with which you are very familiar (e.g. a roll-down, swings, or even an action as simple as walking across the space).*
- *As you move through the action, use your imagination to experience a heightened awareness of either your muscles, your bones or your flesh.*
- *Notice how bringing your attention to one particular body component changes the experience and emphasis of the action.*
- *Try all three ways of moving in turn and notice the difference between them.*

PART B
BUILDING BLOCKS

CHAPTER 3
WEIGHT, TIME, SPACE

THE MOTION FACTORS

Laban identifies just four key factors that reveal how Effort is manifested in all movement. Working with these **Motion Factors** will enable you to unlock the whole range of potential expression that is available through your actions. So, for the actor, understanding them is the ultimate empowerment.

The four Motion Factors are **Weight**, **Time**, **Space** and **Flow**.[1] They combine in varying ways during all types of movement, affecting how the movement is done and what it expresses. Laban explains that movements 'evolve in Space as well as Time . . . and that in this evolution of movement the Weight of the body is brought into Flow'.[2]

When discovering the eight Efforts you work consciously with Weight, Time, and Space as the three key building blocks. Flow is also present, but in this work you let it respond instinctively to the demands of your movement.[3] So our focus is on Weight, Time, and Space.

Motion Factor Elements

Each Motion Factor can be understood as a continuum (a sliding scale) between two polar opposites. These opposites can be referred to as the **Elements** of each Motion Factor:[4]

---

[1] Laban's theory of Effort developed over the course of his working life. The concept of Motion Factors emerges early in his work, but the identification of four precise Motion Factors by these names was an ongoing process. In his earlier writings, the Motion Factors are sometimes referred to by different names (e.g. 'force', 'flux', 'energy', 'tension'). For simplicity, we shall always refer to them as Weight, Time, Space, and Flow as Laban does throughout his later writings.

[2] Laban and Lawrence, *Effort*, p. 66.

[3] Laban explains: 'in a basic Effort Action the Flow remains latent and only the factors of Weight, Time, Space operate. When this is the case we speak of an "Action Drive"' (Laban, *The Mastery of Movement*, p. 79). For more on Flow, see 'The Role of Flow', p. 257.

[4] These Elements are the result of two possible attitudes to each Motion Factor: yielding and resisting. Laban describes them as a 'resisting, constricting, withholding, fighting' attitude, and a 'yielding, enduring, accepting, indulging' attitude (Laban, *The Mastery of Movement*, p. 20). Which of these two attitudes you have affects which Element of the Motion Factors you express: your movement will be different depending on whether you are *resisting* Weight, Time, Space or Flow, or *yielding* to them.

Weight is a continuum between **Light** and **Strong/Heavy**.

Time is a continuum between **Sudden** and **Sustained**.

Space is a continuum between **Direct** and **Indirect**.[5]

A 'specific combination of several of these [...] Elements of movement is observable in every action'.[6] Usually, the combination of Elements being used in a person's movement is an unconscious choice. However, the actor can become conscious of their choices, and investigate how and why a person's movement expresses certain Elements. Developing the ability consciously to choose how Weight, Time, and Space are expressed allows the actor to progress beyond their habitual choices. Limitless movement options become available.

EXAMINING WEIGHT, TIME, AND SPACE

The words Laban uses to identify these three Motion Factors are also used in many other contexts with a subtly different range of meanings, including making reference to complicated scientific concepts. You will have a general – but perhaps hazy – sense of what weight, time, and space 'mean' to you. So it is important to examine your broader understanding of these terms. This will support your discovery of how they can be embodied as Motion Factors. Harnessing some of the knowledge you may already have about weight, time and space will help you to tune into the actor's perspective.

You do not need to memorize or grasp after these concepts. If you were given the opportunity to enjoy a connection with science at school, allow your knowledge to be re-awakened by these thoughts. If not, simply let yourself connect with whichever of these ideas speaks to you and allow yourself to be inspired by the following key italicized statements. The next chapter will take you into working physically to encounter these concepts through your body.

What is Weight?

//Weight is objective: it can be measured
Every person and object is made of a certain amount of matter which we refer to as their mass. The force of gravity works on our mass and we experience this force as weight. On earth we cannot escape gravitational force: we are always being affected by the law of gravity. So, our quantifiable weight remains more or less constant from one moment to

---

[5] The names by which Laban identified these eight Motion Factor Elements also shifted over the course of his working life. For more information, see Appendix B: A Note on Word Choices, p. 264.

[6] Laban, *The Mastery of Movement*, p. 69.

the next because gravitational force remains the same.[7] Both mass and weight have fixed, objective, universally agreed units of measurement. Technically, weight is measured in Newtons.[8] However, in everyday usage we tend to merge our understanding of weight and mass: most commonly, we think of our 'weight' as being the number on a weighing scale that tells us how big or small we are. This colloquial idea of 'weight' tends to be measured in kilograms or pounds (which are, in fact, units of mass).

//*Weight is also subjective*
Our sense of weightedness alters according to how much we choose to fight against or yield to gravity's force. Creating varying resistance through muscular tension or release alters our perception of gravity. So the subjective experience of our weightedness changes all the time, even though our literal weight remains constant. The amount of energy available to engage our muscles in resistance also affects our experience of weightedness: the day after hard exercise you may feel your arms to be unusually heavy as you lift them up to brush your hair, when normally they feel light; or you may begin to run with the feeling that it is easy to move your legs but after a long time you feel you have legs 'like lead'. Our perception of weightedness also shifts according to context. We think of specific things as light or heavy depending on how we relate them to other things: an arm or leg is light compared with your whole body but heavy compared with a finger or toe. Our use of language points to the fact that the thoughts and feelings we are experiencing also alter our perception of weight: for example, we speak of our mood being 'up' (light) and 'down' (heavy).

//*Weight is an ongoing physical experience*
We cannot change the gravitational pull on us. However, we can alter how our body channels gravity, and where in the body we feel our weight to be placed.[9] Our Centre of Gravity can be shifted in any direction. We can use these alterations either to carry us through Lability into movement, or to help retain Stability.[10] Our ability skilfully to shift our Centre of Gravity can clearly be seen in acrobatic hand-balancing. During these acts, the performers are constantly negotiating the exact placement of their weight in order to maintain extraordinary positions, using unusual points of weight-bearing support without falling.

//*Weight can be structured through rhythm*
If the placement of weight changes during an action, an accent (stress) is formed. A swing of the arm, for example, moves through an arc from a feeling of weightlessness

---

[7] If you were an astronaut on the moon, you would be weightless because there is weaker gravitational force there. In outer space, you would be weightless because there is no gravitational force there at all. In each of these locations, your mass would remain the same but your weight would change as the force of gravity alters.
[8] A unit measuring force.
[9] Cf. 'Centre of Gravity', p. 39.
[10] Cf. 'Stability and Lability', p. 40.

(suspension) to weightedness to weightlessness (suspension). As it moves through the bottom of the arc and the expression of weight changes there is an accent. We feel and perceive changes in weight as part of 'Rhythm'.

What is Time?

//Time is objective: it can be measured

Usually, when we think of time it is as an entity that can be measured to tell us when something is happening, or its duration (how long something takes). It is assessed through fixed, objective, universally agreed units of measurement, such as seconds, minutes, hours, etc. This can be referred to as 'clock-time' because they are units of time that we use a clock to measure. Days, weeks and years are also fixed external units of measurable 'clock-time'. We also measure time in terms of speed – the rate at which an action happens, or something moves. Laban identifies the speed with which we act as 'the rate at which we let movements follow one another'.[11] In other words, whether a succession of movements occurs quickly or slowly. This rate can be measured using objective units: we can, for example, say a car is travelling at a rate of so many miles or kilometres per hour.

//Time is also subjective

Clock-time gives us an objective measure of time. However, our perception of time is often subjective and reliant on comparison. For example, we tend to experience speed in general comparative terms of quick (fast) versus slow, rather than through an objective measurement such as miles per hour. Our perception of time also shifts according to context. We think of specific things as fast or slow depending on how we relate them to other things. We have a general understanding that a plane travels quickly but a horse-drawn cart travels slowly. Yet, if we compare a horse-drawn cart to a person on foot our understanding shifts, and we would say that it is the cart that travels quickly and the person who travels slowly. Our use of language points to the fact that the thoughts and feelings we are experiencing also alter our perception of time: we say things such as 'I'm not sure what the mugger looked like, it all happened at the speed of light'; 'the man behind the desk was moving at a snail's pace'; 'as the car hit me everything went into slow motion', etc. The literal speed of action may have changed very little but in each case the speaker's experience of time was radically different from the objective 'reality'. In acting, the term 'Tempo' is often used as a way of referring to this broader, more subjective sensation and expression of quickness or slowness.[12]

---

[11] Laban, *The Mastery of Movement*, p. 39.

[12] Laban identifies Tempo as 'variations between rapidity and slowness' (Laban, *Choreutics*, p. 35). In music, a tempo can be a precisely fixed speed of so many beats per minute and a metronome can be used to accurately set this pace. However, it can also be indicated by means of descriptive terms which suggest a mood, atmosphere or feeling, e.g. *Andante* (at a walking pace), *Allegro* (fast and lively), *Largo* (slow and stately).

//Time is an ongoing physical experience
Our most visceral understanding of time emerges from our embodied presence in the world. Our bodies experience time as an onward progression: the advance of time manifests itself physically in a process of change through ageing, beginning as soon as matter comes together in conception and ending as matter falls apart in the decay of death. This gives us an instinctive sense of time as a threefold reality: past, which exists through memory of what was; present, which exists through our current physical experience; and future, which exists through imagination of what will be. The present moment is measured by the rhythmic processes that occur continuously in our bodies: the beating of the heart and the alternating cycle of the breath. Even our most commonly recognized measurements of time draw on this innate bodily experience: 'in comparing durations of movements we use a conventional unit of time, the second, which corresponds to approximately one heart-beat'.[13]

//Time can be structured through rhythm
We often think of rhythm as a musical term denoting a consciously chosen arrangement of beats, but in fact all movement has rhythm that can be regular or irregular.[14] Rhythmic patterning can range from simple to extremely complex, and it is important to note that we can both hear time-rhythm in sounds and see it in all movement. The same rhythm can be expressed at different speeds: as long as the length of each rhythmic unit remains in proportion, the rhythm will remain the same even if the speed of the whole movement sequence is faster or slower.

What is Space?

//Space is objective: it can be measured
Usually, when we think of space it is as an entity or location within which we exist; something outside ourselves. So we tend to relate to space by identifying where things are placed within it. To discern spatial positioning, we assess the relationship between points (places) in space occupied by specific objects or people. For this we use a variety of different fixed, objective, universally agreed units of measurement such as centimetres, metres, inches, feet, kilometres, miles, degrees, etc. These can be employed precisely to measure spatial variables such as proximity, orientation, facing, level, direction and placement.

---

[13] Laban, *Choreutics*, p. 29.
[14] Laban explains that 'rhythms produced by bodily movements are characterized by a division of the continuous flux of movements into parts, each of which has a definite duration in time. These parts of a rhythm can be of equal or unequal length' (Laban, *The Mastery of Movement*, p. 121).

//Space is also subjective

Although we have objective measures of space, our perception of it often relies on subjective comparison. For this, we have an extensive everyday vocabulary – for example, *proximity*: near, close, far, distant, etc. | *orientation*: upright, sideways, upside down, etc. | *facing*: front, side, back, etc. | *level*: high, mid, low, etc. | *direction*: forwards, backwards, sideways, etc. | *placement*: above, below, opposite, inside, behind, etc. Our perception of space also shifts according to context. A shop may seem far on foot but near if you use a car. Its seeming distance may also alter dependent on the amount of physical energy available to you: it is likely to seem further away when you are tired than when you have plenty of energy. Our use of language points to the fact that the thoughts and feelings we are experiencing alter our perception of space: we say things such as 'are you okay, you're very distant today'; 'his speech was really in your face'; 'we gradually grew apart', etc. These are not literal descriptions of spatial relationships, but rather references to how our relationships in space feel at any given moment.

//Space is an ongoing physical experience

The space in which we move is not simply a void or inert locality but a dynamic entity in and of itself: to a greater or lesser degree, all things are constantly in flux, including the unseen molecules of the air surrounding us or objects which are seemingly still.[15] Space is constituted of 'a superabundance of simultaneous movements'.[16] Descriptions of how we move through space reveal our understanding that space contains moving matter: we speak, for example, of pushing, cutting, slicing, carving or forging through space. Laban concludes: 'movement is the life of space. Dead space does not exist, for there is neither space without movement nor movement without space.'[17]

//Space has a discernible structure

Laban uses detailed analysis to identify a number of innate spatial shapes or forms. They mirror well-known geometrical shapes and solids such as the rectangle, cube and sphere, as well as more complex solids such as the icosahedron (which has twenty faces).[18] These constitute a 'living architecture' that is 'created by human movements and is made up of pathways tracing shapes in space'.[19] They define the space around us and guide our movements in space. In identifying these spatial forms, Laban made a connection between the dynamic structure of our movement in Personal Space and the wider structures of the universe.[20] Laban created many different 'Scales'. They use the structure

---

[15] Cf. 'The Role of Flow', p. 257.

[16] Laban, *Choreutics*, p. 3.

[17] Laban, *Choreutics*, p. 94.

[18] You have already met (and embodied) some of these forms in the previous chapter, when you explored your Kinesphere and the Planes (Cf. 'The Kinesphere', p. 34; 'The Planes', p. 36).

[19] Laban, *Choreutics*, p. 5.

[20] For a detailed summary of Laban's use of geometry to define space, see Newlove and Dalby, *Laban for All*, pp. 23–61.

of geometrical solids to create particular pathways around the body. Moving through these pathways creates 'trace-forms', which help us to visualize and embody the dynamic architecture of the space that surrounds us.[21] This spatial architecture is present in all movement: 'space is a hidden feature of movement and movement is a visible aspect of space'.[22]

---

[21] The complete set of movement scales are a somewhat separate area of Laban's work, so it is not necessary for the actor to have studied them. However, should you be interested in doing so, they will add hugely to your understanding of space. A useful summary of them can be found in the works of Jean Newlove and Valerie Preston-Dunlop.

[22] Laban, *Choreutics*, p. 4.

CHAPTER 4
EMBODYING THE MOTION FACTORS

You will now meet **Weight**, **Time**, and **Space** as embodied **Motion Factors**. This will allow you to discover a specific, practical way of relating to them through the body. As you begin to work with Laban's terminology, let the images, sensations, resonances and associations evoked by each word live in your body. Each word will transform from being merely the description of a concept to become a catalyst for a specific physical experience.

Through focusing on each Motion Factor, you will discover how to shift your subjective experience of Weight, Time, and Space. This is vital for the actor because by altering your own experience, you also shift the perception of others. To alter your experience of Weight, Time, and Space, you have to change how you are expressing them through your actions. This will also change the meaning or narrative of your actions. So conscious articulation of Weight, Time, and Space is a key part of embodied storytelling.

The Motion Factors cannot be removed from any movement. They are 'always inherent in any Effort display, no matter whether it serves a practical purpose or is of an expressive nature'.[1] So, when you are focusing on one chosen Motion Factor, it is not that the others are not part of your movement but simply that you are allowing yourself not to make any conscious choices about them in that moment.[2]

The three Motion Factors of Weight, Time, and Space are explored by embodying each of their two Elements (Light and Strong/Heavy; Sudden and Sustained; Direct and Indirect). It is useful for the actor to work with two clearly defined options for each Motion Factor rather than a full sliding scale. By working with pairs of contrasting Elements, the actor discovers a distinction between the extremes of each Motion Factor. The understanding of an Element is helped by knowledge of its opposite: through a precise understanding of what it is not, you can gain a clearer experience of exactly what it is. So work with the understanding that every Element is expressed at its most intense: Light really is Light (not just a little bit Light but the Lightest it can be), and the same for each other Element.

WEIGHT

Light and Strong/Heavy

The Motion Factor **Weight** can be divided into the two Elements **Light** and **Strong/ Heavy**. In everyday language, when we use the word 'weight' we tend implicitly to mean

---

[1] Laban, *The Mastery of Movement*, p. 14.
[2] For more details, see Appendix C: Focussing the Theory for the Actor, p. 266.

'having Heavy Weight'. It is important to remember that the Motion Factor Weight is a continuum which also encompasses Light (which we might colloquially talk about as 'weightlessness'). When exploring the contrasting Elements, it may be helpful to think about them as expressing either 'a relaxed or forceful attitude to Weight'.[3]

Heavy Weight is an experience of being complicit with gravity. It involves reducing muscular exertion and allowing the body to stop resisting gravity ('release' or 'letting go'). Both Light Weight and Strong Weight, however, are experiences of using muscular exertion to fight against gravity. Laban defines bodily force as 'the degree of energy spent overcoming one's own body weight, or that of an object'.[4] If you employ a greater amount of force through energetic muscular engagement, you are able to work against gravity and Lighten an experience of Heaviness in your body. Alternatively, you can use muscular engagement to turn Heaviness into Strength to move the mass of your own body or that of an external object.

There may be a generalized assumption that expressing Light Weight would be 'easier' or 'less work'. In fact, expressing Light Weight requires just as much commitment as expressing Strong Weight or Heavy Weight – it takes energy to work against gravity.

Video Resource

Weight: Light and Strong/Heavy
https://vimeo.com/251494021

Discovering Light

On earth our bodies are always subject to the force of gravity, so we cannot escape our weightedness. However, by shifting the placement of our weight, we can allow parts of our body to express weightlessness.[5] If, for example, you shift your weight placement across to the left while standing, the left leg becomes the main weight-bearing body part and the right leg is freed to express a greater degree of weightlessness.

We can choose which body parts are weight-bearing at any given moment. Lying at low level on the floor, for example, it is possible to shift the Centre of Gravity up to the top of the body so that weight travels downwards through the shoulder-girdle into the floor. In this 'shoulder-stand', the shoulders become the main weight-bearing body part leaving the pelvis and the legs free to express Light Weight and move upwards into the air.

Whenever the body is expressing Lightness, there will always be some body parts employing just enough Strong Weight to support the mass of the body. These parts can

---

[3] Laban, *The Mastery of Movement*, p. 69.
[4] Laban and Lawrence, *Effort*, p. 63.
[5] Cf. 'Centre of Gravity', p. 39.

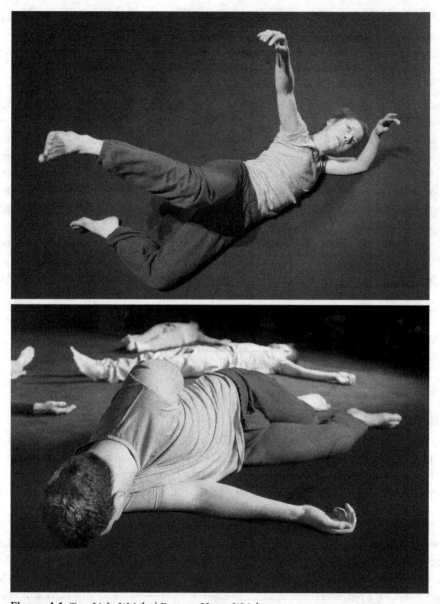

Figure 4.1 Top: Light Weight | Bottom: Heavy Weight.

be employed 'secretly' by the actor (i.e. they are excluded from the expressive story). Parts of some statues are supported by a stick. The viewer knows they are meant to look at the statue and ignore the support because it is not part of the story of the statue. Likewise, it is possible for an actor to employ Strong Weight in some body parts, but for the story that is communicated to be one of total Lightness. In this way, it is possible to feel and communicate an imaginative expression of total Lightness despite being bound by the law of gravity.[6] Remember, we have all had subjective experiences of extreme, all-encompassing Light Weight: this is reflected in our language when we talk about feeling 'light-headed' or 'walking on air'.

- *Lie on the floor and release all your muscles, including the muscles of your face.*
- *Pay attention to your breathing. Allow the in-breath to become more fulsome, without putting any over-emphasis on the action of drawing in more air.* In this exploration you may take in more air than you usually do. If you begin to feel dizzy or faint at any point, simply pause to let your breathing return to normal so the sensation recedes.
- *Feel the Lightness of the air. Imagine that the breath is travelling inside you, all the way down to your toes. Imagine that the whole volume of your body becomes filled with air.*
- *Let the air gradually lift one small part of your body away from the floor and into movement. Take your time and don't move until you really feel the sensation of Lightness in your chosen body part. Make that body part so Light that it feels as if it has no gravity holding it.*
- *Now, let the air move through you to another body part, which then lifts freely into Lightness; and then another, and another.*
- *As the story of the Lightness shifts, identify where you need to support your body-weight to keep discovering Lightness in different places.* You will need to shift the responsibility of weight-bearing around your body so all the different parts of your body can have an experience of Lightness (just not at the same time). Your extremities will sometimes become weight-bearing, so that that the knees, hips, torso or head can also be released into Lightness.
- *Use comparison to find the same Lightness in your core body as you did in your extremities. Can you make your knees as Light as your fingers? Or your pelvis as Light as your toes?*
- *Allow each breath to carry you onwards into more movement, so that you find a way to begin moving in Light Weight through the space. Make sure you do not release into Heaviness or use Strength.*
- *As Light Weight takes over, fully enjoy the imaginative experience of being released from gravitational force. There is no longer any sense of 'up' and 'down'.*
- *Keep this same sensation of Light Weight in your body as you stand and walk around the room. Discover how to maintain the experience in your body whilst hiding it a little, so that you can walk in such a way as to fit into society – so that you are within the limits of what we perceive as socially 'normal'.*

---

[6] Cf. 'The Actor's Imagination', p. 32.

Discovering Heavy

It is vital to disconnect the idea of Heavy Weight in Laban's work from any negative cultural ideas about being 'heavy' or 'overweight'.[7] All bodies can express Heavy Weight and it is an essential part of the actor's palette of expressive choices. The actor should be able to offer an audience a full range from extreme Light Weight to extreme Strong/Heavy Weight.

We have all had subjective experiences of Heavy Weight: imagine being very weary or sad, or dozing in bed and being reluctant to get up. Feel how it brings the sensation of not having the will or ability to lift yourself up; how you become compliant with gravity. These are expressions of Heavy Weight. Common experiences like these are reflected in our language when we talk about feeling 'weighed down' or 'having the weight of the world on our shoulders'.

The centre of our body has more mass than the peripheries. So it can be tempting to assume we are only able to experience Heaviness in our core and Lightness in our peripheries. However, by viewing the body as made up of parts, the actor can access an imaginative expression of Heavy Weight in all areas of the body.[8] All body parts also have their own centre and periphery. For example, working with the hand you can discover that the palm of the hand (centre) is heavier than the fingers (peripheries); or working with the finger, you can discover that the knuckle (centre) is heavier than the fingertips (periphery). With this comparative perception you can begin to access a sensation of Heaviness in any body part, even those which are always going to be, in a literal sense, lighter than others (have less mass).

- *Lie on the floor. Imagine you are lying on sand and it is engulfing you. Slowly, the whole volume of your body is sinking into the sand: it is creeping up your sides and over your hands, until you are semi-submerged.*

- *Then imagine the sand slowly seeping into your body so that it fills up almost all the available Space inside.*

- *Pay attention to your breathing. Use each exhalation to sink you deeper and deeper into the floor.*

- *Imagine gravity weighing you down from above. Feel that you could not lift your body off the floor even if you wanted to.*

- *Try and lift a hip off the floor. Have the ambition to lift the hip but feel the reluctance in your body: it takes a great amount of exertion and soon falls back*

---

[7] In Western society a damaging value judgement is placed on the size ('weight') of the human body. Most people have deeply rooted beliefs about their size ('weight') due to this cultural conditioning. Commonly, being smaller and lighter is viewed as 'better' for women; increasingly, this belief also applies to men, or a belief that being bigger and stronger (muscly) is 'better'. In general, people believe that heavy (i.e. 'fat') is 'bad'. This belief is particularly reinforced in actors who are aware that getting work can rely on conforming to an industry-led ideal of attractiveness. Being trapped by this viewpoint tragically devalues the extraordinary range of humanity, and the uniqueness of each human body and what it can express. Both the actor and the audience have much to gain from experiencing the physical expression of Strong/Heavy Weight.

[8] Cf. 'Working with Body Parts', p. 46; 'The Actor's Imagination', p. 32.

down again. Try lifting a shoulder off the floor. Moving any body part takes a great amount of exertion.

- *Now imagine that there is a tiny part of your body that is not filled with sand. A gentle change in body position causes the sand to begin trickling through your body. It gradually moves into the empty body part, leaving a gap elsewhere. As the sand slowly shifts, the Weight in the body also shifts and movement occurs in response.*

- *Take the time to feel the sand moving inside you. Imagine the sand pouring from place to place, so that once you start moving and the weight of the sand is shifting you can't stop. Include the peripheral body and extremities, as well as the core body.*

- *Let the shifts in your body move you through the space as the sand keeps moving around the body.* It may help you to recall some of the ways of moving Sequentially that you discovered earlier.[9]

- *Begin to explore changes in level, still working with the constant sensation that the sand is weighting you back down towards the floor. Play with movements which take you from lying to sitting to standing.*

- *Keep this same sensation of Heavy Weight in your body as you stand and walk around the room. Discover how to maintain the experience in your body whilst hiding it a little, so that you can walk in such a way as to fit into society – so that you are within the limits of what we perceive as socially 'normal'.*

Discovering Strong

Strength is expressed both as a form of resistance and a response to resistance. If we want to resist force, we engage our muscles to employ Strength (e.g. if someone is pushing us and we do not want to be moved). Likewise, we employ Strength if something is resisting us (e.g. if we want someone to move but they are resisting being pushed).

We also employ Strength to create or overcome resistance within our own body. This occurs when we want to move part of our body but need Strength to move its mass against gravity (e.g. lifting the leg or arm). We also create internal resistance – Counter-tension – through patterns of muscular engagement that generate oppositional forces within our body.[10]

In this exploration, you use the mass of an external object to provide resistance. When you work with real resistance, your body naturally responds with the force of Strong Weight. This allows you to identify the sensation of moving with Strength, which you will then be able to access whether or not you have the stimulus of external resistance. It is possible to use the exertion of muscular force to experience Strong Weight even in the peripheries where the body has less mass. When we push against an external object, the

---

[9] Cf. 'Sequential and Simultaneous', p. 43.
[10] Cf. 'Counter-tension', p. 40.

muscles of the body engage in such a way as to produce an experience of Strong Weight all the way through the arm to the fingertips.[11]

- *Find a large object that you can push across a room.* It should be something which is quite heavy but which you are more than able to slide across the floor, and will not change or collapse if pressure is applied to it (eg. a partly-filled box, or a suitcase on its side).

- *Find the most efficient way of pushing your object into a slide. How can you move it across the room in one pathway of ongoing travel without stopping and starting?*

- *Locate the exact places on the object where you need to apply your Strength. This will keep you from straining yourself. How can you use the weight (mass) of your body to help you exert the necessary force? Notice where exactly in your body you experience the sensation of force and muscular engagement.* This is unlikely to be at the point of contact with the object.

- *Allow your breath to travel throughout your body and support the exertion of this action. To begin with, access the Strong Weight of pushing on a continuous exhalation which naturally engages the muscular support of your core.*

- *Experiment with different ways of moving your object. Your first instinct was probably to bend down and push, using your hands: what happens if you use other parts of your body to push it through the space? Which parts of your body allow you to exert Strong Weight most efficiently? How does the experience of Strong Weight vary, depending on which surface/part of the body you are using to push?*

- *Notice that the floor is also there for you as a surface to resist. Pushing against the floor can help you move your object. Notice how many different points of contact you have for resistance against these two surfaces (the floor and your object).*

- *Now experiment with pulling your object through the space instead. Notice how the direction you are travelling in is different, but otherwise the physical experience of employing Strong Weight to carry out the action is the same.*

- *Find one particular way of pushing or pulling your object and then try the action without your object.* The experience of resistance becomes internalized in your own body through muscular Counter-tension, so that you experience Strong Weight even though you are no longer actually pushing/pulling an external burden.

- *Keep this same sensation of Strong Weight in your body as you stand and walk around the room. Discover how to maintain the experience in your body whilst hiding it a little, so that you can walk in such a way as to fit into society – so that you are within the limits of what we perceive as socially 'normal'.*

---

[11] Laban uses the familiar act of swimming to illustrate this experience: 'the movements of the crawl-stroke are essentially peripheral, reaching out to the periphery of the Kinesphere with the muscular force exerted from the extremities' (Laban, *Choreutics*, p. 44). Although the fingers and the hands have less mass than the core body, as they pull through the resistance of the water they nonetheless express Strong Weight.

Comparing Light and Heavy

Within our body we have a natural cycle of Light and Strong/Heavy Weight: as the breath enters the body we can feel the inhalation as Lightness and, as it leaves, we can feel Heaviness – or Strength if the breath is supported out of the body on an active exhalation.

Heavy Weight has a natural Affinity to moving downwards, and Light Weight has a natural Affinity to moving upwards.[12] Yet it is possible to move downwards with Light Weight and upwards with Strong/Heavy Weight. These explorations allow you to play with Light and Strong/Heavy Weight in relationship to both breath and changes of level upwards and downwards.

- *Stand and lean against the wall. Carefully, allow yourself to slide down the wall until you arrive in a heap on the floor. Use the wall to support your weight so that you can safely change level both slowly and quickly. You can allow your feet to slide a little.*

- *Return to standing. Once more lean against the wall and allow yourself to slide down it, but this time with Heavy Weight. Allow yourself to be complicit with gravity; to give in to it. Notice the sensation the movement provokes: it may involve feelings of sinking, exhaustion, submission, defeat, surrender, etc. Try sliding down the wall on an exhalation and see if you can deepen your experience of Heavy Weight.*

- *Return to standing. Repeat the same action of sliding down the wall but this time with Light Weight. Try sliding down the wall on an inhalation and see if you can deepen your experience of Light Weight.*

- *It is less common to move downwards with Light Weight than with Heavy Weight, so take some time to explore this action: allow the wall to help you fight gravity by supporting your weight as you move downwards, and imagine that you are going up as you descend. Experiment with distributing yourself across more of the wall, with your arms softly extended. Imagine you are leaving a memory of yourself behind.*

Comparing Light and Strong

- *Begin standing. Allow the weight of the head to drop forwards gently. Slowly roll down through the spine.* Each vertebra in turn peels away from the vertical as the head moves downwards towards the floor.

- *As you roll down, keep your weight forward on your feet and allow your knees to bend gently as your body folds the way it wants to (rather than keeping the legs straight and swinging your weight back onto the heels).* Be careful not to let the knees fall inward towards each other – keep them over the toes of the parallel feet. The chest ends folded over onto the thighs. There is no sense during this that you are stretching the muscles of the legs.

---

[12] For more information on Affinity, see 'Use of Affinity', p. 265.

- *At the bottom of the roll-down, experience an acceptance of gravity: Heavy Weight.*

- *Once you have reached the bottom, reverse the action to roll back up through the spine.* Starting from the bottom, each vertebra in turn stacks back up on top of one another to return the spine to the vertical. Once the pelvis has returned to a vertical alignment you can straighten the legs, but make sure the knees are soft up to this point.

- *As you roll back up through the spine, notice how you are using muscular engagement (force) to defy gravity and return to standing.*

- *Repeat the roll-down. This time, as you return to standing, increase the amount of muscular engagement so you are actively expressing Strong Weight as you uncurl the spine. It may help to imagine you are rolling up through a substance thicker than air, which is providing external resistance.*

- *Repeat the roll-down again. This time allow the engagement of your muscles to give you a sense of weightlessness, so that you express Light Weight as you uncurl the spine to return to standing.*

Weight and the Actor: Weight as Metaphor

Heaviness as Gravitas

Many of our commonly used metaphors associate Heavy Weight with responsibility ('work was weighing me down') and Light Weight with freedom from responsibility ('my spirits lightened as I left the building'). This is because the burden of responsibility registers as a real physical experience – we speak of 'carrying' responsibility as if it were a weighty, material object. Each moment of increased responsibility, such as when a child takes over the responsibility of brushing their own teeth, is a tiny incremental shift to a weightier presence on the planet.

Over many years, people who have a lot of responsibility develop a habit of expressing Heavy Weight, a trait which we refer to as 'gravitas'. Although this is mainly associated with age, it can also be the result of sorrow: someone who is 'heavy-hearted' with grief often has an unexpected gravitas for their age.

This exploration uses material objects to manifest the Heavy Weight of responsibilities, and so helps the actor find an altered physicality expressing Heaviness. The potential to express gravitas is vital for the actor. Imagine you are playing a Queen who rules a country. The Weight of the country needs to be visible upon you.[13] The actor in any role

---

[13] You may notice in this exploration how objects carried/draped on the head/around the shoulders begin to make someone look like a person of high-status such as the Pope or the King. We use weighty adornments such as a crown or a sceptre to show responsibility (and therefore power). Similarly, in everyday life people may choose to wear a big statement coat, or a large signet ring. The Heavy Weight of the object becomes a visual metaphor for gravitas. A costume which includes, for example, a heavy cloak or coat can serve as a reminder of the responsibilities your character is carrying and help you to express Heavy Weight in much the same way as this exploration.

also needs the gravitas to command the attention of a large auditorium and confidently hold the gaze of hundreds of audience members.

- This is an exploration for two or more actors. It uses small objects that are to hand in the room (e.g. a book, water-bottle, scarf, bag). Each object represents something that is seen as a burden in life.

- Partner A: *Give the objects to your partner one by one, gradually filling their arms and draping things over them until they cannot keep hold of anything else. As you give each item to them, say to them what it represents. Objects can represent responsibilities such as:*
  - *paying bills*
  - *being on time*
  - *your relationship with your family*
  - *an unfulfilling job*
  - *winning the lottery*
  - *getting dressed every day*
  - *being a parent*
     etc.

  These burdens can include both positive and negative things. Some might be responsibilities that are experienced as good but which are nonetheless a Weight we have taken on. They may also be large or small; sometimes it is the smallest responsibilities which come to feel the heaviest (e.g. selecting our clothes every day, choosing and preparing food, etc.).

- Partner B: *Feel the Weight of the burdens being loaded upon you. You have to accept these burdens: if you need to, you can reposition them to make them fit you. Absorb the sensation of Heaviness into your body. Live with them as part of you.*

- Partner A: *Once your partner has had a few moments to embody the sensation of Heaviness, remove all the objects one by one.*

- Partner B: *Retain the sensation of Heaviness in your body as the burdens are removed. Track through the responsibilities again in your mind and know that you are still carrying them. Your body is living the story of responsibility. The difference is not just psychological: it's an identifiable physical change.*

- Partner B: *Take a walk in the room. Have you retained the sensation of Heaviness in your body? How has it shifted your physical experience?* Remember: many people choose the burdens they carry in life. So don't confuse burdens with inevitable doom and gloom – you may enjoy the sense of identity and responsibility that they give you.

Lightness as Levity

Just as Heaviness can be an expression of gravitas, so Lightness can be an expression of its opposite: 'levity'. This exploration allows you to explore Lightness as freedom from responsibility. The sensation of Lightness may remind you of being a child, when your body had not yet experienced the Heavy Weight that comes with the burden of responsibility. The description of someone who is a 'free-spirit' also has a weightlessness about it. Like gravitas, levity can be experienced as something positive or negative. Some people would not welcome freedom from responsibility. They feel their responsibilities as a desired tether which defines their identity.

- *Repeat the exploration outlined above. However, as the burdens are removed, allow the Heavy Weight your body took on to disappear so that you feel Lighter and Lighter. Track through the burdens in your thoughts and reverse them as they are lifted away (e.g. 'the bills have been paid'; 'my child is well'; 'I no longer have to do a job'). Use your breath to help you: release each burden with an exhalation.*

- *Feel the weightlessness of release – having your burdens removed has left you feeling Lighter than you were before.*

- *Take a walk in the room, and feel how the sensation of Lightness in your body has shifted your physical experience.* Remember: freedom from responsibility may feel like either a positive or negative experience.

Dying is the ultimate release from all responsibility, even the responsibility of our own identity. We may tend to think of dying as becoming 'dead weight' (i.e. falling to the ground with Heavy Weight as our muscles no longer hold up our matter). Yet it is also possible to experience this action with Lightness. It would then be a metaphorical action in which loss of life signals release from the Weight of the world.

- *Explore moving to the floor ('dying') with Light Weight: take a full in-breath with your arms rising upwards as you descend to the floor with Lightness.*

TIME

Sudden and Sustained

The Motion Factor **Time** can be divided into the two Elements **Sudden** and **Sustained**. The expression of Time as a Motion Factor encompasses more subjective experiences of speed and tempo. When exploring the two contrasting Elements, it may be helpful to think about them as expressing either 'a prolonging or shortening attitude towards time'[14] or having 'the presence or absence of rapidity'.[15]

Sudden and Sustained describe Time as a quality, rather than the 'reality' of time. So Sudden and Sustain do not necessarily equate to 'fast' and 'slow'. A racing car, an ocean

---

[14] Laban, *The Mastery of Movement*, p. 69.
[15] Laban and Lawrence, *Effort*, p. 63.

liner and a plane are all fast-moving objects which are Sustained in their movement. They remain on one continuous, Sustained action in order to move through Space. Compared with these forms of transport, a trotting horse or a marching soldier are slow-moving but are both Sudden in their movement. They do many actions to meet the task of moving through Space. It is important for the actor to embody the quality of Time not the objective reality. If you were asked to become a plane, the temptation would be to attempt to recreate the reality of a plane's movement and move very fast. This would result in Sudden movements of your legs as you ran. In fact, to embody a plane successfully, it is more important for the actor to express Sustained movement than it is for them to move 'fast'.

Video Resource

Time: Sudden and Sustained
https://vimeo.com/251494339

Discovering Sudden

It may help to think of Sudden movement as using the breaking up of Time. Sudden expresses itself in short movements, giving a feeling of interruption. It is as if you are doing the beginning and end of a movement with no middle. You reach the end of a movement almost as soon as it began. Imagine an idea popping into your head which you immediately arrest and dismiss, or your hand flinching away from something hot.

For Sudden, it can be helpful to work with the idea that you are breaking each action up into many different actions (i.e. that one action can comprise many different actions, if you identify all its constituent parts).[16] An observer is engaged by Sudden because it never stays the same and constantly offers something new.

- *Create a simple sequence of Sudden movements (e.g. sitting down, folding your arms, looking from side to side).*
- *Repeat the sequence several times.*
- *Make sure you're not making immediate unconscious choices about the other Motion Factors: Sudden can be Light or Strong/Heavy, Direct or Indirect.*
- *Use your breath to help you: feel the starts and stops of your breath as each new inhalation and exhalation occurs.*
- *Be precise with yourself. Don't let any Sustain into the movement. Keep the stakes very high: if it helps, imagine that the world will end if any action carries on for too long.*

---

[16] This could be compared to stop-motion animation (or a classic 'flick-book') in which an object is photographed many times and moved by small amounts between each photograph. When the photographs are run together it looks like one movement, but each action has in fact been broken down into a series of much smaller actions.

- *Identify any moments where the action is no longer Sudden. This is most noticeable if there is an identifiable 'middle' to the action, or a 'revving up' or 'tailing off' rather than a sharp beginning and end.*

- *Keep experimenting until you have been able to do a few truly Sudden movements in a row.* Once you can express Sudden, even for a short duration, you will have an understanding of it in your body. Gradually, you will be able to maintain it over longer and longer periods.

- *You have explored embodying Sudden during a sequence of actions. Now experiment with breaking one action down into many actions through use of Sudden.* This could be one of the actions from your sequence (eg. sitting down).

Discovering Sustained

Sustained movement is continuous and consistent. It may help to think of Sustained Time as offering a quality of endlessness: it is as if you are doing the middle of a movement, with no beginning and no end.

For Sustain, it is helpful to work with the idea that many actions become one continuous, seamless action. So, the present-tense experience of Sustain is of one move that carries on at the same speed forever. When someone uses circular breathing to play an instrument their breath still has an inhalation and an exhalation, but one is indistinguishable from the other. The actions of breathing become one continuously Sustained cycle. Likewise, when snow gently falls the individual action of each snowflake becomes subsumed into the overall Sustained action of blanketing snowfall.

Sustain can be set at any pace, but once you begin the movement it must remain at the chosen pace without speeding up or slowing down. Imagine watching a rocket. As your gaze tracks the rocket, you will be expressing Sustain at a fast pace. Likewise, a tornado moves at a fast pace but is nonetheless Sustained. Whether Sustained is at a fast or slow pace, an observer is engaged by it because it is one ongoing movement: they become hooked and feel compelled to stay with it. The fact that it is one never-ending, unfolding move means it is constantly leading to somewhere anticipated but as yet unknown.

- *Trace a Sustained pathway with your arm.*

- *Start by lifting the arm upwards. The arm can then continue out to the side, or in any direction you choose. Keep the movement very simple.* Remember: once you've set off you are committed, so you need to be able to maintain the pace at which you've started. To begin with, you are likely to find that you will have to move very slowly to maintain the Sustain.

- *Make sure you're not making immediate, unconscious choices about the other Motion Factors: Sustained can be Light or Strong/Heavy, Direct or Indirect.*

- *Use your breath to help you: imagine it as a wave that consistently ebbs and flows but never stops.*

- *Be precise with yourself. Do not let any Sudden into the movement. Keep the stakes very high: if it helps, imagine the world will end if the movement stops.*

- *Identify any moments where the action is no longer Sustained.* This is most noticeable if there is a moment of impulse, indicating the start of a new movement, or a new decision.

- *Keep experimenting until you have been able to maintain the Sustain for a short while.* Once you can maintain Sustained for ten seconds or so, you will have an understanding of it in your body. Gradually, you will be able to maintain it over longer and longer periods.

- *You have explored embodying Sustain during one action. Now experiment with converting a series of actions into one action through use of Sustain.* Choose simple actions like sitting, lying down, or Gestures of the limbs. Challenge yourself to keep the movement going: once you have set off, do not stop or change the speed of the movement. If you feel yourself lose the Sustain, go back to the point you last had it and reconnect.

Comparing Sudden and Sustain

Sudden relates to the finite where Time is broken into shorter moments; Sustain relates to the infinite where Time is without end. Our fundamental experience of existing in Time is paradoxical, as we experience both the finite and the infinite at the same time: we know our life will end (finite), but also that our molecules will carry on existing and transform to something else (infinite). It is vital for the actor to be able to embody this paradox. They must know what it is to be in the present moment within an ongoing journey, and also what is offered by the beginnings and ends of actions.

- *Look at a real horizon.* The further away it is, the easier this exploration will be. You are aiming to achieve a constant gaze.

- *Using Sustained movement, begin to scan the horizon by moving your head without moving your eyes.*

- *Now try scanning the horizon by moving your eyes without moving your head.*

- *Notice what you adjust to achieve a Sustained gaze in each very different movement.*

- *Try scanning a horizon that is slightly nearer, again experimenting with the two versions (moving just the head/just the eyes).*

- *Return to looking at the further horizon. Choose four points on the horizon. Look Suddenly to each one in turn by moving your head without moving your eyes. You are aiming to shift your gaze from point to point.*

- *Now try looking to each one in turn by moving your eyes without moving your head.*

- *Notice what you adjust to achieve Sudden looks in each very different movement.*
- *Try shifting your gaze from point to point on a horizon that is slightly nearer, again experimenting with the two versions (moving just the head/just the eyes).*

Time and the Actor: Time vs. Clock-time

Clock-time is the objective, measurable progression of Time.[17] However, its expression can vary. A second hand on a clock can move Suddenly, 'ticking' from one position to the next. Alternatively, it can move in a Sustained way, sweeping gradually around the clock face. The length of Time in which the hand moves around the clock-face is fixed (one minute), but the quality of its movement is different.

A need to be faster or slower in clock-time does not mean that you need to change the quality of expression (Sudden or Sustained). A director may need you to complete a Sustained action within a certain time-period (clock-time). It is possible to do the action maintaining the same quality of Sustained Time: you maintain the story of lack of rapidity, whilst cutting down the duration of the action in 'real' time.

- *Choose a simple sequence of movements (e.g. sitting down, turning the head from side to side, lifting the arm).*
- *Do your chosen sequence using Sustained movement.*
- *Now, repeat the movement still using Sustained movement, but halve its duration in clock-time (so if, for example, it took thirty seconds, now aim to carry it out in fifteen seconds).* Remember: from the very first moment Sustain carries on indefinitely, without a noticeable change in speed. So to do the movement in less clock-time, you will need to set off at a slightly faster pace that you then Sustain.
- *Do your chosen sequence using Sudden movements.*
- *Now, repeat the series of movements still using Sudden movements but double its duration in clock-time (so if, for example, it took ten seconds, now aim to carry it out over twenty seconds).*

The Difference between Sustained and Slow Motion

Movement that is Sustained may appear as if it is in slow motion. This is not the case. Slow motion is a stylistic effect in which a pre-determined movement or sequence of movements is slowed down considerably to last over a much longer period of clock-time than it initially took. The movement has an unnaturally elongated duration and is no

---

[17] For further explanation of clock-time, see 'What is Time?', p. 54.

longer occurring in 'real-time'. It appears other-worldly because each part of the movement is prolonged in clock-time and so loses its original dynamic and rhythmic qualities.[18] Even Sudden actions will appear Sustained in slow motion. The actions of the actor no longer retain their quality and instead meaning is communicated via the overall theatrical/filmic device. On close examination, movement that has been altered through the device of slow motion will always be distinguishable from Sustained movement.

SPACE

Direct and Indirect

The Motion Factor **Space** can be divided into the two Elements **Direct** and **Indirect**. When exploring these two contrasting Elements, it may be helpful to think about them as expressing either 'a pliant or lineal attitude towards Space'[19] or expressing either 'straightness' or 'roundaboutness'.[20]

It is extraordinary to think that all the spatial complexity in our movement can be broken down into these two simple Elements. Yet if you bring your attention to your own movement now, you can quickly identify how each part of every action is made up of either straight lines or curves.

The word 'Indirect' might lead you to think that it is simply the negative of Direct and so a less important Element.[21] Work against this assumption: the two ends of the continuum are equal.

Video Resource

Space: Direct and Indirect
https://vimeo.com/251494730

Discovering Direct
Direct pathways are immediately identifiable through their linear form. When someone is using Direct pathways, what is visible are straight lines and corners as they cut through the space. Direct knows where it is going and uses the shortest route from A to

---

[18] The same is true of a stylistic 'fast-forward' effect in which a pre-determined movement or sequence of movements is sped up considerably to last over a much shorter period of clock-time than it initially took.
[19] Laban, *The Mastery of Movement*, p. 69.
[20] Laban, *Choreutics*, p. 55.
[21] For more detail, see 'Use of Indirect', p. 265.

B on any given journey. Direct pathways occur in any direction in Space, including up, down, forwards and backwards.

- *Take some time to move freely in the space, frequently changing direction and level.*
- *Begin to think of yourself as 'funnelling' through Space so that all your movements and pathways become linear as you head through your work-space. This includes your gaze.*
- *Eradicate any curvy movements. Make sure each straight line of your movement has a known endpoint: your pathways go from A to B using the shortest possible route. Direct your attention so that it is pinpointed to your destination.*
- *Play with the corners in your movement when you switch from one pathway to another.*
- *Play with different ways of folding down to the floor and back up again.*
- *Play with crawling.* It may help you to refer back to your exploration of Simultaneous movement.[22]
- *Make sure you're not making immediate unconscious choices about the other Motion Factors: Direct can be either Light or Strong/Heavy, Sudden or Sustained.*

Discovering Indirect

Indirect pathways are immediately identifiable by their circular form. When someone is moving using Indirect pathways, what is visible are curves and spirals as they meander through the space. Indirect has no given destination but can still travel through Space, moving up, down, forwards and backwards.

- *Take some time to move freely in the space, frequently changing direction and level.*
- *Begin to think of yourself as 'spiralling' through Space so that all your movements become curvy and circular as you wind through your work-space. Shift your gaze so that your attention is not on any one thing, but you take in everything at once.*
- *Eradicate any straight movements. Make sure your winding pathways do not have a known endpoint. Let your attention wander in the space.*
- *Play with twisting and turning.*
- *Play with different ways of corkscrewing down to the floor and back up again.*
- *Play with rolling.* It may help you to refer back to your exploration of Sequential movement.[23]
- *Make sure you're not making immediate, unconscious choices about the other Motion Factors: Indirect can be either Light or Strong/Heavy, Sudden or Sustained.*

---

[22] Cf. 'Sequential and Simultaneous', p. 43.
[23] Cf. 'Sequential and Simultaneous', p. 43.

Comparing Direct and Indirect

Direct and Indirect use of Space interact in the world all the time. Be careful not to make a value judgement that perceives one as being 'better' or more efficient than the other. They give opposing ways of being in the world, but both are of equal status and use depending on the context.

The built environment often uses Direct forms, which perhaps indicates that Direct movement is more successful or efficient. Yet organic forms are often Indirect (we ourselves have curved bodies and live on a round planet). When a walrus is attacked by a polar bear heading towards it in a Direct line, it evades the Direct blows of the bear by using Indirect rolling motions, and so escapes death.

A combination of Direct and Indirect often provides the greatest efficiency: a punch travels in a Direct line, but has an Indirect twist in the arm as the fist reaches its target. Direct and Indirect are so closely related that one is rarely found without at least the potential for the other.

- *Move through the space in Direct pathways, changing direction cleanly. Travel in straight lines with hard corners. Keep your energy quietly present as you move.*

- *Maintaining the same energy, switch to Indirect pathways: take away the straight lines and hard corners, and make all your pathways curved.*

- *Keep switching between Direct and Indirect movement. Don't blend one into the other: make sure that when you switch you do so instantly.* There should be a clear contrast and an obvious moment of changeover.

- *Notice the difference between the two types of pathway. How do they feel different in your body? Does one type of pathway feel like a release from the other?* You may notice that in Direct you feel more focused with pinpointed attention, whereas in Indirect you have a wider field of attention and expanded peripheral vision.

- *Notice how each type of pathway affects your behaviour.* When you encounter someone or something in your way, if you are moving in Direct you have to stop and make a plan about a changed destination. Moving in Indirect you do not have a plan, so you can just deal with the encounter as it happens.

Space and the Actor: Personal and General Space

Broadly speaking, there are two identifiable areas of Space: Personal Space (as defined by the Kinesphere) and General Space (everything outside your Kinesphere).[24] In these explorations, it is easiest to think of your movements in General Space being your pathways through the room, and your movements in Personal Space being the

---

[24] Cf. 'Kinesphere', p. 34.

other movements of your body, including Gestures. Movements in both Personal and General Space can be either Direct or Indirect. You may be expressing the same Element in both Personal and General Space, or they may differ. So the movement of your body may mirror the Direct or Indirect nature of your pathways, or it may form a counterpoint.

Movement in General Space may be chosen or imposed. The architecture of a city with straight, empty streets between square buildings may force you to move in Direct pathways; or it may be that crowds of people on the streets force you to move in Indirect pathways as you wind your way through and around them.

For the actor, Personal Space expresses the world of the character (their thoughts, feelings, intentions, actions, etc.), while General Space expresses the world of the play (the environment around you, expectations, influences and obligations, etc.). How your use of Personal Space complements or conflicts with your use of General Space tells us something about the character's relationship with the world around them.

- *As in the previous exploration: take some time to move freely in the space, frequently changing direction and level.*
- *Explore being Indirect in both Personal and General Space: make both the movements of your body and your pathways through Space Indirect (curved).*
- *Explore being Direct in both Personal and General Space: make both the movements of your body and your pathways through Space Direct (straight).*
- *Explore being Direct in Personal Space and Indirect in General Space: make the movements of your body Direct (straight) and your pathways through Space Indirect (curved).*
- *Explore being Indirect in Personal Space and Direct in General Space: make the movements of your body Indirect (curved) and your pathways through Space Direct (straight).*

DISCOVERING THE EIGHT BASIC EFFORTS

The three Motion Factors **Weight** (W), **Time** (T), and **Space** (S) combine in different ways to express eight specific qualities of movement: **The Efforts**.[25] The Efforts are both basic actions in and of themselves, and movement qualities that inform how we do all other actions. Each Effort is built using one Element of the three Motion Factors (WTS).

---

[25] The term 'The Efforts' is used here to refer to the eight Efforts of Action Drive (as it does throughout the book). For more information, see 'What are Laban's Efforts?' p.8

Building the Efforts

This short exploration allows you to discover the name and composition of each individual Effort for yourself by working through the body, rather than trying to understand them intellectually.

Laban did not invent the Efforts: he identified and named the movement qualities that already existed in the world. His onomatopoeic names for the Efforts resonate with the movement qualities they describe. It is right that the actor should explore the instinctive connection between each movement quality and its name, and almost begin to believe they discovered and named each one for themselves. The Efforts already exist within the movement vocabulary of each person, so there is inevitably a deep sense of recognition and shared ownership. The eight Efforts will start to emerge as you explore combining different Elements of Weight, Time, and Space (WTS).

- *Choose a Weight Element: Light or Strong/Heavy.*
- *Choose a Time Element: Sudden or Sustained.*
- *Choose a Space Element: Direct or Indirect.*
- *Briefly play with moving in your work-space, changing direction and level. Embody each of your three chosen Elements. Experience the sensation of the movement in your body.*
- *Find the word that seems to describe this quality of moving: what would you name this movement?*
- *Check the list below. Did you also come up with any of these words which Laban uses in relation to each Effort?*[26]
  - *strew, stir, stroke*
  - *pat, tap, shake*
  - *pull, pluck, stretch*
  - *shove, punch, poke*
  - *crush, cut, squeeze*
  - *flip, flap, jerk*
  - *beat, throw, whip*
  - *smooth, smear, smudge*
- *Now, check Table 1 below to find out what name Laban gives this movement quality.*
- *Return to moving in the space. Again, embody each of your three chosen Elements but now with an awareness of Laban's name for this Effort. How does this alter, clarify or inform the movement?*
- *Choose a different combination of three Elements and repeat the same steps.*
- *Keep exploring until you have briefly experienced each of the eight Efforts. Keep your explorations short, playful and liberated.*

---

[26] Laban called these 'Derivatives'. For more information, see 'Derivatives', p. 269.

The Efforts

Table 1 outlines how the Elements combine to create the eight Efforts: **Floating**, **Dabbing**, **Wringing**, **Thrusting**, **Pressing**, **Flicking**, **Slashing**, and **Gliding**.[27] To recall the Elements that make up each Effort, you need only remember that each Effort is made up of Weight, Time, and Space (WTS). The name of the Effort will then help you work out whether it is Light or Strong/Heavy; Sudden or Sustained; Direct or Indirect.

Table 1: The Eight Efforts

	WEIGHT	TIME	SPACE
FLOATING	Light	Sustained	Indirect
DABBING	Light	Sudden	Direct
WRINGING	Strong/Heavy	Sustained	Indirect
THRUSTING	Strong/Heavy	Sudden	Direct
PRESSING	Strong/Heavy	Sustained	Direct
FLICKING	Light	Sudden	Indirect
SLASHING	Strong/Heavy	Sudden	Indirect
GLIDING	Light	Sustained	Direct

The Efforts can be listed in any order – there is no hierarchy. They are different ways of existing in the world but no one Effort is more expressive than another. It will be difficult to keep believing this when you immediately encounter compelling moments in some and not others. The experience of this is persuasive. However, rather than favouring the Effort that instantly feels visceral and eloquent, trust that they are equal. The next section (Part C) offers a process through which you develop a deep and personal connection to all the Efforts by exploring each one in turn. As their full potential is revealed, you will find that each Effort is just as exciting as any other. Each has its own unique power.

---

[27] Each of these Efforts is expressed with Flow, which might be either Free or Bound. The actor does not make conscious choices about the expression of Flow. It fluctuates as part of an instinctive response dependent on the level of control the movement requires at any given point. For more on Flow, see 'The Role of Flow', p. 257.

PART C
DISCOVERING THE EFFORTS

CHAPTER 5
ABOUT THE DISCOVERY PROCESS

Part C outlines a practical process which is the core part of learning the Efforts for use as an actor. It is called the **Discovery Process** (or sometimes simply referred to in shorthand as 'the Process'). You work through the same process eight times, focusing on one Effort each time. This allows you to encounter each of the eight Efforts individually and so discover every Effort in depth. Ultimately, it will give you ownership over the Efforts by embedding a deep understanding of each one in both your mind and body.

It is referred to as a process because it follows a progression of necessary stages. These take you from discovering each Effort in the whole body to the first steps in applying the Efforts to character development. Once you have worked all the way through the Discovery Process with each of the eight Efforts, you will be ready to apply them in all sorts of acting contexts.

FOLLOWING THE DISCOVERY PROCESS

Reading through Part C will give you some idea of the potential of each individual Effort. However, to discover it in full you will need to take the time to do some practical sessions.

- **Work through Chapter 6(a)**, which guides you through the Discovery Process for the first Effort you will discover: Floating.

- **Follow the italicized guidelines** to do the practical explorations.

- Once you have discovered Floating, **repeat the Process for each different Effort** in turn. To do this, work through Chapter 6(a) again. Wherever there is a number [**X**], turn to the numbered information in Chapter 6(b) in the section that is specific to the Effort you are currently exploring.

You can work on the Efforts in any order. However, the recommended order of study is: Session 1: *Floating* | Session 2: *Dabbing* | Session 3: *Wringing* | Session 4: *Thrusting* | Session 5: *Pressing* | Session 6: *Flicking* | Session 7: *Slashing* | Session 8: *Gliding*.[1]

---

[1] This is because the Efforts are related to each other, so the order in which you chose to study them has a significant effect. The order recommended here allows you to build your skills in an efficient progression. In this order, you can draw on the bank of skills you have already developed with previous Efforts as you go back through the Discovery Process to embody each new Effort in turn.

Plan your practical sessions in the knowledge that for each you will need a workspace in which you have enough room to move freely (a studio, or a living room with the furniture pushed back) and, ideally, time to undertake a whole session.[2]

DISCOVERY PROCESS OVERVIEW

For a quick overview of the Discovery Process, you can refer to *Table 2*. To help you plan your sessions, this table also contains some guidelines as to the approximate amount of time you should allocate to each stage.

The length of your explorations will depend on the Effort (Slashing explorations will, for example, need to be shorter than those for Floating). Where the guidelines indicate for you to 're-enter your exploration' or state 'for a short while', this implies an exploration of less than five minutes.

Table 2: Discovery Process Overview

A) PREPARATION *(30 mins)*	D) THE EFFORT AS CODE *(25 mins)*
Targeted Warm-Up	Single-Celled Amoeba (Improvisation)
Body Reference	E) A JOURNEY (GUIDED IMPROVISATION) *(45 mins)*
Initial Experience	Phase 1: Single-Celled Amoeba
Using Imagery	Phase 2: Adding Human Condition
Using Music	Phase 3: Effort Archetype
B) MEETING THE EFFORT *(20 mins)*	Phase 4: Internalised
Sampling the Effort	Phase 5: Physical Action
Capturing your Immediate Response	Follow Up
Identifying the Effort Default	F) EFFORTS IN THE WORLD *(ongoing)*
Comparing the Effort	Everyday Existence
Locating Control	Point of View
Identifying Your Affinity	
Noticing Your Associations	
C) MAPPING THE EFFORT *(60 mins)*	
Working Technically	
Adding Sound	
Targeted Exploration: Working with an Agenda	
Meeting Challenges	
Solving Common Conundrums	
Reimagining the World as Playground	
Using the Walls and Floor	
Working with Obstacles	

---

[2] When following this Process in a conservatoire setting, actors are gifted the opportunity of exploring one Effort for a session of three hours working through all the stages of the Discovery Process from start to finish. They repeat this for each Effort in turn, with a rest and reflective period between sessions. So, in total, this equates to eight full practical sessions of three hours each (either undertaking one or two Efforts a day; or, in a more spacious time-frame, per week). Not everyone has the time to dedicate to working in this way. It is fine to break down the Process and plan your practical sessions according to the time you have available.

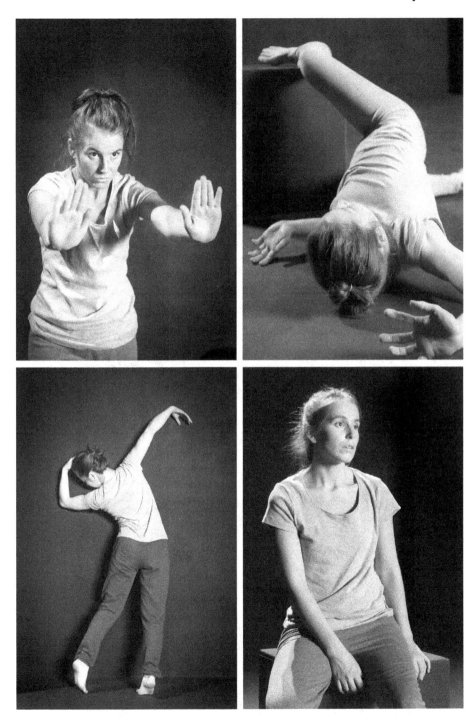

Figure 5.1 Clockwise from top left: The Default (*Pressing*) | Single-celled Amoeba (*Wringing*) | Internalized (*Floating*) | The World as Playground (*Floating*).

Figure 5.2 Top to bottom: Adding Human Condition (*Floating*) | Responsive Physical Action (*Slashing*) | Passive Physical Action (*Floating*).

BASIC PHILOSOPHIES

Some **Basic Philosophies** provide overall guidance on how to approach your practical work. It is worth keeping them at the forefront of your mind. They will become easier to understand as you progress through a series of encounters with each individual Effort. If they seem abstract at first, return to them later once you have begun your movement explorations. You will gradually become increasingly attuned to what they mean in practice. You will then be able to use them to demand more of yourself when undertaking the practical explorations.

When you begin the Process for a new Effort, it can be useful to re-visit the Basic Philosophies. Once they have become familiar to you, just remind yourself of the key italicized statements. If you are working with a Buddy, you can read the key statements aloud, so that there is a vivid reminder of them in the room as you begin your session.

//Trust the immediate inspiration of Laban's chosen words
The words Laban uses to describe each Effort and its Elements (WTS) can be an anchor to keep you connected to what you are doing. Remind yourself of the words which relate to your current movement exploration. Do not be afraid to draw on your instinctive and immediate responses to them, as well as your ongoing insight as you learn more.

//Don't 'do' the Effort, become the Effort
You may have previously encountered the Efforts in such a way that you feel you can 'use' or 'do' them. The aim of this process is to *become* the Effort. By learning how to embody the Efforts fully, you discover how they can enable you to express completely different ways of being – to transform. If you can only 'use' the Effort, then you are always present as the actor and the work will show. Aim to stop (over)doing and start being; seek for the body to be fully present and engaged in action. Let the Effort drive you.

//Embrace the struggle to be precise
The Efforts should always maintain their distinct forms with the detailed clarity of their specific Elements (WTS) intact. If they become blended, generalized states, they lose their power. Difference between things is exciting; contrast is dramatic. The Efforts are composed from the Motion Factors being embodied at the furthermost points on their continuum. Each Element is an identifiable extreme. So, for example, Sudden is as Sudden as the body can possibly be and Sustained is its total opposite. There is no room for middle ground. This precision is a significant challenge, particularly at first. Yet acting is an art that portrays the conflicts inherent in being alive. So the struggle for precision within each Effort is a useful part of the expressive story. Visible moments of struggle as the actor lives through conflict should be embraced as a vital part of the work itself.

//Work without self-consciousness
In living things, the Efforts usually work in dialogue with one another, interacting and co-existing to create a recognizable harmony of expression. A solo Effort reads as one

part of the usual range of human expression becoming excessive and out of balance, so it may appear disconcerting or strange. We tend to relate it to experiences of someone's mental or physical equilibrium being affected through illness or substance abuse. When you are exploring the Efforts, don't be afraid of appearing to be something or someone 'mad'. An ability to work without inhibition is vital for the actor. The actor recognizes in themselves, and in the characters they play, the possibility for overwhelming and extreme emotion. This is normally kept hidden underneath a social veneer of 'acceptable' behaviour, but we are closer to it than we think. Often, a character in a play will tend not only to display their 'everyday' Efforts, but will enter into heightened, altered or disinhibited states in response to the impact of narrative events. Embrace the sense of liberating yourself to express something that is normally kept 'boundaried' or hidden. The actor expresses the potential for extreme emotion or 'madness' that lies within us all.

//Stay with it

If you study a musical instrument, you will have experienced that it is relatively easy to get to a stage where you can play, yet incredibly difficult to progress to playing really well. This is the same with the Efforts. Laban has given us something which seems so simple that it can be misunderstood as only an easy 'tool' or 'shortcut'. Being simple is not the same as being easy. Each Effort is immediately physically available, so you can quickly get to the first stage where you feel you've got it and are enjoying the initial experience of the Effort. At this point, be careful not to de-sensitize your body, imagining you have arrived. It takes commitment to reach the next stage of experience (*being* the Effort) and then to be able to offer that experience to an audience. Yet if you stay with the work you will be rewarded.

//Notice how you are learning and progressing

It is impossible to 'mark' or half-do the Efforts: full, embodied articulation *is* the Effort. Once you begin exploring the Efforts, you may leave a session with a memory of them having been 'effortful' (as, of course, they are). In many ways, this is no different to the feeling of ambivalence or tiredness that can arise in response to the sheer amount of energy it takes to accomplish anything worth doing. If this is the case for you, it is important to get past this feeling so that it does not become a barrier. Before each session, remember that there is an ease in channelling the Efforts rather than working at them. Afterwards, notice and remember how you are being fed. Take time to reflect on what is now firmly in your knowledge bank (and therefore feels much easier and more readily accessible), rather than solely focusing on what still seems puzzling or challenging.

CHAPTER 6(a)
THE DISCOVERY PROCESS WITH FLOATING

STARTING POINTS

Identifying the Effort

You are preparing to discover a whole new Effort. Take a moment to remind yourself of the three Elements (WTS) of this Effort that you are about to explore. **[1]** *For Floating*: Floating is Light in Weight; Floating is Sustained in Time; Floating is Indirect in Space. To Float is to be Light, Sustained, Indirect.

Video Resource

There are short videos which follow actors working through the Discovery Process in each Effort. You may choose to watch the relevant video before or after your practical session, or to refer to it as you go. **[2]** *For Floating*:

Video Resource

Floating
https://vimeo.com/251496135

(A) PREPARATION

Targeted Warm-up

It is vital to start your practical process with the right **preparation**. Presence of both body and mind allows you to approach the work with ease and efficiency. A time of physical and mental preparation is also essential for preventing injury.

The term 'warm-up' describes the preparation done by an actor before beginning work. What this means is hugely variable, and the term can be misleading because a 'warm-up' should do far more than simply making sure that the actor is physically warm. A **targeted warm-up** will not only fulfil basic safety needs but also leave your body and mind in a state of full readiness for the specific tasks you are about to face, as well as allowing you to re-connect to yourself as an actor. It should be an experience which gives you confidence. No group warm-up can ever fully meet the needs of all the participating actors, so you should create a warm-up tailored to both the situation and your individual needs.

- *Do a targeted warm-up at the start of each practical session.*[1] *This should ensure you have prepared in a way that:*
  - *brings awareness to your breath*
  - *makes a range of energy available and ensures a raised heart rate (even if only for a short time)*
  - *eases your joints, releases excessive tension and awakens all your muscles through mobilization and stretching*
  - *reawakens the senses and a conscious connection to space*
  - *connects you to imagination and reminds you of your expressive range*
  - *allows you to do exercises to your own Agenda (e.g. specific strengthening or mobilization exercises to manage ongoing physical conditions or injuries).*
- *Build exercises into your warm-up that specifically prepare you for the Effort you will be exploring.* [3] ***For Floating:*** *Build exercises into your warm-up that:*
  - *mobilize individual joints*
  - *move the whole body through circular pathways*
  - *involve Sequential movements*
  - *mobilize your torso and prepare you to move off-centre.*

Ways In

The second half of your preparation helps you access relevant experiences for the Effort you are going to be exploring. These '**Ways In**' ease you towards working in the Effort itself. They give you a way of beginning to build (or re-find) the particular skills that will help you most as you enter into your encounter with the Effort.

Body Reference

A '**Body Reference**' is an instinctive movement that your body knows how to do. You will find that your body already knows how to embody the Effort perfectly through its inbuilt repertoire of movements. These can be used as a physical reference point: they will always be able to give you an immediately accessible experience of an Effort.

- *Recall the sensation in your body when the following natural action or reflex occurs.* [4] ***For Floating:*** *Recall the sensation in your body when you feel nauseous. Notice how the experience of nausea is Light, Sustained and Indirect: Floating.* Nausea is a sensation that we all have from time to time and it is a natural Float. So, you already know how to embody Floating perfectly. Once you have undergone the whole Process exploring Floating, your Float should become as beautifully Light, Sustained and Indirect as the known experience of nausea is already.

---

[1] If a thorough warm-up is something which does not feel familiar to you, then take a look at the sample warm-up available at www.labaneffortsinaction.com

Initial Experience

This exploration gives you an **initial experience** of the Effort you are discovering. Allow the existence of responses triggered by the movement: thoughts, feelings, sensations, wants, desires, difficulties or struggles. However, stay in the present tense – don't stop to react to your experience or any of your responses. Make sure the quality of the movement is exact. Keep it just to the Effort: avoid framing it in the context of all sorts of other movement.

- *Embody the following experience. Let it suggest the Elements of the Effort to you.* [5] *For Floating: Play with defocusing the eyes:*
  - *Allow your eyes to Float. Don't land your gaze on anything: you can look at things but just move over them. Put into your mind the idea of seeing everywhere and nowhere at the same time. Allow the face to Float, too, so that your expression is not fixed.*
  - *Now, Float the neck. Whilst doing this, try making a list or a plan. Notice how hard it is to think Directly or to organize your thoughts.*
  - *Gradually allow the rest of the body to join in the Float along with the eyes, head and neck.*

Using Imagery

Your actor's imagination can help you to access the sensation of each Effort. By **using imagery** and creating a particular imagined experience, you stimulate your body to respond naturally in the Effort.

- *Take a moment to imagine each image before allowing yourself to embody it, using full-body movement.* [6] *For Floating: Explore the following images:*
  - *Imagine you are silk billowing in a gentle breeze.*
  - *Imagine you are a jellyfish in tranquil waters.*
  - *Imagine you are smoke curling upwards into the air, or heat rising off the desert.*
  - *Imagine a landscape of visible air. Move through the air without disturbing it: you are moving through cloud but without re-shaping, scattering or destroying it.*

N.B. If you are exploring Flicking or Slashing, work through [6](b) 'Additional Explorations' on pp. 155–157 before you continue.

Using Music

Using music can help you. You will not have to work with the music for long. Once you are *en route* to accessing the quality of the Effort, you will be able to retain the sounds that help you connect to the Effort without having to hear the music.

- *Choose a piece of music that evokes the Effort.* For help, refer to the list of Effort-related music examples in Appendix D.[2]

---

[2] Appendix D: Music Suggestions, pp. 271–274.

- *Play your chosen music and briefly just listen, before beginning to move. Notice the sounds that provoke each of the Elements (WTS) of the Effort.* [7] **For Floating:** Useful types of music to work with include: Ambient Electronica and Pastoral (Classical).

(B) MEETING THE EFFORT

Everything you have done as a 'Way In' has been to help you find something of the Effort Quality. You now **meet the Effort** itself. First, you have several short periods of time in which you move freely whilst embodying the three Elements (WTS) of the Effort you are currently exploring. There is no story, character or even emotion; just full body movement.

The guidance provides you with a structure that alternates short periods of active exploration with breaks for self-reflection.[3] Whenever you re-enter the same physical exploration after a period of reflection, aim to go straight back in from where you left off. Each period of physical exploration should be neither too long nor too short.[4]

Remember the Basic Philosophies:
Trust the immediate inspiration of Laban's chosen words | Don't 'do' the Effort, become the Effort | Embrace the struggle to be precise | Work without self-consciousness | Stay with it | Notice how you are learning and progressing.

Experiencing the Effort

Sampling the Effort
To begin with, you are just **sampling the Effort**. It is a first taster; a process of discovery. Have confidence that there is no 'right' or 'wrong' way to embody an Effort. You will uncover your own unique physical understanding of it through experimentation and play.

- *Remind yourself which Elements (WTS) make up the Effort.*

- *Recall your Body Reference.[5] Relate this to the Effort. Then begin to find the Effort in other parts of your body.*

- *Begin to move freely, aiming to embody all three Elements (WTS). Let your whole body take you on a journey.*

---

[3] For more information, see 'Pattern of Work' p. 16; 'Self-reflection', p. 259.
[4] For guidance as to how long each phase of the Process should take, see Table 2: Discovery Process Overview, p. 82.
[5] Cf. 'Body Reference', p. 88.

- *Keep the words for the Elements in your mind as you move. Be specific about embodying Weight, Time, and Space equally. Make sure you are not neglecting any of the Motion Factors.*

- *Pause to reflect. What have you experienced as you sampled this Effort?* [8] **For Floating**: You will have experienced some of the following:
The body is off-centre; Labile and asymmetrical. The Light Weight of Floating challenges the body's relationship to gravity so you may not have begun from an upright position.
The Sustained Time of Floating means that there is only one continuous ongoing movement: once you have started moving, you cannot stop to start again.
The Indirect Space of Floating means that there is no movement in any pre-determined direction; there is no plan to the journey.
The power that Floating possesses is not in force or push. It is in its endless ability to keep changing, as well as its immaculate perception of delicacy and sensuality.

Capturing Your Immediate Response

It is vital to capture your **immediate response** to first meeting the Effort. It will give you clues about what this Effort is to you personally: when and how you use it in your life, how you relate to it, and what it already means to you. You can never experience an Effort for the first time again. So make sure you note down your initial response at the time you experience it.

- *Capture your immediate response by asking yourself:*
  - *Do I love this Effort or hate it?*
  - *Why do I feel this way about it?*
  - *What does it remind me of?*
  - *Are there natural examples of this Effort that spring to mind?*

Examining the Effort

Identifying the Effort Default

A first attempt to move in an Effort will almost certainly lead to the **Effort Default**.[6] This is a small selection of movements to which the Effort most easily lends itself. It varies from Effort to Effort and comprises some of the most common ways the Effort is likely to manifest itself in human movement. Each Effort has its own distinct Default, and it is important to ask yourself what it is and how it emerges in your body. Later, you will use your knowledge of the Default to learn how to avoid excessive repetition of

---

[6] This term did not originate from Laban. It was coined in the studio to describe the immediately accessible and recognizable expression of an Effort.

certain types of movements. For now, simply identify the Default and notice how you're working within it.

- *Re-enter your exploration of the Effort for a short while. Begin to move freely, aiming to embody all three Elements (WTS). Let your whole body take you on a journey.*
- *Pause to reflect. Identify the Default by asking:*
  - *Am I mainly doing large-scale or small-scale movements?*
  - *Is it easier to move the core or periphery of the body?*
  - *Have I ended up moving mainly at low-level (on the floor) or mid/high-level (standing)?*
  - *Am I mainly doing contracting/Gathering or expanding/Scattering movements?*
  - *Am I mainly moving in the Door, Wheel, or Table Plane?*
- *Compare your answers to the following description of the Default.* [9] **For Floating:** The Default is:

  Large-scale, peripheral, Scattering: Lightness naturally occurs at the edges of the body where there is less mass. So Floating often starts with seeking the desired Lightness through the limbs: arms and legs open outwards, expanding in the mid-area through the *Door Plane.* It is spacious but without using the full stretch of the limbs.

  Low-level: On the floor it is easier to be off-centre. Here, Indirectness can express itself in Lability, and Sustain can be sought without danger of stepping from foot to foot; the body can roll and spiral, finding Expansion as it moves through the *Table Plane.*

Comparing the Effort

As you repeat this Process for each Effort, you will have experience of an increasing number of Efforts. You can begin to refer back and **compare the Effort** with those you already know. This will allow you to use the discoveries you have made when working on other Efforts. Understanding the interrelationship between the Efforts can help you to embody each Effort with precision and make clear distinctions between them. It also lays a good foundation for later work in which you will shift between all eight Efforts.

- *Re-enter your exploration of the Effort for a short while.*
- *Pause to reflect. Identify how this Effort relates to the Efforts you already know. With which Efforts you have previously encountered does it share one Element? Two Elements? Which Effort is its opposite (i.e. all three Elements are different)?* [10] **For Floating:** You don't yet have anything with which to compare Floating. You will soon begin to discover how it connects to the other eight Efforts.

Locating Control

The actor's job involves telling the story of wildness, danger or extreme freedom. However, there is always **control** and the actor must know where it is located in any given situation.[7]

It is the actor's proper expression of Weight and/or Time and/or Space which keeps the movement in control when working with the Efforts. In Slashing, for example, you are powerfully throwing yourself off-centre. Yet the task of precisely embodying Sudden as part of Slashing demands that the movement is continually arrested through stops and starts. To meet this challenge, you will instinctively make your Flow more Bound, which keeps you in overall control. By meeting the inherent challenge of expressing Sudden, the movements are controlled. So we can say that in Slashing, control is partly located in the Element of Sudden. In Thrusting, the expression of Strong/Heavy Weight means moves are done with force. Yet a clear focus on expressing Strong/Heavy Weight leads to the instinctive activation of Counter-tension. This prevents forceful movements from taking the actor off-balance into unwanted Lability or falling. So we can say that in Thrusting, control is partly located in the Element of Strong/Heavy.

It is important to have a quick method of identifying and checking where control is located. This will mean you know how to allow your expression to go to its maximum, offering the seemingly 'uncontrolled' whilst actually having complete control. Identifying which Element(s) of the Effort is allowing you to be in control of your movement, leaves you free to embody the Effort trusting it can and will regulate its expression safely.

- *Re-enter your exploration of the Effort for a short while.*

- *Pause to reflect. Locate control by asking: in which Element(s) is control located for this Effort? How can expressing this Element with precision allow you to be more in control as you move? Which other Element(s) can now be expressed more fully?* **[11]** **For Floating**: Control is located in: Light (Weight) and Sustained (Time):

   Sustain demands that you move continuously without stopping; it requires you to shift your centre of gravity gradually but continuously. Although

   there may be a feeling of falling, Sustain demands that it is controlled so that there is never an end-point. There is nowhere to stop; no arrival. Embodying Sustain enables you to undertake an ongoing action of falling: falling without ever landing.

   Lightness demands that you work against gravity: the movement must be controlled, a landing would involve Strong/Heavy Weight, which is not an option in Floating.

---

[7] Cf. 'Control', p. 260.

Identifying Your Affinity

Some Efforts will feel easier than others to find or maintain. This is because your relationship to each Effort will vary depending on your natural physical tendencies and learned habits: your **Affinity**.[8]

We each have a unique way of moving in the world and habitually use some Efforts to the exclusion of others (which Efforts they are will be different for each person). Working to experience each Effort in isolation highlights which Efforts you regularly embody, and which you do not. You have an innate understanding of the Efforts you already use regularly in your everyday life because you know them inside out. This means that these familiar Efforts are easier to access and feel instinctively like the 'right' or only way to move. These are the Efforts with which you have an Affinity. Others will not be part of your everyday physical vocabulary in the same way. They are the Efforts with which you do not have a natural Affinity, and will probably feel strange and be harder to access.

The exploration of an Effort with which you have an Affinity becomes a celebration of specialism – you have a specialist understanding of that Effort as it is an instinctive, owned part of your unique physical expression. However, the actor needs access to a full range of expression. So the aim is to work towards being a specialist in all eight Efforts, not just those with which you have an immediate Affinity. Each time you work on the Efforts, you will gradually increase your ability to progress beyond from your embedded habits. This will expand your range as an actor.

When working in just one Effort for a whole session, even the most determined actor will experience the body demanding that it 'needs' to experience an opposite or different quality. This feeling is particularly apparent when working in an Effort that is outside your natural Affinity (and so feels harder to maintain in the first place). Notice this desire for change but don't allow any other Effort to intrude. If you do, it denies you the opportunity to embody fully the Effort you are currently exploring: you will end up consistently dropping back into your personal, habitual Efforts and never move beyond your own Affinity.

However, it is not a moment to be ignored because it tells you something important about your own Effort habits. The specific Effort your body is wanting to switch into for a 'rest' is likely to be the Effort with which you have the strongest Affinity. This new experience will never happen again with such clarity, so make sure you have an immediate moment of analysis before it is lost.

- *Re-enter your exploration of the Effort for a short while.*
- *Note the body's desire to switch Effort. As you move, take a short pause to ask yourself:*
  - *What move am I involuntarily aching to do?*
  - *Which Effort(s) would intrude if I let it? Which Effort is 'banging at the door' (i.e. asking to be let in)?*

---

[8] For more detail regarding the word 'Affinity', see 'Use of Affinity', p. 265.

Noticing Your Associations

Your natural Affinity – and therefore how easy or hard you find an Effort – can also affect your emotional response to it. Be careful, as it is easy to start to think or speak of a particular Effort as 'good' or 'bad'. Attaching a label or category to an Effort is restricting. It provides a mental block to exploring all eight Efforts equally and limits what you believe it is possible to communicate in an Effort. It can also lead to an over-simplistic understanding of their potential: Thrusting as solely 'aggressive'; or 'Floating' as 'poetic'; etc.

Enjoy the recognition of the connections you are making: they give you an immediate understanding of when in the past you have had a clear experience of that Effort in your body. Then bank these **associations** so that you can go on to discover all the many thoughts and feelings the Effort can express beyond the limited ideas you have of it. Every Effort is a vehicle through which any thought or feeling can be transmitted: Thrusting can be poetic; Floating can be aggressive; etc.

- *Re-enter your exploration of the Effort for a short while.*

- *Pause to reflect. Ask yourself:*
  - *How do I view this Effort? What are my immediate associations?*
  - *How can I grow to love and understand this Effort? What can this Effort help me to discover?*

- *Use the following description of the Effort to help clarify your answers.* [12] *For Floating:*
  Floating doesn't arrive on time, or stop to make clear-cut plans, or win arguments through logic, or write concisely worded emails. So it is predominantly viewed as non-productive.
  It has become an Effort associated with the ways in which we seek release from the pressures of our hectic everyday lives. It may seem other-worldly and hard to attain; an experience that fades out of reach too soon. Your first impression may be to associate it with being drunk, high on drugs, or delirious with nauseous fever; or with practices such as meditation.
  Floating is not a lazy Effort. True Floating takes exquisite commitment. This applies to all the Efforts, but with Floating it needs to be clearly understood because the general perception can suggest otherwise. Make no mistake: Floating is not lazy. Floating is just Floating – Light, Sustained and Indirect – trust that the Float can express anything.

(C) MAPPING THE EFFORT

Building a Vocabulary

Working Technically

Now you have registered your first impressions, it is time to begin finding out how to really embody this Effort. **Working technically** allows you to examine the mechanics of how the three Elements (WTS) work together in the Effort, and how your body expresses them.

This mode of work is different from improvising, or purely physical exploration. It allows your analytical brain to be present so that you can assess what you're doing as you work. Whilst moving, you notice what is happening, identify things which are not yet working, then go back and re-try them. This allows you to try things several times, or in different ways.

The aim is to build a register of information (vocabulary) about how to embody the Effort: when something works you 'bank' it and then try something new. Once you have 'banked' something, you have consciously added it to the remembered experience of being in this Effort. Your body memory will recall the movements you have banked for later use.

Your ongoing analysis will guide the progression of movements you are trying out. Working technically offers an important opportunity to grapple with any problems that you have identified for yourself. By the time you progress from working technically, you will be able to remain in the Effort as you move forwards, backwards and sideways; change direction; change level; interact with obstacles, walls and the floor.

- *Re-enter your exploration of the Effort. Move in the Effort you are exploring, keeping a clear reference of the three Elements (WTS) in your mind.*
- *Take a short while to explore what it means to work technically:*
  - *Identify and solve a problem as you encounter it.*
  - *Go back and try a movement again.*
  - *Figure out how to make movements work in this Effort.*

  Make sure you don't get caught up in improvisation or skim over movements that are not working.
- *'Bank' things that work and then try something new.* You do not need to keep repeating movements that you have found easily, or that are now working.
- *As you continue to work, check that you haven't just gone with your idea of the Effort. Keep engaging with the specificity of the three Elements (WTS).*
- *Pause to reflect.*

Adding Sound

Part of our physical expression is the movement of air in and out of the body to create sound. To gain a full understanding of an Effort, you therefore need to include a vocal expression of it by **Sounding** as you move. You will now start to vocalize sound during each exploration. Sound is 'movement made audible':[9] the sound shares what is being expressed through your body. This means you will be able to hear the quality of your movement reflected in the sound.

Sounding will help you to maintain the precise expression of the Effort. It allows detection of any unwanted shifts from one Element to its opposite. If the quality of the sound shifts away from the Effort you are currently exploring, then you know your expression of the Effort is no longer exact.

Ensure you are simply allowing the sound to emerge and are not working from a place of tension. Tension can be unsafe in any body part, including the voice. So it is important that you are not constraining any of your physical impulses, including those of your breath and voice. If Sounding makes you feel self-conscious, use the relevant 'Soundtrack' Audio Resources.[10] This is a sample of a group of actors working in the given Effort. Play this as you work so that your sound becomes part of a tapestry.

Once you have added in Sounding, make sure you sound throughout the rest of the process. If you go silent, you may not be fully expressing the Effort because your breath and voice should always be an integrated part of your physical expression.

- *Re-enter your exploration of the Effort. Continue working technically. This time allow the Effort Quality to be expressed vocally as you move.*

- *Hear how the movement of your body is mirrored in the sound of your voice.*

- *Remember that breath has both an inhale and an exhale.* Sound happens primarily on the out-breath, but don't ignore the in-breath completely. It can also express the Effort Quality.

- *Discover a voice that is united with the movement of the Effort. Find the sound that helps you; the sound your body wants to do. Use the following guidance to help you discover the sound of the Effort.* **[13] For Floating:**
  Floating gives you a good opportunity to experiment with the relationship between breath and sound, as Floating uses Sounding which is right on the boundary between voiced and unvoiced breath.
  You will discover that the sound of Floating is so Light that it may be almost imperceptible to an external ear, or even to you yourself – it is going to be on the tip of the breath. Even if there is only the smallest sound – or just the sense of a sound – coming from inside your body, there is still a voice that is connected to the Floating movement.

---

[9] Laban, *A Life for Dance*, p. 87.
[10] The relevant resource is referred to in each Effort section, or can be found in the complete list of Audio Resources on p. 285.

If it helps, use the Floating Soundtrack to accompany you as you work:

Audio Resource

Floating Soundtrack
https://vimeo.com/251646519

Expanding Your Vocabulary

Targeted Exploration: Working with an Agenda

At first, the Effort Default feels like the outer limit of how the Effort can be expressed.[11] However, you can create a far fuller expression of the Effort through **targeted exploration**. This allows you to progress beyond certain expressive limitations and actively expand your vocabulary beyond the Effort Default. In this next stage, you will gain technical expertise, supported by imagination. Your next set of explorations will encourage you to find out how the Effort can be expressed in an infinite variety of ways.

You will continue working technically to expand your movement vocabulary. Now, however, you choose something specific to work on each time: **an Agenda**. This is set in response to your analysis and reflection between explorations. Ongoing feedback guides the series of choices about what to focus on next.

Ultimately, progressing beyond the Default will open up different choices when you create new characters. It will let you make specific choices about how each unique character expresses the Effort, rather than simply expressing the Effort in a generic way.

- *Re-enter your exploration of the Effort. Continue working technically. This time, set yourself an Agenda before you begin.* You will find a list of **Suggested Agendas** below.

- *Find new movements by focusing only on your chosen Agenda.*

- *Make sure you are still working technically: you can stop, think, and try things out more than once.*

- *Aim to collect the largest movement vocabulary you can for the Effort.* Remember: the aim is to build a map of movements in your body – once you have found a movement that works, 'bank' it and then turn your attention to finding others.

- *Pause to reflect. Articulate what new discoveries you have made. Think about what types of movement still seem challenging or inaccessible in this Effort.*

- *Choose a new Agenda that will help you to explore the movement which does not yet feel accessible. Refer to the list of Suggested Agendas to help you.*

- *Do a series of short explorations according to a different set Agenda each time. Pause to reflect after each short exploration to keep track of what you are discovering.*

---

[11] Cf. 'Identifying the Default', p. 91.

Suggested Agendas:

//Including the face and releasing the breath
Make sure your face is mobile, with the potential for the facial muscles to move and change. Allow the Effort to be expressed through the whole face, even if this amount of facial movement feels unusual. Include the eyes and the inside of the mouth. Check that you are not holding your breath, or only allowing a shallow inhalation or partial exhalation. It is easy to forget to include your face in full-body movement, and/or to allow the breath to become held in concentration.

//Relating to breath
Notice the connection between your breath and movement. Explore the range and variety of your breath. Explore moving the Effort on the in-breath as well as on the out-breath. Changing the relationship between your breath and your movement can expand the ways in which you express the Effort.

//Using all body parts[12]
Notice the parts of the body that don't immediately get involved in the Effort. Track through the body; concentrate on different body parts and give them equal focus in turn. Discover how every body part can express the Effort in a number of ways. Then return to full-body movement. Use your new vocabulary to ensure the Effort is expressed throughout the body. Without this detailed level of exploration, it is hard to express an Effort in body parts where it does not feel as 'natural' (e.g. hips would never Float; ribs would never Thrust).

//Finding small-scale and large-scale movements
Notice whether your movements are tending to be small or large. Explore the ways in which you can access a whole range of different size movements. Then practise switching between movements of all sizes.

//Finding core and peripheral movements
Notice whether your movements tend to be at the periphery of your body (using mainly the limbs) or at the core (using the torso and/or pelvis). Work technically to find each type of movement in turn until both feel equally accessible. Then practise switching between the two.

//Changing level
Notice whether you are tending to work at low, mid or high level. Work technically to make sure you can move in the Effort at all levels. Then explore different ways of changing level; moving in and out of the floor from lying to standing, and vice versa.

---

[12] Cf. 'Working with Body Parts', p. 46.

//Changing Plane[13]
Notice which Plane(s) you are using most. Work technically to make sure you can move in the Effort in all three Planes (Door/Wheel/Table). Then explore ways of switching between the Planes as you move.

//Using contracting/Gathering and expanding/Scattering[14]
Notice whether your movements tend to be contracting/Gathering or expanding/ Scattering. Work technically to find each type of movement in turn until both feel equally accessible. Then practise switching between the two.

//Shifting awareness of body components[15]
Try moving with a varying sense of your body: first as 'muscly', then 'bony', and then 'fleshy'. Changing to different perceptions of your body as you work can expand the ways in which you express the Effort.

//Shifting tempo[16]
Play with the possibility of moving at various different tempos. Each Effort will always be either Sudden or Sustained. However, the tempo of your movement can still vary whilst remaining clearly Sudden or Sustained.

Meeting Challenges

Each Effort presents specific **challenges**. It is important to meet these challenges in order to discover a fuller expression of the Effort.

- *Continue working technically and do another series of short explorations according to a different set Agenda each time. Pause to reflect after each short exploration to keep track of what you are discovering. When you no longer feel restricted by any of these challenges, it is time to progress to the next stage.*

- *Use the following guidance to help you set Agendas specific to the challenges of the Effort.* **[14]** *For Floating:* Specific Agendas include:

//Don't reverse or repeat a move
You can't come back out of a movement the same way you went in because stopping to change direction breaks the Sustain. Keep moving through to see if you can find pathways that endlessly evolve, rather than doing and undoing. Floating does not break the journey up into bite-size pieces but always continues on. Not to move on would not be Floating, but would instead be 'wafting' or 'waving'. To 'waft' or 'wave' is a piecemeal action that involves stopping and changing direction to reverse or return.

---

[13] Cf. 'The Planes', p. 36.
[14] Cf. 'Gathering and Scattering', p. 42.
[15] Cf. 'Body Components: Bony, Muscly, Fleshy', p. 47.
[16] Cf. 'Time and the Actor: Time vs. Clock-time', p. 72.

If you are 'wafting' or 'waving', this also implies that the Float is only being expressed through Gesture, with an over-emphasis on movement of the arms and hands. Avoid holding the limbs in mid-air and making them the focus of your movement. Move beyond use of peripheral Gestures and enter into a whole-body journey which carries you ever onwards through General Space.

//Remember: Sustain is not slow motion

As you learn, Floating will be at a very slow pace, as you do not yet have an extensive vocabulary to feed the movement and keep it going without pausing or stopping (the faster the pace, the more vocabulary you need).

However, make sure that you do not think of the Effort as 'slow motion':[17] it is not a progression through moves which are preconceived but then deliberately slowed down. The movement emerges in the ongoing moment of the Float.

//Embodying Indirect in the line of the neck

Holding your head in a straight line with your body (i.e. maintaining an expression of Direct through the line of the neck) will mean your thoughts feel logical in their progression.

Instead, allow the head to meander off-centre, drifting into a sensation of curve in the neck. The body and the mind are released from having a plan, you enter Lability, and the Float begins to emerge.

A sensation of unease or motion sickness indicates a struggle between the Effort and your thoughts – your mind still wants to decide where your body will move in Space. As soon as you trust the Float and release the need for decision-making by allowing your body to live the Indirect, this will dissipate.

//'Chewy' Floating is not true Floating

When you discover moments of Floating, there is a desire to cling on to them. Yet in trying to retain the experience, it is easy to dip into Stronger Weight; an almost imperceptible shift in which the quality is lost to a markedly different movement that has a 'chewiness' about it.

Instead, trust yourself to find and re-find the Effort, allowing it to emerge moment to moment. In the present tense, the body expresses the movement quality anew; the Effort is continually renewed as the movement progresses.

//Floating is not 'drugged'

It is easy to begin accidentally playing an experience commonly associated with Floating (e.g. Floating as though you are drunk or drugged). This is to be avoided, as you would then be playing the associations you have with this Effort, rather than expressing the Effort itself.

---

[17] Cf. 'The Difference between Sustained and Slow Motion', p. 72.

Solving Common Conundrums

Each Effort throws up **Common Conundrums** that everyone will encounter. These puzzles occur when technical expertise is required to negotiate a conflict between the physical rules of your body/the world and the desired communication of a seemingly impossible expressive story.

Solving these Common Conundrums involves a negotiation between imagination and practicality: an actor, for example, who is imaginatively embodying the experience of defying gravity in Floating is, of course, simultaneously dealing with the actual experience of gravity working on their body. The actor has to discover how to use technical skill to support their imagination. They can then communicate an expressive story that takes them far beyond the physical limitations of the body: an actor who inevitably remains subject to gravity can give the appearance of being released from it.[18]

Some of the Efforts bring up the same Common Conundrums. So, as you progress through the different Efforts, you may already have some solutions which can be applied from your previous work.

- *Continue working technically and do another series of short explorations according to a different set Agenda each time. Pause to reflect after each short exploration to keep track of what you are discovering. When you no longer feel restricted by any of these Common Conundrums, it is time to progress to the next stage.*

- *Use the following guidance to help you set Agendas specific to the Common Conundrums presented by the Effort.* **[15]** *For Floating*: Specific Agendas include:

//Shifting your Centre of Gravity

There is no fixed Centre of Gravity in Floating.[19] Gradually and continuously shifting your Centre of Gravity is what allows you to move through Space without breaking up the journey into pieces or losing balance.

The Sequential travelling of the movement through the body, as well as the body through the space, never allows the placement of weight in the body to become fixed. Follow the Float by placing the movement in a specific body part and then tracking it to another body part, and another, and so on.[20]

Discover how progressively shifting your Centre of Gravity as you move in Sequential spirals and twists helps you move fluidly through positions where you at first felt 'stuck'. You will discover that the continuous movement of Sustain will lead you into problem positions but it can also enable you to pass through them.

//Using one point of gravitational support

You will need to discover ways of supporting weight through different parts of the body. Usually, we support ourselves through our feet (walking or standing), pelvis

---

[18] Cf. 'The Actor's Imagination', p. 32.
[19] Cf. 'Centre of Gravity', p. 39.
[20] Cf. 'Explorations of Sequential Movement', p. 44.

(sitting) or back (lying down). Yet other body parts might also be used, such as the hands or the head (e.g. in handstands or headstands). We consider using other parts of the body to support our weight to be more unusual, or gymnastic. However, as you begin to move in Float, you will discover that the spirals and turns of your motion allow you organically to access support through other parts of your body – you might take the weight of the body through a hand, shoulder, your side, upper arm, knee, hip, etc. For a moment this becomes the point of support which takes your weight, allowing as much of the rest of the body as possible to express the Effort.

The supporting part is continually changing. Make sure you are clear where the necessary point of gravitational support is at any given time. If you're uncertain where it is, this might be because you are using multiple points of gravitational support. Identify and play with one dominant point of gravitational support which continually shifts.[21] Enjoy how a clear sense of where the point of gravitational support is located allows you to Float even the heaviest parts of your body (e.g. shifting the weight through your shoulders can allow you to Float the heavy bones of the pelvis).

//Experiencing Lightness as release from gravity
In Float there should be no sense of gravitational pull. Imaginatively, every direction becomes equal: without a sense of gravity there is no up or down. When you move downwards, you are not sinking but continuing an ongoing experience of perpetual Lightness.

You can imagine that you are in the air and have a perspective of distance as though you're looking from an aeroplane. Each small detail could be vast: patterns on the floor are fields and a tiny bit of dirt might be a house or a whole factory. The vast spaciousness which is all around you can enter inside your body as all parts of the body become Light.

By using your imagination to re-configure the space around you, an infinite variety of movements become possible: you will discover it makes as much sense to have your feet in the air as your arms because there is no fixed sense of the vertical in which the arms need to be above the legs, or the rib-cage above the hips. Re-imagining the space through which you are moving will help as you begin to explore supporting your weight through different body parts.

Moving in the World

Re-imagining the World as Playground
You are now ready to focus on discovering vocabulary that allows you to travel through your work-space and interact with the world around you. We are used to perceiving our

---

[21] You may have multiple points of contact with the floor, but still only one dominant point of gravitational support (e.g. your arm and leg may both be touching the floor, but the leg is the main weight-bearing support and the arm is simply aiding balance, or vice versa).

environment in terms of vertical and horizontal placement: the floor is below us, the ceiling above us, the walls around us, etc. We place ourselves in the world according to habit and perceived possibility: we sit on the floor or a chair; we change direction when we meet a wall; and we tend to keep our gaze at more or less eye-level.

When embodying the Effort, you no longer travel and encounter objects in this usual way. You imaginatively re-define your relationship to the world around you. So the way you relate to the space and objects within it adjusts: you are as able to move along the floor as at standing-height; you can travel one way whilst facing another; your gaze can be directed anywhere; you can travel over or under objects, not always around them, etc.

The world in which you are existing becomes a **playground** that you can relate to and move through in an infinity of different ways, freed from the material realities of the physical world. In the imaginative world within which you are working, a wall could become the 'floor' that is supporting your weight as you move along it; or you might lie on the floor imagining it to be the ceiling, as the actual ceiling becomes the 'floor', which is now far beneath you. This is in itself a useful practice for the actor, whose job is always to create and inhabit imaginative worlds.

- *Re-enter your exploration of the Effort. Take a moment to celebrate what you have already found.*

- *Begin to move through your work-space. There will be physical shapes that have kept re-occurring as you move in this Effort. Work technically to discover different pathways in and out of these now-familiar shapes. Let these pathways lead you to new shapes, which in turn lead you to more new pathways, and so on. Aim to make significant journeys in and around your work-space.*

- *You are still working technically. Bank the fresh shapes and pathways as they occur. Combine them in a variety of ways to keep expanding your range of possibilities.* This is not to be confused with choreographing: you are seeking new ways to travel in this Effort, not creating forms or sequences.

- *Make sure you are exploring all forms of travel according to what the Effort demands: rolling, sliding, crawling, jumping, etc.*

- *Pause to reflect.*

Using the Walls and Floor

Exploring how you **relate to the wall and floor** can help you clarify your expression of the Effort you are exploring. In some Efforts, you might identify with the wall and floor's solid bulk, and/or ongoing length, and/or straight lines and angles. In others, you might feel alienated by them. This exploration helps you to identify when you are experiencing similarity to the walls and floor, and when you are experiencing difference. The floor and walls become surfaces with which to interact, as you choose to move with or against them.

- *Re-enter your exploration of the Effort but this time start close to a wall. You will need to pay attention to safety:* in Slashing, for example, you cannot Slash in the direction of a nearby wall. However, you can spring or bounce off a wall as you would off the floor in jumping; or you can keep one part of the body, such as an arm, in contact with the wall while the rest of the body is Slashing.

- *You are still working technically. Ask yourself:*
  - *How can I relate to the wall in this Effort? How do I feel about the relationship of my body to the wall? Do I want to move near it or up close against it? If so, how?*
  - *What can the wall help me to do? (e.g. change level; turn myself (or the world) upside-down; travel; change direction or facing; express an Element more precisely; etc.).*
  - *How am I experiencing the surface of the wall? (e.g. touching it; using it to bear your weight; moving along it; bouncing off it; etc.).*
- *Pause to reflect.*

Working with Obstacles

This exploration deepens your understanding of how to move in relationship to your surrounding environment. For this, you create some **obstacles** to transform your empty work-space into a more diverse world through which to move.

It is possible to move freely through an 'obstacle course' in every Effort. If you are struggling with something – such as how to get over or under a particular object without slipping out of the Effort – keep experimenting until you work out how to do it. When you have banked enough moves to get you through the obstacle course, your body will begin to draw on these moves instinctively. It will become much easier to negotiate moving through the world.

- *Create an obstacle course through which to move by placing some large objects into your work-space. These can be any objects that are sturdy enough to bear your weight and don't have sharp corners (e.g. tables, chairs, garden furniture, sofas, etc.). The walls of the room in which you are working are also part of this obstacle course. Corners, ledges, window-sills, etc. can all provide interesting environments in which to play.*[22]

- *Re-enter your exploration of the Effort. This time explore travelling through the obstacle course on a journey that takes you from A to B. Make sure you are playing with ways over, under, through, around, along, etc. You are still working technically, asking questions and discovering movement vocabulary. The aim is to find ways to travel through the created world – to bank enough vocabulary to enable you to complete your journey.*[23]

- *Pause to reflect. Articulate what new discoveries you have made. Think about what types of movement through the obstacle course still seem challenging*

---

[22] Always make sure that you are working with focus so that you relate safely to the environment in which you are moving.

[23] Laban identifies three main phases to physical contact: preparation, actual contact, release (Laban, *The Mastery of Movement*, p. 66). It might be helpful to think of these three phases as you learn how to interact with obstacles.

or inaccessible in this Effort. Set an Agenda in response to any challenges you identify.

- *Do a series of short explorations according to a different set Agenda each time.* When you feel you have banked enough vocabulary to move through the obstacle course with ease, it is time to progress to the next stage.

(D) THE EFFORT AS CODE

Working through Improvisation

You now progress to working in the Effort through **improvisation**.[24] This lets you test out the information you have discovered through technical work by letting it 'live' in the body within a given imaginative context.

Allowing yourself to be fully in the improvisation will teach you different things to working technically. Improvisation lets you discover what your body now knows without you needing to be consciously in charge. As with any improvisation, belief in the context is vital. You can then simply allow your movement to respond to the context in any given moment. Through the imaginative play of an improvisation, you will find yourself solving challenges that may have seemed completely impossible when approached using your technical brain.

Stay in the present moment and don't try to correct things while you are improvising. It is not possible to work technically and improvise at the same time. Continue using the practice of reflection and analysis after each exploration, but as you work do not self-monitor, interrupt yourself, or make any predetermined decisions about how you move.

If you do find your technical brain is interrupting the improvisation, it may mean that you are not quite ready to begin this stage. That is fine. You can go back to the previous stage of working technically, and explore whatever it is you have discovered to be a problem. If you are uncertain whether you are yet ready to progress to improvisation – or you find it hard to let go – then begin improvising with a shorter time frame. Keeping the length of your improvisation short to begin with will help you to commit to the experience completely.

Discovering the Effort as Code

In Actor Movement, the term '**Code**' refers to a set of rules which amount to a particular recognizable behaviour or way of being. Codes may be physical or social. Physical Codes

---

[24] As an actor you have probably had experience of working through improvisation. However, if you would like to learn more about how to improvise, see Chris Johnston, *The Improvisation Game: Discovering the Secrets of Spontaneous Performance.*

are innate rules which affect all human bodies in particular contexts (e.g. old age, being drunk, illness, etc.). Social Codes are made from externally imposed rules, such as etiquette or manners specific to a given cultural or historical period. Both Social and Physical Codes are instantly communicated through physical expression, and the Code is apparent even when the character is at rest. A character may embody more than one Code at a time (e.g. old age and drunk; or old age, drunk and a seventeenth-century woman).[25]

The following improvisations lead you into working with the **Effort as Code**. Each Effort can be clearly identified as a Physical Code: they are defined ways of being which follow a pattern of specific rules (dictated by the Elements (WTS) of the Effort). Understanding that the Effort is a Code, and trusting in the rules of that Code, allows you the liberation of easily transforming into a way of being different to your own.

Single-celled Amoeba (Improvisation)

In this improvisation, you transform into a simple living organism: the **single-celled amoeba**.[26] This is a version of the Effort Code that gives you freedom to move through the space differently from when you are thinking of yourself as a human body. It helps you access full-body expression: unlike in a human or animal form, there is no hierarchy within a single-celled organism so everything expresses the Effort equally, including your face. Accepting yourself as this living breathing organism will enable you to improvise with the movement of the Effort in very simple terms. You can travel without relying on a definite body shape, or considering limbs as having certain roles.

The amoeba moves through the world because to keep travelling is to survive. It is important that you perceive this single-celled organism as a success. It is not 'just' a simple organism but an incredibly skilled survivor. In fact, a better survivor than other more complicated forms of life, and likely to carry on existing on the planet long after human beings have become extinct.

Unlike more complicated life forms, the amoeba doesn't move towards obstacles in order to interact with them; they just happen to be in the pathway of its ongoing travel. So at first you work without the obstacle course. This allows you to find the amoeba's motivation to travel (an innate instinct to move through the world), rather than unconsciously relying on the obstacle course to give you a reason to move. Using the vocabulary you have banked during the previous stages of technical work will allow you to move through the space as the amoeba and prevent you from getting stuck on the spot.

In this improvisation, you are just a vehicle for the Effort Code (WTS). Simply set the Code and let it inhabit you. Allow everything the movement brings but don't stop to react to your experience. Trust yourself and live one move, then the next. Don't over-indulge what you imagine the Effort might be for you. Allow yourself to *be* the Effort, honouring what the Effort is moment-by-moment. Let it teach you.

---

[25] More on Codes can be found in Ewan and Green, *Actor Movement*, pp. 228–243.
[26] This is usually one of the first organisms we learn about in school. It is with that childlike view that we use it as a means to humble ourselves and transform into something simpler with awe and respect.

- *Create as empty a work-space as possible (no obstacles). Using all the vocabulary you have banked, re-enter your exploration of the Effort.*

- *Now, imagine you have transformed into a single-celled amoeba.* Moving in this way there is no thought or feeling but there is an existence: life is maintained in the form of the Effort. You simply move through your work-space, surviving on the planet.

- *Don't take any stops or 'time out' from the Effort Quality.* You are now existing in the form of a single-celled Effort organism. You cannot break out of the improvisation, or come back to yourself as actor to think of a new movement or phrase before doing it. The moves you have banked during your technical work will help you: you already have ways of moving through the world in this Effort stored in your body memory.

- *Remember:*
  - *keep all three Elements (WTS) of the Effort precise: don't get stuck in the Default*
  - *involve all body parts, including the face*
  - *move through the world*
  - *change direction and level*
  - *allow yourself to sound.*

- *Once you are sure that you have discovered the amoeba's innate instinct to move through the world, pause to reflect.*

- *Replace your obstacle course and repeat the same improvisation but now moving through this more varied world as your single-celled Effort organism.* Create a world for yourself by negotiating the obstacles which your amoeba would acknowledge, and imaginatively altering or ignoring the things it would not recognize.

- *Once you have discovered how to exist in this world, pause to reflect.*

(E) A JOURNEY (GUIDED IMPROVISATION)

The final exploration is a guided improvisation of about ten to fifteen minutes: the **Journey**. You are given instructions to respond to as you improvise. An Effort Journey does not impose a context. The instructions can be understood as an inner monologue. They offer prompts of thoughts and feelings for you to experience, and samples of what it is to be 'you' from the logic of the Effort. You supply the context in each moment: where you are, what you are doing and why you are there.

Each phase of the extended improvisation has a specific purpose: they take you through different modes of expressing the Effort, and provoke a range of thoughts and feelings. The prompt constantly changes, enhances or deepens your experience, challenging you to access a diverse range of expression in each Effort. You experience the same Journey with each different Effort. This deepens the understanding you are already beginning to have that for you as an actor all thoughts, feelings and physical actions are possible in any Effort.

The Audio Resources offer just one example of an Effort Journey, but there are an infinite number of possible Journeys that could be constructed using a similar structure. Any Journey should enable you to be in the present tense and safely take you through a range of experiences.

Following a Journey

The Journey is exploratory not performative. It is a **framework** for making discoveries (and mistakes). There will be moments of the improvisation that really work and moments that are less successful. Don't carry mistakes with you or allow them to frustrate you; just carry on playfully maintaining the improvisation.

As with any journey, you have to give yourself up to what it offers you in the moment to experience it fully. You cannot hold the whole Journey as you go but must surrender to the shifting landscape of thoughts and feelings. You've got to want to go where the Journey takes you. Your previous technical work will support this: you no longer need to think about how to move in the Effort but can allow yourself to exist in it in the present moment. This is an improvisation in which you can rediscover that the world is a bigger place than your version of it.

Each phase of an Effort Journey has a specific purpose. The phases are outlined below, as it is useful to understand why the Journey improvisation is structured in a certain way. However, you are encouraged to do the improvisation first so that you will have your own practical experience to refer to as you read.

- *Use the audio to guide you through an extended Effort Journey improvisation.*[27] Towards the end of this improvisation you will drink from a bottle of water, so make sure you have one ready. The Effort will shape and carry whatever you are expressing so you don't have to work at anything: let the Effort become the vehicle for whatever it is that you are feeling, thinking and doing. Trust the guidance, and trust the Effort. **[16]** *For Floating*:

Audio Resource

A Floating Journey
https://vimeo.com/251647354

- *Read through the information below to understand more about an Effort Journey improvisation*:

Phase 1: Single-celled amoeba
First, you return to existence as the single-celled amoeba.

---

[27] Alternatively, this guidance is also available as a written framework of instructions at www.labaneffortsinaction.com

Phase 2: Adding human condition

Improvising as the single-celled amoeba, you gradually add 'human condition' – the presence of thoughts and feelings. You remain amoeba-like (i.e. the scale of your full-body movement remains the same and is still liberated from the hierarchical body organization of the human form) but start to allow thoughts and feelings to motivate and affect your improvisation. At first, it is better to work with extreme thoughts and feelings because these are easier to identify and express. So the instructions ask you to locate whatever the automatic thought or feeling happens to be and take it further, to its extreme.

Phase 3: Effort Archetype

An Effort Archetype emerges organically from the expression of thoughts and feelings in the Effort Quality. It is a more human form than the amoeba, but still uses full-body movement to express the Effort. There are eight Archetypes: one for each Effort.[28]

The Effort Archetype is a 'larger than life' character, as it is a physical expression of only one Effort.[29] It is a learning device that deliberately uses just one Effort for expression, so that the actor can discover the different possibilities for personality (and ultimately character) inherent in the specific Effort they are exploring. Using a solo Effort is the easiest first point of access for transforming into a human being who has a completely different Affinity to you.

//Discovering personality through Gestures

As you work in the Archetype, you are encouraged to find moments when Gestures can emerge from a particular thought or feeling. Gradually, they amount to a sense of distinctive personality. Thoughts and feelings are expressed through gestural movement in all the different parts of the body.[30] You might mull over a thought with your ankle, or feel an emotion in your jaw. Someone else should be able to look at you and know what you are thinking and feeling just from your Gestures. Your sounds may also start to change into exclamations, words, and sentence fragments.

//Effort Archetype experienced as trap and comfort

We experience our character-traits as positive or negative according to context. Single-mindedness, for example, may enable someone to maintain focus and

---

[28] You may have come across other ways of working with Archetypes. Versions of different Archetypes are found in genres such as Commedia Dell'Arte, and widely used in mask-work by practitioners such as John Wright. The Effort Archetypes are also a way of working with universal and instantly recognizable character types but should not be confused with any other Archetypes you may have encountered.

[29] In everyday movement, most people access many Efforts. So, ultimately, for a full character portrayal, an actor would want to employ a combination of Efforts.

[30] For more detailed explanation about the intended meaning of the term 'Gestures', see 'Working with Gestures', p. 260.

achieve great things, but also make them unable to take into account other people's priorities. Each Archetype can experience the innate characteristics of the Effort Code as both a comfort (positive) and a trap (negative). Sustain, for example, might be experienced as an ability to keep going, to be constant; or as an inability to ever finish anything, or face an ending. The same Effort is the vehicle for both of these opposing experiences depending on your current focus or perception. By experiencing the Archetype's perception of some tendencies as negative or distressing, you can understand the particular neuroses that arise from their struggle to accept their own inborn characteristics. You begin to perceive the ways in which the Effort Archetype is both funny and endearing in their unique way of existing in the world, with all their very particular beliefs, survival mechanisms and habits.

Phase 4: Internalized
You now take your Archetype's entire range of full-body movement and hide it inside – internalize it. This reflects the way in which we contain and hide our inner drives once we become socially conditioned adults. The powerful movement of our thoughts and feelings still occurs inside but we fight to maintain a socially appropriate exterior. The extremes of our internal landscape are revealed only in times of heightened emotion (anger, love, fear, etc.) or times of disinhibition (madness, drunkenness, dementia, etc.). In Phase 2, when you embody the Effort in the form of a single-celled amoeba with human condition (presence of thoughts and feelings), the inner drive is expressed externally through full-body movement. Now, the inner drive is hidden back inside: internalized.

You first internalize the Effort through a moment of stillness. The residue of the Effort movement will remain clearly visible within you. The simplicity of stillness and looking should not be confused with being 'frozen' or tense. You are the protagonist – alive and ready – with the Effort internalized in your body.

//Telling a joke
Responding to a joke reminds you that the Archetype can express a whole range of emotions, including those which are 'frivolous' or 'light-hearted'. A particular joke might appeal to the Archetype because of the phrasing or logic of the joke. Make sure that an element of performance doesn't creep in: your response may range from gentle amusement to full-scale hilarity but the laugh must be genuine (provoked in the moment). Laughter reminds you to include breath and sound as your Archetype, as well as all the Gestures that usually accompany it.

//A moment of dancing
Finding the way this Archetype would dance allows feelings and thoughts to exist freely in the body. It should feel fun to do and not be taken too seriously. It might be that the Archetype dances from the need to be with the music: a sensation that there is meaning in the moves and that it expresses their true

self. Perhaps imagine being alone on a moonlit beach with headphones. Or it might be that the Archetype dances from the desire to express their personality: a sensation that the moves are performative (aware of self) and fill a communicative function. Perhaps imagine being at a social function, such as a wedding disco.

Phase 5: Physical Action

You now take a moment to find the way in which the Effort Archetype engages in action.

//Passive Physical Action: going to sleep

After sitting for a while, you begin to do an essentially 'passive' action (e.g. reading, doodling, sunbathing, daydreaming, etc.). This includes allowing your Archetype to fall asleep and begin to dream. In **Passive Physical Action**, we have the best understanding of our interior movement of thoughts and feelings because our actions are initiated from within, rather than as an interactive response to the world.

An Alternative Journey

It is also possible to do an **Alternative Journey**: an Effort Journey improvisation which uses a story. This leads the actor through a condensed narrative in which you encounter a series of events. Take everything that is offered to you in the story as hyper-real: keep the stakes very high, and do not censor any thoughts and feelings that occur but allow them to be as extreme as they seem to you in the moment. Again, the Audio Resources offer just one example of an Effort Journey which uses a story, but there are an infinite number of possible Journeys.[31]

- *You may also wish to do an Effort Journey which uses a story. This audio offers a framework of instructions which can be used when exploring any of the eight Efforts:*[32]

Audio Resource

An Effort Journey Using a Story
https://vimeo.com/251652620

---

[31] For more examples visit www.labaneffortsinaction.com
[32] Alternatively, this guidance is also available as a written Framework of Instructions at www.labaneffortsinaction.com

Follow-up

After you have completed the Effort Journey, allow yourself a short break (about five minutes) before you return into your work-space to undertake two short **follow-up** improvisations.

Fundamental Physical Action

Fundamental Physical Actions are movement staples of most characters – sitting, standing, lying, walking, running, etc. Some of these will have been experienced during the Journey, others you may not yet have encountered. This exploration allows you to ask how does your Archetype walk? Or run?, etc. Doing a Fundamental Physical Action such as sitting will allow you to see how embodying this Effort has changed your own patterning.

- *Take a sitting position. You are not doing anything other than simply sitting, thinking and feeling.*
- *Make sure that you are empty of all Efforts, other than the Effort of your Archetype.*
- *Let the Effort Quality dictate the way you choose to sit in the space (e.g. curled up on the floor; squarely on the chair; etc.).*
- *Have something in your mind that triggers thoughts and feelings so you have an active internal landscape.*
- *Let your movement occur instinctively. Without feeling any pressure to 'do' movements, allow the exploration to take you gradually into simple everyday actions such as standing and walking. Do as little as possible.*
- *Take some time to analyse and reflect.*

Responsive Physical Action: Having a Drink

Responsive Physical Actions are a negotiation between the Effort in which we desire to do an action and the inherent demands of the action itself. Ultimately, our interface with the world demands certain physical actions of us, regardless of our natural Effort Affinity. Opening the lid of a water bottle, for example, demands that it is unscrewed. Even a person working in a Direct Effort will have to turn the lid, creating a necessary compromise between their Affinity to Direct movements and the needs of the task in hand (which demands an Indirect movement). A brief moment of negotiation occurs and the Effort Quality is momentarily altered to complete the task.

Playing with Responsive Physical Action is the first moment of interface between your Effort Archetype and the world. The character meets the world and the demands of the world interfere with the Effort expression of the character. Through this, you discover how the Effort Archetype engages and interacts with the external world. Unconsciously, we seek for the moments in physical action when we feel we can 'be ourselves'. This means the parts of any action that fit most easily with the natural Affinity of our given Effort are indulged or celebrated, and the moments of negotiation are skirted over. When you are working with a Direct Effort, for example, you will still have to unscrew the lid (necessary circles) but would take much more pleasure in lifting the bottle to your mouth (straight line). As your Archetype meets the challenges of the world, enjoy the small moments of drama that occur in the conflict between the Effort Quality you want to indulge and the Effort Quality that the action demands.

Video Resource

Responsive Physical Action
https://vimeo.com/251505925

- *As your Effort Archetype, re-visit the action of taking a drink from a bottle.*
- *Notice the moments which your Archetype indulges or celebrates, and the moments in which they have to negotiate the demands of the action.*
- *Take some time to analyse and reflect.*

(F) EFFORTS IN THE WORLD

Everyday Existence

After working extensively in this solo Effort, it will reside in the body and affect your habitual patterns of movement expression during your **everyday existence**. If it is not overshadowed by other stimuli (e.g. a different kind of intense movement activity), this shift should last for the rest of the day.

- *Pay attention to your movement, particularly through the rest of the day after your work session. Ask yourself: what actions am I doing differently? How has my relationship to the world around me shifted?*

You can use your daily interaction with the world around you as an opportunity to carry on playing with this Effort. This will deepen your ability to embody it fully in a variety of different actions and contexts.

- *Carry on exploring how to move in the Effort: choose to do your daily routine in the Effort you're currently discovering (e.g. brushing your teeth, getting dressed, making your bed, or eating part of a meal).*

Point of View

You may find you have a temporarily altered or expanded **point of view** on the world: perhaps you are noticing things that would not have caught your attention before, or finding a new sense of Affinity with unexpected things. After discovering Floating, for example, you might find yourself experiencing anew the circular pathway of the spoon in your coffee, or enjoying the Lightness of a butterfly lifting up into flight.

- *Be aware of the life of things around you. Allow yourself moments of observation.*

- *Ask yourself: what is catching my attention? Why is it of interest to me? How is the newly discovered Effort affecting my current point of view?*

[Now go back to the beginning of Chapter 6(a) and repeat this Process with the next Effort. Remember to refer to the numbered sections in Chapter 6(b) where prompted.]

Figure 6.1(a) Stages of a Floating Process.

Figure 6.1(b) Stages of a Floating Process (cont.).

CHAPTER 6(b)
DISCOVERY PROCESS INSERTS: THE OTHER SEVEN EFFORTS

Note: These sections provide the additional guidance for completing the Process when exploring each Effort in turn. Reading them will give you a flavour of each Effort. However, to work practically, **follow the complete instructions in the main text of Chapter 6(a) and only turn to these pages where prompted**. These sections are written in the quality of each different Effort to help you remain in the Effort at all times as you work, including when you are reading the guidance.

DABBING

[1]   Dabbing is Light in Weight;
Dabbing is Sudden in Time;
Dabbing is Direct in Space.
To Dab is to be Light, Sudden, Direct.

[2]

Video Resource

Dabbing
https://vimeo.com/251497202

[3]   *Build exercises into your warm-up that:*
- *are spatially organized*
- *efficiently move individual body parts while keeping the rest of the body calm*
- *involve Simultaneous movements*
- *prepare your feet and knees to jump.*

[4]   *Bring your attention to your eyes until you become aware that you are blinking all the time without realizing it. Notice how the experience of blinking is Light, Sudden and Direct: Dabbing.* Blinking is a reflex we all have and it is a natural Dab. So you already know how to embody Dabbing perfectly. Once you have undergone the whole Process exploring Dabbing, your Dab will become as beautifully Light, Direct and Sudden as the familiar action of blinking is already.

[5]   *Play with the idea of Dabbing at a spill:*
- *Imagine using a cloth to gently Dab at a red wine spill on a white carpet.*
- *Move around the room. Use your hands to Dab places and things which catch your attention. Make the target you are Dabbing very specific: a mark on the wall, the corner of a window, etc.*
- *Begin to Dab places and things with your feet and other body parts. Find out how to Dab with parts of your body for which it doesn't feel as easy.*

[6]   *Explore the following images:*
- *Imagine delicately and exactly potting a snooker ball that is hovering over the pocket. Do this with different parts of your body.*
- *Imagine you are light rain landing on the surface of water.*
- *Imagine that each molecule in the air is a tiny target that can be Dabbed. Choose a body part and Dab the molecules of the surrounding air with it.*

[7]   Useful types of music to work with include: Funk, Old School Rap and Klezmer music.

[8]   You will have experienced some of the following:

The core body is upright and centred; Stable and symmetrical.
The Direct Space of Dabbing makes it clear in its linear movement.
Each move carries the purpose of Direct: it has a known end-point.

The Sudden Time of Dabbing means that it starts and stops.
Dabbing is lots of fresh beginnings and crisp endings.
The Dab is changeable: a series of pocketed moments in Time.
Moves begin and end. There are no middle bits.

The Light Weight of Dabbing means it does not know exhaustion.
Pinpointed attention without fatigue gives Dab its power.

[9]   The Default is:

Small-scale, peripheral:
Sudden tends to express itself in smaller moves;
these are easier to start and stop.
Lightness occurs naturally at the edges of our body.
There is less mass at the periphery.
So Dab tends towards movements of the extremities:
repetitive moves of head, hands, elbows, feet, knees.

High-level: Directness is Stable.
Suddenness allows for stepping.
So to stand upright on two feet is easy.

There is no instant need to find moves on the floor.
The *Wheel Plane* and the *Table Plane* come into use.
Arms move from the elbow.
The body bends at the hinge of the hip.

[10] Dabbing shares:
the Lightness of Floating.

[11] In Dabbing, control is located in:
Light (Weight), Sudden (Time), and Direct (Space).

Dabbing feels inherently controlled.
Movements are Sudden yet Light:
there is little force so they are easy to stop and start.
The movements are swift and short; easily contained.

Dabbing is Direct, and therefore innately Stable.
Direct movement has an inherent relationship with Stability.
There is little need to work to control balance.

[12] Dab feels bite-sized and palatable.
Dab likes order and is not invasive.
It is an Effort society often asks of us.
The Dab arrives on time and makes lists.
It seems not to demand commitment.
Dabbing does not force a point.
It happily changes its opinion.

Dabbing may seem tentative.
The Dab can't commit to its Direct intention.
It does not have the force of Strong/Heavy Weight.
It does not have the relentlessness of Sustain.
Yet it is not inherently timid, faltering or shy.
Make no mistake: tentative is not Dabbing.
Dabbing is Dabbing: Light, Sudden and Direct.
Trust that the Dab can express anything.

[13] Start by finding a Light, Sudden, Direct breath.
Begin to allow the breath to carry a sound.
Words, or sounds that are formed like words, appear.
They are monosyllabic.
They begin and end Suddenly with the pop of a consonant.
Repetition of the word 'Dab' sounds like Dabbing.

So your Dab may say 'Dab, Dab, Dab, Dab . . .' as you move.
This may become 'Dab, dib, dob, bib, bob, cob, fob, fab', etc.

The shortness of the words may cause you to over-commit.
How can the sounds be deftly made, but remain Light?
Focus on Direct will help you.
Give the words pinpointed intention, without Strong/Heavy Weight.
The sounds will nimbly pitter-patter out of your mouth.

If it helps, use the Dabbing Soundtrack as you work:

Audio Resource

Dabbing Soundtrack
https://vimeo.com/251647668

[14]   Specific Agendas include:

//Knowing where you are going
Dab knows where each move is going.
It gets there using the shortest route.
See the ending before you begin.
Set off and arrive with the same precision.
Dab can jump. It knows where it is going in the air.
It knows where it is landing.
Both parts of the action are Dabs.

//Maintaining the Effort Quality in the stillness
You are always embodying the Dab:
both in the moves and in the pauses between moves.

//Finding a variety of moves
Repetition of moves is needed to master and bank them.
Yet in Sudden it is easy to get into a repetitive pattern.
Don't forget that each Dabbing move is singular.
Avoid repetition of the same action over and over.

//Using both wide and narrow moves
In Dab, Direct Space is paired with Sudden Time.
A sense of restriction sometimes emerges.
This can cause a narrowing of movement.
Remember: moves can be wide as well as narrow.

//Avoiding one repetitive rhythm
Dab can feel less expressive than the other Efforts.
This is because the movement is so controlled.
Be careful: don't buy into this trap.
Dabbing is not necessarily robotic.
Yet if you Dab in one repetitive rhythm it will be.
Find Dabbing at different tempos.
Retain precision as you ask:
How fast or slow can Dabbing be?
Rhythmic variation will help.
It unlocks Dab's expressive potential.
Dab can have emotional significance.
Don't bypass its potential.

[15]   Specific Agendas include:

//Direct movement has no circularity
We can't move without circles occurring.
Our joints move through rotation.
Our bones have curves.
Our anatomical structure is innately Indirect.
But our body can express the story of Direct.
Remember: your eyeball is curved.
Yet your natural blink is a Dab. It expresses Direct.
Focus on expressing the story of Direct in Dabbing.
Discover linear pathways in Space.
Do not indulge sensations of curve.
Investigate how to change direction in Space.
Can you change direction without expressing 'turning'?
Imagine corners where two straight lines in Space meet.
Shift facing from one Direct pathway to the other.
Use your knowledge of the Planes to help you.[1]

//Sudden movements have no 'middle'
Every move has a beginning, middle and an end.
Even very fast moves.
Yet in Dab the expressive story is of Sudden.
So the feeling is of starts and stops. Nothing in-between.
Focus on succinct ends and beginnings.
This will highlight the Suddenness of Dab.
Is it taking you longer to stop the movement than start it?

---

[1] Cf. 'The Planes', p. 36.

Or to start the movement than stop it?
Eradicate the blurring of Sustain in both the stop and the start.
Seek exactness; precision.
Tell the story of a move with no middle.

[16]

Audio Resource

A Dabbing Journey
https://vimeo.com/251647766

Figure 6.2(a) Stages of a Dabbing Process.

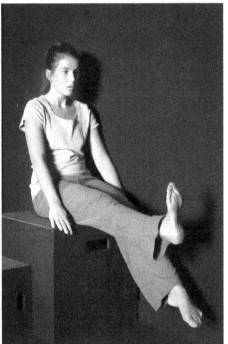

Figure 6.2(b) Stages of a Dabbing Process (cont.).

WRINGING

[1] Wringing is Strong/Heavy in Weight;
Wringing is Sustained in Time;
Wringing is Indirect in Space.
To Wring is to be Strong/Heavy, Sustained, Indirect.

[2]

Video Resource

Wringing
https://vimeo.com/251497956

[3] *Build exercises into your warm-up that:*
  - *mobilize individual joints*
  - *move the whole body through circular pathways*
  - *involve Sequential movements*
  - *demand full breath and commitment.*

[4] *Recall the sensation in your body when you do a big yawn that fights its way out of your body. Notice how the experience of this type of yawn is Strong/ Heavy, Sustained and Indirect: Wringing.* Yawning is a reflex we all have and it is a natural Wring. So you already know how to embody Wringing perfectly. Once you have undergone the whole Process exploring Wringing, your Wring will become as beautifully Strong/Heavy, Sustained and Indirect as the familiar action of a big yawn is already.

[5] *Play with the idea of Wringing out a wet cloth:*
  - *Imagine you are wringing out a wet cloth – it requires a significant amount of applied Strength, so both your hands and arms are involved in the action.[2]*
  - *Now imagine that you want to squeeze the twist of the cloth even tighter: feel how your shoulder girdle, torso and core muscles start to become involved in the action.*
  - *Allow the rest of the body gradually to join in the Wring along with the hands, arms, torso and core.*

[6] *Explore the following images:*
  - *Imagine you are wrestling through the gut of a boa constrictor.*

---

[2] Some actors may never have done or observed this action, which used to be such a large part of everyday life when water had to be squeezed out of washed clothes by hand. If you are unfamiliar with the action of Wringing out clothes, try it for yourself by soaking some clothes or fabric in water and then squeezing it out by twisting the cloth.

- *Imagine your blood is made of chewing gum.*
- *Imagine you are wrapping yourself up in elastic string; entangling and disentangling.*

[7]   Useful types of music to work with include: Ballads, North American Country Music, Gospel and Opera.

[8]   You will have experienced some of the following:

The body is off-centre; Labile and asymmetrical. The Strong/Heavy Weight of Wringing changes the body's relationship to gravity drawing you inwards and downwards, so you may not begin upright.

The Sustained Time of Wringing means that there is only one ongoing movement: once you have started moving, you cannot stop to start again The movement is always different, continually emerging. The Indirect Space of Wringing means that there is no movement in any pre-determined direction; there is no plan to the journey.

The power that Wringing possesses is in the progression of one constantly evolving movement. The inevitability of the spiralling Sustain captivates and satisfies. Wringing can teach us about the beauty of spirals and twists; their capacity to coil and uncoil, bind and unravel. It can find itself passing through extraordinary shapes, constantly unearthing new possibilities.

[9]   The Default is:

Large-scale, whole-body, Gathering: Strong/Heavy Weight naturally occurs in the core body where there is more mass, so Wringing often starts with Strong/Heavy movements of the torso, pelvis and spine that draw the arms and legs inwards.

Low-level: On the floor it is easier to be off-centre. Here, Indirectness can express itself in Lability, and Sustain can be sought without stepping from foot to foot; the body can roll and spiral, finding Expansion as it moves easily through the *Wheel Plane* and the *Table Plane*.

[10]   Wringing can be felt as: a Strong/Heavy version of Floating, and the opposite to Dabbing.

[11]   In Wringing, control is located in: Strong/Heavy (Weight) and Sustained (Time):

Strong/Heavy Weight demands committed muscular engagement to create force. Engaging your muscles in an expression of Strength facilitates power with control, and will help you remain in Lability without over-balancing into an uncontrolled fall.[3]

Sustain demands you move without stopping; that it is controlled, so that there is never an end-point. It requires you to shift your Centre of Gravity gradually but continuously. There is nowhere to stop; no arrival.

The expression of this onwards progression of movement facilitates muscular engagement and shifts in Flow which prevent you from falling, and allow you to be safely in Lability. Embodying Sustain enables you to undertake an ongoing action of falling: falling without landing.

[12] Wringing cannot readily change its standpoint from one moment to the next, although it does not have a clearly articulated plan. It is easily understood as intense, gloomy or preoccupied with self. Your first impression may be to associate it with the internal tightening of anguished crying or creeping fear. Yet there is the potential for freedom in the Wring, as the body surrenders to the unending, Sequential pathways of the movement which maintain one action whilst constantly discovering new things.

Wringing can be viewed as ineffective because it is both committed and uncommitted at the same time: Wringing is a powerful, Sustained commitment to going nowhere as Indirect pathways journey onwards with no planned destination. Except 'nowhere' can also be everywhere. So Wringing can be a powerful Sustained commitment to grapple at scale with everything, everywhere. Make no mistake: Wringing is not ineffective. Wringing is just Wringing – Strong/Heavy, Sustained and Indirect – trust that the Wring can express anything.

[13] The sound of Wringing is never-ending, guttural and deep. It can seem quite extreme at first. You may feel you want to scale down or diminish the sound but instead ask: how can you stay Strong/Heavy? Let the sound wind and twist its way out of you just as the movement spirals and turns. The face and jaw can help you masticate the sound, chewing it out of the body.

In Wring there may be a tendency to strangle the sound, adding a painful excess of tension. This is not necessary and should be avoided. Constriction is an indicator of stasis: movement which is held not Sustained. It is only painful if you hold the sound. Go with it rather than fighting through or against it; allow the sound to Wring with the movement of the body and breath.

---

[3] Cf. 'Counter-tension', p. 40.

If it helps, use the Wringing Soundtrack to accompany you as you work:

Audio Resource

Wringing Soundtrack
https://vimeo.com/251647886

[14] Specific Agendas include:

//Don't reverse or repeat a move
In Sustain you can never undo or redo your movement. As you twist in and around yourself, don't give in to the temptation to stop and rewind your movement by reversing the pathways which took you into a certain position. In Sustain there is only ever one constant action that carries you onwards, without stopping.

//Avoiding stepping
As much as possible, avoid stepping as a means of travelling: steps are a series of the same move rather than one continuous movement, and therefore are more likely to express Sudden than Sustain. The limbs and spine can be used Sequentially as you move through the space. Be aware of your peripheries and your core, and the connection between the two; feel the connection between the toes and the fingertips. Find ways to solve the problem of travelling through Space, which will help you to maintain Sustain. Experiment with rolling, spiralling, twisting, turning, etc.

//Remember: Sustain is not slow motion
Do not try to pre-plan a movement progression, but rather be present in the moment and allow the movement to emerge – to happen to you – at a pace you can maintain indefinitely.

//Embodying Indirect in the line of the neck
Notice if you are allowing the back of the neck to be in Direct line with the body. Instead, let the head meander off-centre so that full-body Wringing emerges as different pathways carry you through perpetual Lability.

//Maintaining Strong movements in the peripheral body[4]
Outward movements tend to get Lighter at the periphery where there is less body mass, but expression of Strong Weight in the peripheral body is possible. Imagining that the air around you is thick can help create a sense that you are working against something and so create resistance.

//Wringing is not only contracting
Wringing can easily draw inwards on itself in contracting spirals but this is not the only possibility. Discover how Wringing can also expand outwards to meet the world.

---

[4] Cf. 'Discovering Strong', p. 63.

[15]   Specific Agendas include:

//Shifting the Centre of Gravity
Progressively shifting your Centre of Gravity as you move in Sequential spirals and twists helps you move fluidly through the space.

//Using one point of gravitational support
Enjoy how a clear sense of where the point of gravitational support is located allows you to Wring the parts of your body that are normally preoccupied with supporting weight (e.g. the legs and hips).

//Re-imagining vertical and horizontal
Re-imagine the space through which you are moving as you begin to explore supporting your weight through different body parts.

[16]

Audio Resource

A Wringing Journey
https://vimeo.com/251648002

Figure 6.3(a) Stages of a Wringing Process.

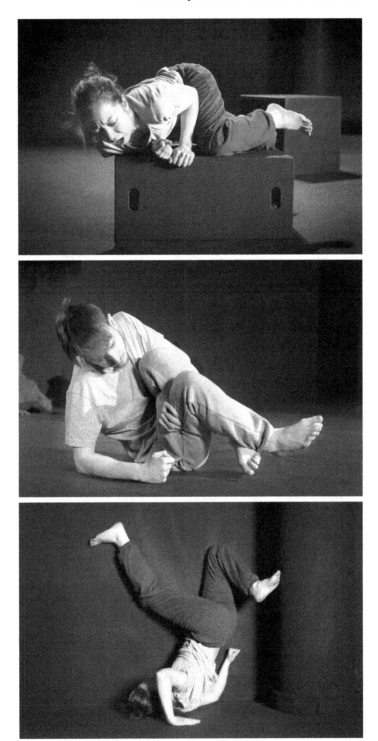

Figure 6.3(b) Stages of a Wringing Process (cont.).

THRUSTING

[1] Thrusting is Strong/Heavy in Weight;
Thrusting is Sudden in Time;
Thrusting is Direct in Space;
To Thrust is to be Strong/Heavy, Sudden, Direct.

[2]

Video Resource

Thrusting
https://vimeo.com/251498690

[3] *Build exercises into your warm-up that:*
- *are spatially organized*
- *efficiently move individual body parts while keeping the rest of the body calm*
- *move the whole body and demand full breath and commitment*
- *involve Simultaneous movements*
- *prepare your feet and knees to jump.*

[4] *Recall the sensation in your body when your core muscles contract with force.* This will be familiar to you from when you have vomited, or if you have given birth. *Notice how the first moment of the contraction is Strong/Heavy, Sudden and Direct: a Thrust.* It is part of a reflex that we all have. So you already know how to embody Thrusting perfectly. Once you have undergone the whole Process exploring Thrusting, your Thrust will become as beautifully Strong/Heavy, Sudden and Direct as the familiar action of contracting is already.

[5] *Play with the idea of bouncing a ball:*
- *Imagine you are bouncing a basketball or netball very close to the floor.*
- *Notice how the movements in your hand and arm, torso and knees are all Strong/Heavy, Sudden, Direct: Thrusting.*
- *Find this same quality of movement with other body parts.*

[6] *Explore the following images:*
- *Imagine you are the pistons in an engine.*
- *Imagine you are a stampede of cattle.*
- *Imagine you are blasts of lava erupting out of rock.*

[7] Useful types of music to work with include: Military music, Dubstep, and Techno.

[8]   You will have experienced some of the following:

Thrust is Stable, symmetrical.
The core body is upright, centred.
Thrust expresses through linear movement.
Directness in Space reads as clear purpose.
Each move has a known end-point.
Strong/Heavy Weight doubles commitment.
Sudden Time means moves start and stop.
There are no middle bits; begin and end.
Moves explode. Power is in Directed force.

[9]   The Default is:

Large-scale, peripheral, Scattering:
Strong/Heavy Weight powers large, outward moves.
Sudden explosions of force away from the body.
Thrust often starts with violent moves of the arms.
A rigid torso holds the body upright.

High-level: Thrust is Direct and so Stable.
To stand upright on two feet is easy.
Thrust is Sudden: it can step.
There is no instant desire to find moves on the floor.
The *Wheel Plane* and the *Table Plane* come into use.
Arms drive forward.
The body bends at the hinge of the hip.

[10] Thrusting shares:
the Strength/Heaviness of Wringing.
It can also be felt as:
a Strong/Heavy version of Dabbing;
the opposite to Floating.

[11] In Thrusting, control is located in:
Sudden (Time) and Direct (Space).

Strong/Heavy Weight combines with Sudden Time.
So Thrusting movement has explosive force.
This might feel overly powerful: uncontrolled.
Yet Sudden demands that each movement is finite.
Every move has a clear beginning and ending in Time.
Focus on the precise start and stop of the Sudden.
Muscular engagement and shifts in Flow will occur.
Each stop and start allows you to regain and reassert control.

Thrusting is Direct and so innately Stable.
In Thrust there is little need to work to control balance.

[12] Thrust has Strong opinions.
It makes firm decisions. But they can change with force.
One moment, one plan.
Another moment, a new plan.
Thrust does not take much time to listen.
Thrust can seem bull-headed:
very certain, only to change its mind.
Thrust is dominant and tough.

Thrusting may seem aggressive.
The Thrust commits to its Direct objective.
Strong/Heavy Weight backs this up with force.
Sudden brings stops and starts.
Each one is a new explosion of Directed energy.
Yet it is not innately violent or antagonistic.
Make no mistake: aggressive is not Thrusting.
Thrusting is just Thrusting: Strong/Heavy, Sudden and Direct.
Trust that the Thrust can express anything.

[13] Start by finding a Strong/Heavy, Sudden, Direct breath.
Begin to allow the breath to carry a sound.
Monosyllabic words occur.
They begin and end Suddenly with the hit of a consonant.
Repetition of the word 'Thrust' sounds like Thrusting.
Your Thrust might say 'Thrust, Thrust, Thrust . . .' as you move.
This may start to become 'Thrust, thrast, hast, hust, blust', etc.
The sounds will blast out of your mouth to a pinpointed place.

In Thrust there may be a tendency to shout.
The Thrusting sound will be loud.
Yet there should be no constriction.
Use your muscles to support the breath.
Take care to release unwanted tension.
Keep the voice open.
The sounds should be Strong and clear.

If it helps, use the Thrusting Soundtrack as you work:

Audio Resource

Thrusting Soundtrack
https://vimeo.com/251649112

[14]   Specific Agendas include:

//Knowing where you are going
Thrust has definite starts and stops.
Set off and arrive with the same precision.
Thrust can jump. Both parts are Thrusts.
It heads to an exact point in the air.
It knows where it will land.

//Maintaining the Effort Quality in the stillness
Don't Sustain the pauses between the moves.
You are still in Thrust as you pause.
Thrust in the stillness is not tense.
It is committed with ease to its focus and power.

//Finding a variety of moves
Excessive repetition becomes automatic. It loses its point.
The brain no longer works together with the body.
Explore how many different Thrusts your body can do.

//Using both wide and narrow moves
Don't restrict yourself to narrow moves.
Use your knowledge of the different Planes.[5]
This can help you venture sideways into width.

//Thrusting is not tense
Too much tension can cause Thrusting to be robotic.
Move efficiently to find ease even in exertion.
Make sure you let yourself breathe with the Thrust.

//Avoiding punching and stamping[6]
A Thrusting arm Gesture can seem like a punch.
Yet a punch has Indirect within it.
The action uses curved fingers. The arm twists.
So Thrusting is not punching.
Keep your Gestures Direct.
Seek how the arms can Thrust.
Just as Thrust is not a punch, Thrust is not a stamp.
Stomping dissipates energy. It can become Indirect.
Creating noise is a shortcut to feeling moves are Strong.
But bangs cannot tell the story of Thrust for you.
Strength must be found in the body.
Contact sound may occur but it is not the task.
Keep force in the body (not wasted on objects or the floor).

---

[5] Cf. 'The Planes', p. 36.
[6] Cf. 'Use of Thrusting', p. 266.

The task is to Thrust. Don't make the story about the floor.
The story is Thrusting. It has humanity.
Don't bypass its potential.
Thrust can have emotional significance.

[15]   Specific Agendas include:

//Direct movement has no circularity
Discover linear pathways in Space.
Do not indulge sensations of curve.
Change direction without expressing 'turning'.

//Sudden movements have no 'middle'
Focus on succinct ends and beginnings.
Tell the story of a move with no middle.

[16]

Audio Resource

A Thrusting Journey
https://vimeo.com/251650062

Figure 6.4(a) Stages of a Thrusting Process

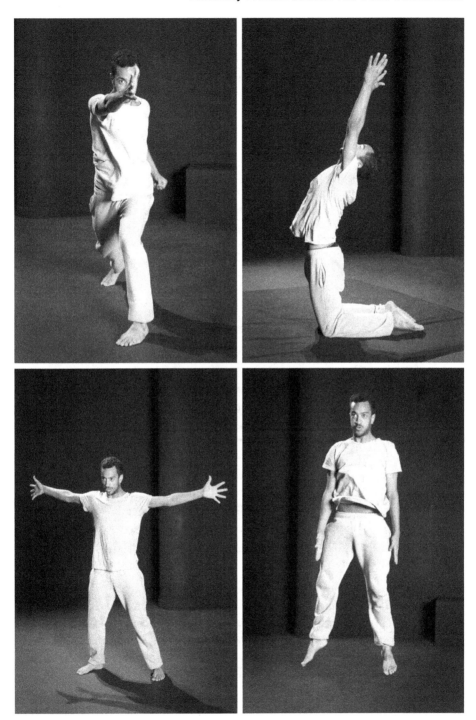

Figure 6.4(b) Stages of a Thrusting Process (cont.).

PRESSING

Safety point: Pressing takes a significant amount of energy. Pay particular attention to your energy levels – it is fine for you to feel the exertion of Pressing, but make sure you alternate short explorations and reflective pauses as you feel necessary. There should be no muscular tremors or reverberation in your Pressing. These would alert you to unnecessary muscular tension or overwork.

[1]   Pressing is Strong/Heavy in Weight;
       Pressing is Sustained in Time;
       Pressing is Direct in Space.
       To Press is to be Strong/Heavy, Sustained, Direct.

[2]

Video Resource

Pressing
https://vimeo.com/251499214

[3]   *Build exercises into your warm-up that:*
       • *are spatially organized*
       • *efficiently move individual body parts while keeping the rest of the body calm*
       • *move the whole body and demand full breath and commitment*
       • *involve Simultaneous movements*
       • *shift energy throughout both your core and peripheral body.*

[4]   *Straining/squeezing:* In movement work, to 'strain' implies an overwork that can lead to injury. So we cultivate ease and efficiency instead. However, it can be useful to recall the sensation briefly. Single-minded endeavour naturally produces straining. A woman strains to press down through a contraction to birth a baby. When a baby is on the potty, you can also see their whole body driven by a natural impulse to Press down. The sensation is of a directed squeeze and it will be a familiar experience to you.

Recall the sensation in your body when you use a directed squeeze. Find the sensation of a directed downwards squeeze in your abdomen. Notice how the experience of this type of squeeze is Strong/Heavy, Sustained and Direct: Pressing. Squeezing is an action we all do from time to time and it is a natural Press. So you already know how to embody Pressing perfectly. Once you have undergone the whole Process exploring Pressing, your Press should become as beautifully Strong/Heavy, Sustained and Direct as the familiar action of squeezing is already.

[5]   *Play with the idea of Pressing Blu-tack into a wall:*
- *Imagine you are Pressing Blu-tack (or putty) into the wall with your thumb, and then the heel of your hand.*
- *Now, move around the room and use your hands to Press against places and things which catch your attention.*
- *Begin to Press against places and things with your feet; and with other body parts. Find out how to Press with parts of your body for which it doesn't feel as easy. Use your body weight to enable you to push away / off / up from different things.*

[6]   *Explore the following images:*
- *Imagine the walls, floor and ceiling are closing in on you and you need to Press them away using different parts of your body.*
- *Imagine you are walking out to sea, pushing and dragging your legs through the water; or you are on a flat mountain top and the wind is so strong that you can lean into it. Move different parts of your body against the wind.*
- *Imagine the air as thick blocks which hug your body. Choose different body parts and use them to Press against the surrounding air.*

[7]   Useful types of music to work with include: Tango, Drum and Bass, and Heavy Metal.

[8]   You will have experienced some of the following:

The core body is in an upright and centred position, allowing it to be both Stable and symmetrical. The Direct Space of Pressing means it is clear in its linear movement. The Press has a known end-point so the movement is purposeful. Strong/Heavy Weight doubles commitment as you constantly move towards the destination.

Sustained Time means that there is only one continuous, ongoing movement: once you have started moving, you cannot stop to start again – it is one movement which is constantly progressing. Pinpointed intention guiding the unyielding advancement of one unfolding Strong/Heavy movement gives Press its power.

[9]   The Default is:

Large-scale, whole-body, expanding: Pressing is often first expressed through the Gesture we think of as 'pushing': a mid-space Gesture forwards through Space with the arms, supported by a whole-body engagement of the muscular core. Even for gestural movements of the periphery (arms), the core body engages to provide Counter-tension for expression of Sustained Strong/Heavy Weight. The result is use of full core-body activation and big movements.

Mid-level: a mid-level stance allows expression of Sustain together with Directness. At low-level it is harder to maintain Directness (it is challenging to move through angles on the floor). At high-level it is harder to maintain Sustain (stepping breaks Sustain into Sudden). Here, the legs power a fully activated core giving Stability as the body moves primarily through the *Wheel Plane*, with additional use of the *Table Plane* and the *Door Plane*.

[10] Pressing shares: the Sustain of Floating and the Directness of Dabbing. It can also be felt as: a Direct version of Wringing; or a Sustained version of Thrusting.

[11] In Pressing, control is located in: Strong/Heavy (Weight) and Direct (Space).

Strong/Heavy Weight demands committed muscular engagement to create force. Engaging your muscles in an expression of Strength facilitates power with control.[7]

Pressing is Direct and therefore Stable. However, expressing Direct Space with Sustained Time may challenge balance in certain movements. Direct demands that you know where you are going in Space and do not deviate from that pathway. So focusing on Direct can help Stabilize you and keep you from overbalancing into unwanted Lability.

[12] Pressing can be viewed as emotionally hard work: oppressing and repressing.[8] Your first impression may be to associate it with holding in emotion. Yet Pressing is also impressive: teaching us about the beauty of a powerful, forging, unstoppable force, as the body connects with Strength to infinite lines in Space. It can be consumed in mono-directional focus that removes everything in its path to manifest the possibility of an everlasting journey.

Pressing is often used to repress socially 'unacceptable' thoughts and feelings. The Press works as a tight lid which pushes thoughts and feelings inside and keeps them hidden. However, although it is often used this way, it can express any thought or feeling. Make no mistake: Pressing is not only an oppressor. Pressing is just Pressing – Strong/Heavy, Sustained and Direct – trust that the Press can express anything.

[13] The sound of Pressing is guttural and deep, and remains on one pitch and tone. It can seem quite extreme at first. You may feel you want to scale down or diminish the sound but instead ask: how can you stay Strong/Heavy? The face and jaw can help you propel the sound out of the body.

Avoid any 'strangling' of the sound (the addition of a painful excess of tension), particularly if the Press feels like an imposition of an Effort that is oppressing the sound. This is not necessary and should be avoided. Make the Press active,

---

[7] Cf. 'Counter-tension', p. 40

[8] Notice how these assumptions are even built into the roots of our vocabulary: each of these words contains the word 'press' within it.

not passive: the sound itself is Pressing, not resisting a Press. It is only painful if you hold the sound. Go with it rather than fighting through or against it; allow the sound to Press with the movement of the body and breath. It will propel its way out of you in the same way the movement forges through Space.

If it helps, use the Pressing Soundtrack as you work:

Audio Resource

Pressing Soundtrack
https://vimeo.com/251650203

[14]   Specific Agendas include:

//Avoiding the lure of body design
In Pressing, there can be a temptation to reduce the movement to body design: a focus on the shape of the body. This can result in the movement becoming a series of static body shapes that are being manoeuvred around the space like statues, without true Sustain. The experience that Press offers is that of the line of energy travelling through Space without the interruption of Sudden (starts and stops).

//Don't reverse or repeat a move
Allow yourself an embodied understanding of our human journey; as we move through Time there is no true return, moments pass away and we cannot re-enter them. Pressing and the other Sustained Efforts understand this.

//Avoiding stepping
Find ways to travel through Space which help you to maintain Sustain throughout the body. Explore how bringing parts of your body towards or away from each other, or shifting level, can help move you through Space.

//Remember: Sustain is not slow motion
In Sustain, your movement may need to be slow, but don't fool yourself by confusing Sustain with slow motion.[9] Live inside the pace set by the Sustain as the Press indefinitely pursues its goal.

//Resisting a desire to use diagonals
You may be experiencing a desire to use diagonal movements. These can be Direct but they do not extend or mirror the vertical and horizontal lines of the body, nor are they on the Planes.[10] So they tend to have a sense of deviating from the straight and are likely to indicate a leaning towards becoming Indirect.

---

[9] Cf. 'The Difference between Sustained and Slow Motion', p. 72.
[10] Cf. 'The Planes', p. 36.

//Resisting the urge to make it 'interesting'

The Press makes linear shapes in Space, and some people associate this with being dull. It can result in attempts to make Pressing more 'interesting', but this is likely to lead to Indirect movement. Inhabit the Press with precision to discover what is remarkable about Pressing. You will find the beauty in its powerful, unrelenting commitment.

//Maintaining Strong movements in the peripheral body

Keep focusing on Strength when movements occur in the peripheral body and out towards the edges of the Kinesphere. Do not allow the Weight to Lighten but remain committed to the force of Pressing.

[15] Specific Agendas include:

//Direct movement has no circularity

Discover linear pathways in Space and do not indulge sensations of curve. Find ways to change direction without expressing 'turning'.

//Sustain never reaches an 'end-point'

As you move outwards in Sustain, you will find that you come to the inevitable 'end-point' of a movement (e.g. when your arm or leg arrives at full reach). You cannot curve the pathway of the movement because you are working in Direct. So, when the movement 'runs out' in this way, you will feel a need to break the Sustain by starting a new move to take the body part in a different direction. Instead, shift the main location of the Press before the movement has run out: if, for example, the arm is Pressing out to the side, the pelvis can begin to Press downwards before the arm movement reaches completion. In this way, the experience is of Pressing that never stops and the overall story is of ongoing Sustained movement. This is not the same as tracking through the body using neighbouring body parts to Press one after the other. Rather, it uses an understanding of Simultaneous movement to help you work with more than one unrelated body part at a time in order to shift the location of the Press around the body.[11]

[16]

Audio Resource

A Pressing Journey
https://vimeo.com/251650517

---

[11] Cf. 'Sequential and Simultaneous', p. 43.

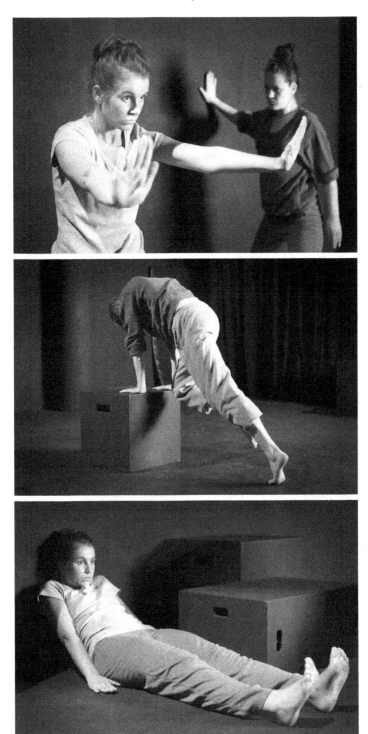

Figure 6.5(a) Stages of a Pressing Process.

Figure 6.5(b) Stages of a Pressing Process (cont.).

FLICKING

Safety point: When you are discovering Flicking, it is important to stay working technically for a significant amount of time. This will let you carefully bank enough vocabulary to improvise in Flick safely. When you are first discovering Flicking, keep your periods of exploration short. Do a greater number of these short explorations with pauses for reflection in between. This will prevent you getting over-tired and doing careless or uncontrolled Flicking.

[1]   Flicking is Light in Weight;
      Flicking is Sudden in Time;
      Flicking is Indirect in Space.
      To Flick is to be Light, Sudden, Indirect.

[2]

Video Resource

Flicking
https://vimeo.com/251501834

[3]   *Build exercises into your warm-up that:*
   - *engage individual body parts while keeping the rest of the body calm*
   - *move through circular pathways, including Swings*
   - *use rotation to mobilize each joint; particularly those to soften your neck, ankles and knees*
   - *mobilize your torso and prepare you to move off-centre*
   - *prepare your feet and knees to jump.*

[4]   *Starting/flinching/jumping:* Our bodies have an inbuilt mechanism called the 'Startle Response'. It occurs when we encounter stimuli that are unexpected or threatening. We use different words to describe the effects of this physical response: a loud sound occurs unexpectedly and makes you 'jump'; a big insect lands on your arm causing you to 'start'; or you 'flinch' away from someone threatening to tickle you.

   Imagine the sensation in your body when you 'jump', 'start' or 'flinch'. Notice how the first moment of all these actions is Light, Sudden and Indirect: a Flick. It is part of a reflex that we all have, so you already know how to embody a Flick perfectly. Once you have undergone the whole Process exploring Flicking, your Flick will become as beautifully Light, Sudden and Indirect as the familiar actions of jumping, starting and flinching are already.

[5]   *Play with the idea of Flicking a piece of dust:*

- *See a piece of dust on your arm. Use your fingers to Flick it off. Make sure you are Flicking something away from just the surface of your sleeve or arm.*
- *Now, move around the room and use your hand to Flick pieces of dust off places and things which catch your attention.*
- *Begin carefully to Flick places and things with your feet; and with other body parts. Find out how to Flick with parts of your body for which it doesn't feel as easy.*

[6]   *Explore the following images:*

- *Imagine you are wearing a grass skirt and use your hips to Flick the grass skirt to and fro.*
- *Imagine you are a dog in the rain shaking the water out of your coat.*
- *Imagine that each molecule in the air is a tiny target which can be Flicked. Choose different body parts and use them to Flick the molecules of the surrounding air.*

[6B] *Additional Explorations*: Once you have worked with these images, **take some time to ease into a full experience of Flicking**. You can do this by revisiting 'Discovering Lability' (p. 42), and/or using mats as described in 'Working Towards Full Body Slashing' (p. 156).

[7]   Useful types of music to work with include: 1920s dance music such as Charleston and Boogie Woogie.

[8]   You will have experienced some of the following:

The body is Labile;
asymmetrical. So start
in an off-centre
position. Sudden
Time means the Flick starts
and stops. It has sharp beginnings;
endings. The Flick
is not a mess or blur; it
changes; moment by
moment. Lightness allows
it to adapt cleanly,
simply. Flitting
from one movement
to the next requires
precision. Changeability

gives Flick its power. It
can bring a feeling
of liberation.

[9] The Default is:

Small-scale, peripheral, Scattering:
Less mass at the body's edges
lets Lightness occur
there easily. So Flicking appears
in the extremities;
we often use Flick
in our Gestures. Sudden
moves tend to be small, as
small moves
are easier to start
and stop.

High-level:
Fast, asymmetrical,
Labile moves are
more accessible when standing;
there is no immediate
motivation to discover Flicking moves
on the floor. Arms Scatter
outwards in the
Door Plane and *Table Plane*.

[10] Flicking shares:
the Indirectness of Wringing;
and the Suddenness of Thrusting.
It can also be felt as:
a Sudden version of Floating;
an Indirect version of Dabbing;
or the opposite to Pressing.

[11] In Flicking, control is located in:
Light (Weight) and Sudden (Time).

Sudden Time combines with
Indirect Space. So Flicking
is asymmetrical; Labile. Moves
tilt the body. It can feel wild; out
of control. Yet, Lightness
demands that each movement

has little force. Focus on
Lightness means brief moves
are easy to begin
and end. They can be efficiently
controlled whilst still
Labile and uninhibited; shifting
the body to and
fro in Space. If you feel you might
fall, heighten your attention
on expression of Lightness. Don't
let yourself give in to
gravity.

Sudden demands that
each move
is finite; every
move has a clear beginning
and ending in Time. Focus
on the precise start and
stop of the Sudden. Muscular
engagement and shifts
in Flow will occur. Each stop
and start allows you
to regain and reassert
control.

[12]   Flick likes novelty and never
remains in one
place, or sticks
to one activity. Flick
has a dash of vitality, a
flair that can seem
frivolous, or harmlessly
chaotic. Flick
seems more suited to parties
than offices. Flick
does not make lists, or
complete tasks on
time. It does not force a
point, and is happy to
change its opinion.

Flick may seem to lack
solemn intent; there is no

Direct end-point or
destination; no force of
Strong/Heavy Weight; continuity is
broken, as one new Sudden move
follows another. Yet, Flick
is not inherently flippant.
Make no mistake: frivolous is not
Flicking. Flicking is just
Flicking: Light, Sudden and
Indirect. Trust that the Flick can
express anything.

[13] Start by finding a Light, Sudden,
Indirect breath. Begin
to allow the breath to carry
a sound. Words,
or sounds that are formed like words,
appear. They are monosyllabic, and begin
and end Suddenly with the
clip of a consonant. Don't let
the sounds become
fuzzy around the edges. Repetition
of the word 'Flick'
sounds like Flicking. So your
Flick may say 'Flick, Flick,
Flick . . .' as you move.
This may start to branch out into
'Flick, flack, flock, tock,
tick, pick', etc.

The shortness
of the words may cause you to
over-commit. A crisp beginning
and end is needed for their Sudden
delivery in Flick. Form
the words with precision, but
remain Light. Keeping
it in your upper
register or head voice
will help. The sounds will
deftly flit out of
your mouth.

If it helps, use the
Flicking Soundtrack as you work:

Audio Resource

Flicking Soundtrack
https://vimeo.com/251651084

[14]   Specific Agendas include:

//Finding a variety of moves
Find out how many
different Flicks your body
can do. You will then
build a large bank of Flicking
moves. Switching between
a range of moves in
Flick will be
easier. You won't
need lots of repeats of a
move. You will have enough
vocabulary to embody Sudden
at a fast pace.

//Releasing the need to make decisions
Repetition can signal
that the actor is falling into
a pattern, plan, or rhythm.
Remember, Indirect
movements and thoughts are not
pre-planned; in Flick,
end-points happen
unexpectedly through the
stops of Sudden
Time, not through
pre-planned decisions of
direction and
destination made in
Space.

//Maintaining the Effort Quality in the stillness
Every part of your movement is
Flicking. You are still in
Flick as you pause.

//Avoiding a series of held shapes
Make sure you are not
accidentally Sustaining held
body shapes. Flick is an
unpredictable, ever
changing, rapid
progression of irregular
movements. Let Sudden beginnings
and endings carry you from
one move to
another. Don't keep centred
by holding body shapes
with your head in line with
your body.[12] Flicking is not
Stable. Do not return to
Centre: enter into
Lability.

//Using all parts of the body
When beginning to
Flick there is a tendency not
to use the legs; they remain stuck
to the floor, Heavy. Find
Lightness in the lower
body as well as the upper to
allow the legs to
Flick. Then Flick
without your arms and legs: Flick
with your torso, using
your breath and all
your innards. Try Flicking
your heart, your lungs, your gut
and then gradually
add your arms and legs
back in.

//Progressing beyond Gesture
Make sure your
Flicking includes both
Gestures and weight-bearing

---

[12] Re-read these important safety points if you need a reminder of how to take care of your neck when working in Lability, p. 42.

moves of all sizes. Allow Indirect
thought and
movement to take
you through
General Space. You will
arrive in places you wouldn't have
found, had you been moving in
a Direct way.

//Flicking is not 'flopping'
There should be no
mess or sloppiness in the
Flick. Make sure
you don't add Heavy
Weight leading to
flopping; or Sustained
Time leading to
blurring. Each
Flick is precise.

[15] Specific Agendas include:

//Sudden movements have no 'middle'
Focus on
succinct beginnings and
ends. Tell the story of a move with
no middle.

//Shifting the Centre of Gravity
There is no fixed
Centre of
Gravity in Flicking.[13] Repeatedly
shifting your Centre
of Gravity is what allows you to be
Labile, and to
Flick without losing
balance. Shift focus from
one body part to
another. Keep
moving: when you try to
hold a shape, to keep
balance, then you fix the Centre
of Gravity and cannot

---

[13] Cf. 'Centre of Gravity', p. 39.

be Labile. If you are not
Labile, you are not
Flicking.

[16]

Audio Resource

A Flicking Journey
https://vimeo.com/251651300

Figure 6.6(a) Stages of a Flicking Process.

Figure 6.6(b) Stages of a Flicking Process (cont.).

SLASHING

Safety point: Slashing is similar in its energy to dance styles that have been done for years to certain genres of music, and labelled with names such as 'moshing', 'slamming', 'pogoing', 'skanking' and 'head-banging'. These amateur movers can dance in this way but still avoid muscle injury even though the moves are vigorous. This is because in a social, happy situation the body is relaxed, with no adverse tension. When you begin to explore Slashing, you must keep in mind that working from a sense of relaxation is vital. Unnecessary tension will prevent freedom of movement and work against the moves you are trying to do. **Releasing tension will allow you to Slash safely.**

It is recommended that you explore Flicking before Slashing. Slashing shares two Elements with Flicking (Sudden Time and Indirect Space). A Flick can be felt as a Light Slash; or a Slash as a Strong/Heavy Flick. So many of the technical discoveries you have made about Flicking can therefore be applied to Slashing. When you are discovering Slashing, stay working technically for a significant amount of time so that you can carefully bank enough vocabulary to improvise in Slash safely.

Apply the following guidance throughout your exploration of Slashing:

- *Make sure that you are warmed up with a supple, alert body and mind.* You must be well-prepared and ready to work.

- *Allow the body to move freely with its own momentum.* This can be done by trusting yourself, moving without hesitation, and buying into the expression of the Effort Quality.

- *Ensure there is no hint of additional tension.* Make sure you are not holding your breath and keep the muscles soft and loose (released).

- *Keep your explorations short, dynamic and focused.* Don't carry on moving for too long without adequate pauses for reflection and rest. Slashing takes a great deal of energy and so you will tire more quickly in this Effort than in some of the others. Do a greater number of short explorations with pauses for reflection in between.

- *Don't let your explorations become a runaway train.* If you feel you're racing and somewhat out of control, then just stop for a few moments. Locate control before continuing.

- *Work in a clear open space, with conscious awareness of your body.* Don't throw your body with such abandon that you end up bruising yourself through impact with the floor, stray objects or other parts of your body.

- *Make sure you're not wearing any unsafe items of clothing* (e.g. long trousers that are going to trip you up, socks that are going to cause you to slip, or jewellery that might get ripped out or cut you).

[1]   Slashing is Strong/Heavy in Weight;
Slashing is Sudden in Time;
Slashing is Indirect in Space.
To Slash is to be Strong/Heavy, Sudden, Indirect.

[2]

Video Resource

Slashing
https://vimeo.com/251502316

[3]   **Safety point:** A particularly rigorous targeted warm-up is essential for Slashing. Slashing is demanding and poses specific challenges for the body. You should aim to be loose and released in your movement, without unnecessary tightening or holding of energy anywhere in your body. Focus on preparing the body parts that will be most challenged. Especially vulnerable to strain or injury is the neck.

Build exercises into your warm-up that:
- *engage individual body parts while keeping the rest of the body calm*
- *use rotation to mobilize each joint, particularly those to soften your neck, ankles and knees*
- *move through circular pathways, including Swings*
- *mobilize your torso to prepare you to move off-centre*
- *prepare your feet and knees to jump*
- *move the whole body and demand full breath and commitment.*

[4]   *Recall the sensation in your body when you do a big, surprising sneeze. Notice how the experience of this type of sneeze is Strong/Heavy, Sudden and Indirect: a Slash.* Sneezing is a reflex that we all have and it is a natural Slash. So you already know how to embody a Slash perfectly. Once you have undergone the whole Process exploring Slashing, your Slash will become as beautifully Strong/Heavy, Sudden and Indirect as the familiar action of a big sneeze is already.

[5]   *Play with the idea of escaping from spider webs:*
- *Imagine you are covered in sticky, unpleasant spider webs. Try to shake and brush them off your arms.*
- *Also try and get them off the rest of your body by moving your legs and other body parts.*
- *Now, move around the room trying to get away from webs that surround you.*

[6]   *Explore the following images:*
  - *Imagine you are a colt on an ice rink.*
  - *Imagine that your clothes are on fire.*
  - *Imagine your limbs are made of knives.*
  - *Imagine hurling furniture about the room.*

[6B] **Additional Explorations:** Once you have worked with these images, **take some time to ease into a full experience of Slashing** using the explorations outlined below.

//Upper Body/Lower Body Slashing
This exploration divides the body so that only one half moves at a time, whilst the other offers support. This gives an initial technical understanding of Slashing in both the upper and lower body. Before you begin, **remind yourself of the safety guidance** outlined at the top of the Slashing section (p. 153).

  - *Take a solid, Stable chair or large wooden box to a clear space in the room. Make sure you have plenty of room in which to work.*
  - *Sit on the chair.*
  - *In short bursts of about thirty seconds, embody Strong/Heavy, Sudden and Indirect in your lower body to discover different Slashing movements and positions. Your torso, upper body and head remain as normal.*
  - *Let the Stability of the chair hold you, whilst the movement of your legs rocks your body diagonally into different positions on the chair (forward/back/side to side). Find out how expressive your legs can be with Slashing.*
  - *Hold on to different parts of the chair with your hands and arms to give you greater support. This allows you to make bolder choices and shift into true Lability.*
  - *Don't race through the movement. Keep it clear. Allow the stops to be a source of active rest.* Each stop allows you to discover new positions for the body that result from Slashing. You should find yourself in some exciting, dynamic shapes.
  - *Now, embody Strong/Heavy, Sudden and Indirect in the upper body (torso and arms). The lower body remains as it is normally. At this point, don't involve the head or neck but work from the chest downwards through the trunk: Slash with the hips, the chest, the shoulders, the arms.*
  - *Remember to work in thirty-second bursts and give yourself enough rest in between bursts.*
  - *As the moves of your upper body draw you off-balance into Lability, trust that the chair anchors you safely and use your legs for additional support.*
  - *Take weight into your legs, so that you briefly stand as you allow the Slash to take you away from the chair for small moments before returning to sitting.*

- *Switch back to Slashing with the lower body only.*
- *Find moments when the Slashing in the lower body can allow for weight-bearing and move you away from the chair.* The chair remains as a support, and you can use your arms and hands to connect to it for security.
- *Switch between upper body movement only and lower body movement only. Allow your Slashing to move you on, off and around the chair.*
- *Remove the chair to create a large, clear space where you can work freely. Continue to switch between upper body movement only and lower body movement only. Don't Slash the head or neck but work from the torso down the body. If you have any concerns about safety, stop immediately – take a pause, and then start again with a clear focus.*

// *Working towards Full-Body Slashing*

This exploration requires thick mats so that you can experiment with Sudden Lability. This allows you to bank movements which are safe to repeat when you are no longer working on mats. It will help you safely discover the sensation of full-body Slashing.[14] Pay attention to keeping yourself safe. If you are working with a Buddy, take turns on the mats whilst the other observes.

- *Re-visit experimenting with moving from one Labile body position to another.[15] Start with the positions you have already discovered and then begin to add to them.*
- *Imagine that with each movement you are shifting where the Centre of Gravity is within the body.* Each position will be asymmetrical and you should feel that you are not Stable; that you are off-centre.
- *To start with, just give yourself a little time to realize that it's fun and that you can keep yourself safe.*
- *As your confidence increases, start to experiment and bank useful body shapes and movements.* You can then translate what you discover to different levels and orientations.
- *Resist becoming manic: use the stops and starts of the movement, and find active pauses.*
- *Play with off-centre moves at every level.* Moving between positions at mid and low level allows the legs and core to be as involved in the movement as the upper body and arms. Finding different points of contact with the mat allows you to support your body weight in various ways, thereby enabling a greater freedom of movement in all parts of the body.
- *Discover how to change level.* If changing level is hard, try thinking about it as one action broken up into different pieces: moving into the floor, for example, can be experienced as a fall that is broken up into a

---

[14] It can also be a useful exploration to discover the sensation of full-body Flicking.
[15] Cf. 'Discovering Lability', p. 42.

sequence of quick-changing freeze-frames, like a flick-book.

- *Make being Labile your key focus; think solely about moving your Centre of Gravity off-centre.* The mats are useful because they allow you to experiment safely with just how far off-centre you can go at every level.
- *Change facings on the mat as you move, and look at different places in the room to release the back of your neck.* Using your eyes will aid engagement of the natural, muscular support system of the neck and shoulders to help you move the head, neck and upper body safely. Remember: there should never be any hint of tension. Your muscles need to be released.
- *Make sure you are including the face in your movements. Avoid any sense that the face is 'watching' the body, or that you are observing your movements from the outside. Focus on experiencing the movement.*

[7]　Useful types of music to work with include: Hard Rock, Punk and Reggaeton.

[8]　You will have experienced some of the following:

The body is Labile;
asymmetrical. So start in
an off-centre
position. Sudden
Time means the Slash starts
and stops. The Slash
is not a mess; not a blur; it
changes; moment by
moment. Strong/Heavy
Weight brings force
in Space. Harsh beginnings and
endings require commitment. Each
movement is charged
and fierce. Slash is intense and
unruly; in this lies
its power. It brings
a sense of radical
unleashing.

[9]　The Default is:

Large-scale, peripheral, Scattering:
Strong/Heavy Weight powers
large moves. Sudden
explosions of force throw

the limbs away
from the body. Slash often starts
with violent moves
of the arms and
legs.

High-level:
Fast, forceful, asymmetrical,
Labile moves are
more accessible when
standing; there is no immediate
motivation to discover
Slashing moves
on the floor. Arms Scatter upwards and
outwards in the *Door Plane*; the
upper spine moves forward
and backwards
in the *Wheel Plane*.

[10] Slashing shares:
the Indirectness of Floating;
the Suddenness of Dabbing;
and the Strong-Heaviness of Pressing.
It can also be felt as:
a Sudden version of Wringing;
an Indirect version of Thrusting;
or a Strong/Heavy version of Flicking.

[11] In Slashing, control is located in:
Sudden (Time).

Strong/Heavy Weight combines with
Sudden Time and
Indirect Space. So Slashing
is asymmetrical; Labile. It can feel
explosive and
chaotic. Its force might feel
overly powerful; out
of control. Yet, Sudden
demands that each move
is finite; every
move has a clear beginning
and ending in Time. Focus
on the precise start and
stop of the Sudden. Muscular

engagement and shifts
in Flow will occur. Each stop
and start allows you
to reassert
control.

[12]   Slash
        can seem violently
        unruly, uncommunicative
        and fierce. It has a
        wildness that flings
        itself in seeming chaos, here
        then there. Slash has Strong opinions
        but no concern for structure,
        order, logic. Slash does not fix
        on one task, or stay
        in one place. Slash is a
        whirlwind: it seizes
        opportunity, then slings
        it away; breaks into
        places and sets the world
        alight.

        The Slash may seem
        frenzied: there is no
        Direct end-point or
        destination, but Strong/Heavy
        Weight takes moves to where they
        go with force; continuity is
        broken, as one new Sudden move
        follows another. Yet Slash
        is not inherently frantic.
        Make no mistake: frenzy is not
        Slashing. Slashing is just
        Slashing: Strong/Heavy, Sudden
        and Indirect. Trust that the Slash can
        express anything.

[13]   Start by finding a Strong/Heavy, Sudden,
        Indirect breath. Begin
        to allow the breath to carry
        a sound. Words,
        or sounds that are formed like words,

appear. They are monosyllabic, and begin
and end Suddenly with the
force of a consonant. Repetition
of the word 'Slash'
sounds like Slashing. So your
Slash may say 'Slash, Slash,
Slash . . .' as you move.
This may start to branch out into
'Slash, clash, bash, thrash,
bosh, bish', etc.

Fight to commit with force
to the consonants that book-end
each word. Sound explodes
from the mouth
powered by Strong/Heavy Weight, but
ends as soon as it begins,
stopped by Sudden Time. Form
the words with precision. Don't
let the sounds become blurred around
the edges. The sounds will be flung
out of your mouth.

If it helps, use the
Slashing Soundtrack as you work:

Audio Resource

Slashing Soundtrack
https://vimeo.com/251652226

[14]   Specific Agendas include:

//Finding a variety of moves
Use the bank of
moves that you discovered in
Flicking. Let this liberate
you from repetition.

//Releasing the need to make decisions
Avoid falling into
a pre-conceived pattern, plan or
rhythm. Separate
your attention into two
parts as you move: retain focus on

Indirect and
Sudden as two distinct
impulses. Find out how
to control stops in Time, without
needing to plan your direction or
end-point in
Space.

//*Maintaining the Effort Quality in the stillness*
Don't switch off in
the pauses. The pauses between
the moves will
re-energize you but
you're not pausing to build up
energy to do
a Slash. You remain in
Slash throughout.

//*Avoiding a series of held shapes*
Slash moves
on quickly from
body shape to body shape. Feel
how each move can
stop in a place which isn't
planned. The train does not
stop at the stations but
unexpectedly at points part way
along the track. Transitions through
off-centre will materialize, as you shift
Suddenly from move to
move in asymmetrical
Lability.

//*Progressing beyond Gesture*
Let Slashing take
you on a journey with
no plan as to where you are
going. To help you travel in
Slash, mix up
the size of moves, using
tiny moves as well as
large moves; and shift between
levels. Ultimately, travelling in
Slash should be easier than
staying on the spot.

//Maintaining control
If it's too
hasty, Slashing
will feel as if it's happening
to you, rather than being your
chosen movement: you will become
a 'victim' of the movement. Locate
control over what you're thinking and
feeling, so that you are in
your element and
it's an expression of you. Don't
let your Slashing become a
runaway train: if you feel you're
racing and somewhat out of
control, then just stop
for a few moments, retaining a
sense of Sudden in the
pause, whilst allowing yourself
time to think.

//Maintaining Strength and Heaviness[16]
Strong/Heavy Weight at
the Kinesphere's edge takes
focus and energy. So moves flung
outwards with no
end-point tend to get
Lighter. Maintain Strength and
Heaviness at the
ending of moves. The beginning and
end are both Strong/Heavy. The move stops
and starts with the
same Weight.

[15]   Specific Agendas include:

//Sudden movements have no 'middle'
Focus on
succinct beginnings and
ends. Tell the story of a move with
no middle.

---

[16] For more information on Strong/Heavy Weight in the peripheral body, see 'Discovering Heavy', p. 62; 'Discovering Strong', p. 63.

//Shifting the Centre of Gravity
Repeatedly
shifting your Centre
of Gravity is what allows you to be
Labile, and to
Slash without losing
balance.

[16]

Audio Resource

A Slashing Journey
https://vimeo.com/251652338

Figure 6.7(a) Stages of a Slashing Process.

Figure 6.7(b) Stages of a Slashing Process (cont.).

GLIDING

[1]   Gliding is Light in Weight;
      Gliding is Sustained in Time;
      Gliding is Direct in Space.
      To Glide is to be Light, Sustained, Direct.

[2]

Video Resource

Gliding
https://vimeo.com/251502819

[3]   *Build exercises into your warm-up that:*
      - *are spatially organized*
      - *move individual body parts while keeping the rest of the body calm*
      - *efficiently move the whole body*
      - *involve Simultaneous movements*
      - *shift energy throughout both your core and peripheral body*
      - *involve expansive movements of the arms and rotate your torso.*

[4]   *Emotional release*: When a letting go of repressed emotions occurs, there
      is a physical sensation of purification and liberation that emerges as a
      Glide.[17] It often appears after a long, lightening exhalation; and tends
      to involve a softening of the gaze, along with a sense of the heart lifting.
      A similar sensation occurs as you arrive at the top of a high hill to
      an expansive view of the sea; or you might have experienced it in
      activities such as prayer, meditation or gazing at a painting or object of
      beauty. It is often accompanied by a sense of awe, or an experience of the
      sublime.

      Recall the sensation in your body when you experienced a sense of emotional
      release in this way. Notice how the experience is Light, Sustained and Direct:
      Gliding. Emotional release is an experience that we all have from time to
      time and it emerges as a natural Glide. So you already know how to embody
      Gliding perfectly. Once you have undergone the whole Process exploring
      Gliding, your Glide will become as beautifully Light, Sustained and Direct as
      the familiar experience of emotional release is already.

---

[17] This sensation is part of *Catharsis*: a fierce cleansing that enables emotional release and is central to Tragedy.

[5] *Play with the idea of smoothing a cloth:*
- *Imagine smoothing a satin cloth on a long, flat surface with your hands.*
- *Use the palm of your hand to experience the flatness of different smooth surfaces (e.g. a table-top, window-sill, a wall). Maintain a smooth line as you move your hand from one place on the surface to another. Experiment with how Lightly you can maintain the contact.*
- *Now, imagine that you are the cloth that is being smoothed out and allow the movement to spread through your body. Flatten your body against the surface of the wall or the floor.*

[6] *Explore the following images:*
- *Imagine scanning the line of the horizon where a calm sea meets a clear sky.*
- *Imagine feeling your way through a room in the dark.*
- *Imagine the projected line of your arm is a beam of light which extends through your fingers and out into Space, far beyond the edges of the room. Experience it as a laser beam that can travel through any object it hits and so carries on its straight pathway endlessly.*

[7] Useful types of music to work with include: Renaissance Choral Music and Plainsong.

[8] You will have experienced some of the following:

The core body is in an upright and centred position, allowing it to be both Stable and symmetrical. The Direct Space of Gliding means it is clear in its linear movement. The movement is focused and purposeful as you constantly move towards a destination, although Lightness means the commitment is persistent but not forceful.

Sustained Time means that there is only one ongoing movement: once you have started moving, you cannot stop to start again – the movement is continuously developing. Pinpointed intention guiding the tireless progression of one unfolding movement gives Glide its power.

[9] The Default is:

Large-scale, peripheral, expanding: Lightness occurs naturally at the edges of our body where there is less mass, so Gliding often starts with an expression of Lightness through the limbs. The arms expand forwards in the mid-area through the *Wheel Plane.*

Mid-level/High-level: A mid- or high-level stance allows expression of Sustain together with Directness. At low-level it is harder to maintain Directness (it is challenging to move through angles on the floor). The legs power a fully activated core, giving Stability as the body moves primarily through the *Wheel Plane*, with additional use of the *Door Plane* and the *Table Plane*.

[10] Gliding shares: the Sustain of Wringing, the Directness of Thrusting and the Lightness of Flicking. It can also be felt as: a Direct version of Floating; a Sustained version of Dabbing; a Light version of Pressing; or the opposite to Slashing.

[11] In Gliding, control is located in: Light (Weight) and Direct (Space).

Gliding is Direct and therefore Stable. However, expressing Direct Space with Sustained Time may challenge balance in certain movements. Direct demands that you know where you are going in Space and do not deviate from that pathway. Focusing on Direct will stabilize you and keep you from overbalancing into unwanted Lability.

Expression of Lightness also works to counteract any sensation of overbalancing. Lightness demands that you work against gravity, so focusing on Lightness facilitates muscular engagement and shifts in Flow that keep the movement controlled.

[12] Gliding can be perceived as simple and pure; other-worldly. It contains a sense of Expansion and connects readily to visions of the infinite. This might bring positive associations with calmness and peace; or might be seen as dull, remote or non-emotional. Yet the Glide holds a key to the discovery of power in Lightness. Its beauty is in its confident persistence as it moves steadily onwards, following a plan without haste or force.

The simplicity of the Glide is deceptive. It takes great control to maintain the Lightness of the Glide in combination with a Direct and Sustained intention in Space and Time. It has an uncommon combination of enduring decisiveness together with the lack of any need to impose its will through force. It holds a great challenge for the actor and is an extremely valuable mode of expression once it is mastered. Make no mistake: Gliding is not simplistic. Gliding is just Gliding: Light, Sustained and Direct. Trust that the Glide can express anything.

[13] The sound of Gliding is so Light that it may be almost imperceptible to an external ear, or even to you yourself. It is going to be on the tip of the breath. Gliding gives you a good opportunity to experiment with the relationship between breath and sound, as it uses Sounding that is right on the boundary between voiced and unvoiced breath.

Even if there is only the smallest sound – or just the sense of a sound – coming from inside your body, there is still a voice that is connected to the Gliding movement.

If it helps, use the Gliding Soundtrack as you work:

Audio Resource

Gliding Soundtrack
https://vimeo.com/251669808

[14]   Specific Agendas include:

//Avoiding the lure of body design
In Gliding, the body passes through extraordinary dynamic forms, but without ever stopping in any held shape; the movement is constantly progressing. Imagining how the lines of the body join the infinite lines of the Dimensional Cross and the Planes helps provoke the linear organization and simplicity in the body which is essential for Glide, and prevents the body becoming trapped in a series of static forms.[18] Extend the long finger-bones to project the line of the body into Space. If the fingers are curled inwards, you are not connected to the surrounding Space and are likely to be shape-making.

//Don't reverse or repeat a move
If you find yourself reversing a move, it means the Sustain has ceased and needs to be re-established.

//Avoiding stepping
Aim towards one endless, Sustained action. Steps break the action into stages of advancement, disrupting the Sustain. Explore how shifting through different levels can help you to move through Space.

//Remember: Sustain is not slow motion
You are Sustaining one unfolding plan, and not progressing through a pre-planned sequence of moves.

//Resisting a desire to use diagonals
There is an infinity of Direct movements to be found without using diagonals. At this point use of diagonals will be because you want them, not because the Effort needs them.

//Resisting the urge to make it 'interesting'
Don't ask 'how can I be interesting?' but rather, ask: 'what is remarkable about Gliding?' You will discover the beauty in its pinpointed attention; its gentle yet unyielding commitment.

//Don't 'zone out'
The Lightness and Sustain of Gliding can lead to a sense of 'zoning out'. Be careful not to fall into this trap. Gliding is not drifting: the Glide is Direct, so

---

[18] Cf. 'The Planes', p. 36.

it has a sense of pinpointed purpose in Space. If you do not keep attentive and end up mentally vacating the movement, you will no longer be expressing the hugely charged quality of Gliding. Your whole being should be taken into the Glide – demanded by the Glide – making the experience limitless. Keep your attention present and enjoy living the self-perpetuating story of the Glide from moment to moment.

[15]   Specific Agendas include:

//*Direct movement has no circularity*
Discover linear pathways in Space and do not indulge sensations of curve. Find ways to change direction without expressing 'turning'.

//*Experiencing Lightness as release from gravity*
Without a sense of gravity there is no up or down. The vast spaciousness that is all around you can enter inside your body, as all parts of the body become Light.

//*Sustain never reaches an 'end-point'*
Shift the main location of the Glide throughout the body.

[16]

Audio Resource

A Gliding Journey
https://vimeo.com/251670444

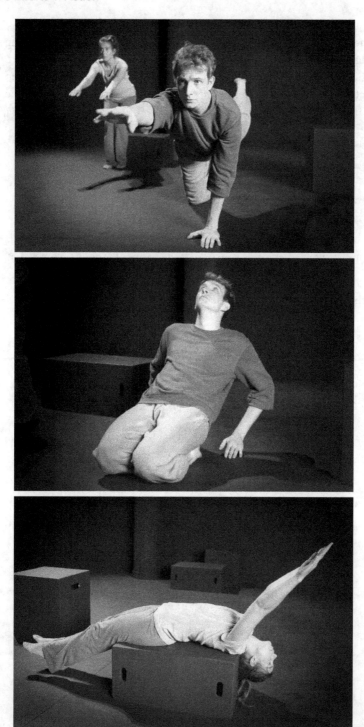

Figure 6.8(a) Stages of a Gliding Process.

Figure 6.8(b) Stages of a Gliding Process (cont.).

PART D
THE EFFORTS AT PLAY

CHAPTER 7
THE EIGHT EFFORT ARCHETYPES

WHAT IS AN EFFORT ARCHETYPE?

An **Effort Archetype**[1] expresses everything through just one Effort. So that singular Effort defines them. To embody an Effort Archetype, you have to obey the rules of its Effort Code (WTS) during all forms of action, including thought and feeling. The Archetype is a simplified expression of a person because someone would usually express several Efforts simultaneously. Yet, by expressing everything through one Effort, a recognizable 'type' of character emerges (the Archetype) which is useful for the actor to explore.[2] You have already begun to discover the eight Effort Archetypes through your Journey improvisations.[3] So all eight Archetypes are now available for you to play with through improvisation. The following improvisations will lead you to a deeper understanding of how the Archetypes build the foundation for sophisticated character work.

EMBODYING THE EIGHT EFFORT ARCHETYPES

Using Improvisation

When playing the Archetype, you only have the option to respond to everything that emerges through your one Effort. So Archetype improvisations are painted with bold, distinct colours. Invest fully in the simplicity of the one choice you have: by remaining true to themselves and their overriding Effort, each Archetype has an inherent openness and integrity. If the actor can commit wholeheartedly to the work, each Archetype also has the power to express something fundamental about the human condition, which is, ultimately, both recognizable and very moving.[4] It is vital not to mistake the simplicity of the Effort Code as the Archetype being simple-minded. The Effort Archetype does not lack in capability, or range of thought and feeling. Each has the potential to express everything that humans can express.

---

[1] This term did not originate from Laban. It was coined in the studio to describe this particular way for actors to work with the Efforts.
[2] Laban suggests that 'characterization can be rough yet typical of masses of persons, or refined and related to an individual' (Laban, *The Mastery of Movement*, p. 99). The Effort Archetypes are an example of the former.
[3] If you'd like to remind yourself of the details of the eight Effort Archetypes, see pp. 175–190.
[4] If you have experienced the clowning work of practitioners such as Jacques LeCoq and Slava Polunin, you might also wish to try parts of the following Effort Archetype Improvisations using the red nose and working in a group.

Improvisation Set-up

These improvisations all share a similar design. They do not rely on lots of spoken dialogue. Rather, they aim to create a playground in which the actor has space to exist without the pressure to create a complex, forward-moving narrative (act out a 'story'). Each improvisation set-up deliberately provokes certain types of action for you to explore.

Make sure that you do each improvisation a number of times so that you have the opportunity to experiment with different Effort Archetypes in the same scenario, and to play different roles. You may wish to set a timer for however long you want each improvisation to run so that you don't allow it to drag on, or to die out too early.

Guidelines for Improvisation[5]

For those working with other actors, there are some simple guidelines that will allow you to play:

- *Move the improvisation forward by offering new possibilities.*
- *Always accept an offer (don't respond to an offer with negativity or 'shut down' the other actor).*
- *Allow the situation to go where it wants to go.*
- *Keep the stakes of the situation high.*
- *Don't be afraid of silence (you will speak, but these improvisations are not about exploring conversational dialogue).*
- *Use all of your senses.*

It is helpful to name the Archetype you are working with 'Ms. Thrust', 'Mx. Slash', 'Mr. Float', etc. This is to remind yourself that you are working with a form of character whose physical expression is fully defined by one Effort Code.

Stay within the context of the improvisation and your role as the Archetype. The Archetype is not a creative launch-pad for you to discover a different improvisation: you cannot say, for example, 'I'll start with Floating', discover that this makes you feel flirtatious, and then shift the improvisation to being about flirtation. If your Archetype is Mr. Float, stay with Floating and respond to the situation through the Float. An improvisation might start with flirtation then move to hilarity, and then to sadness, and so on – all of which can be expressed on a Float, or whichever Effort Archetype you are currently playing.

---

[5] If improvisation is something with which you are not that familiar, or if you would like to learn more, see *Impro* by Keith Johnstone for an in-depth guide to the wonders of improvisational play.

Observation, Analysis and Reflection

After each improvisation take time to analyse and reflect, and perhaps to watch some footage of your work. Don't let yourself sit back and be entertained but actively look for the opportunities in the improvisation which are being picked up, and those which are being missed.

You will notice that, as observers, the moments we love are when the actor is really letting their given Effort take them. A delight is triggered in the audience when an improvisation ends up taking a particular pathway because of the very specific Effort Archetype to whom the situation is happening, and how they respond because of who they are. These are the moments that move us, and in which we feel most connected to the humanity of the Effort Archetype. The Archetype has the consistency of always being themselves and responding through a predictable Effort Quality, which can be very satisfying to watch.

Identifying the Game

As the actor, it is useful to be able to identify the game you are playing. You can then stay with that game and carry it forward to develop the improvisation in a satisfying way. If you have an audience, one way of identifying the game is to notice what it is that appeals to them. There are many games you could be playing: games that play with expectation (e.g. we expect Ms. Thrust to be unsympathetic but she turns out to be highly emotional); conflict (e.g. Mr. Float is forced to answer rapid-fire questions); repetition and development (e.g. Mx. Press needs to answer a phone which keeps ringing, but every time is so slow to get there that they miss the call), etc. If on reflection you identify the potential for a game that was missed, you can always re-visit the improvisation to experiment with the pathway that was not taken the first time round.

Effort Archetype Improvisations

A Heightened Scenario: At the Hairdresser's

Stylistic choices about hairstyle and dress are a manifestation of your movement Affinities. We wear things because of who we are – because they have a particular line, shape and way of interacting with the body that appeals to us. So this improvisation centres around both actors seeking how an Effort Archetype would favour a particular hairstyle over another. A Wringing hairdresser who loves long, tightly wound wringlets might come into conflict with a Gliding client who wants beautifully straight hair; or a Slashing hairdresser might argue for a spiky, punky hairdo when all a Thrusting client wants is a simple short-back-and-sides.

The improvisation should lead to some outcome of a changed hairstyle, however subtle. This is the material outcome of the way in which Effort Quality affects the aesthetic choices and Physical Actions of the hairdresser. Create the hairstyle using brushing, tying and pinning of hair and/or accessories such as headscarves, clip-on extensions and hairclips. For the hairdresser, the handling of equipment such as brushes, combs and hairbands provides an opportunity for you to deepen your understanding of Responsive Physical Action.[6] For the client, sitting gives the opportunity to deepen your understanding of Passive Physical Action.[7]

The hairdresser's can be an emotional place. The Physical Action of the hairdresser results in an irrevocable outcome for the client, so the stakes are high. Neither party wants to get it wrong. The client may think they have the power of being the paying customer, but the hairdresser has the power of the scissors, hair-dye and perming chemicals. Both parties are vulnerable. Agreeing that this is a high-end, very expensive salon increases the stakes for both parties. Also, play that the client is not just coming in for a routine appointment but for a change – a new look, or a style for an important event. There are an infinite number of ways in which two actors can unfold this situation together as the hairdresser and the client do a delicate dance around each other, hiding feelings that might eventually spill over.

Video Resource

Effort Archetypes Improvisation: At the Hairdresser's
https://vimeo.com/251508375

- This is an improvisation for two actors.
- *Set up a chair facing a real or imagined mirror. Make sure that any brushes, hairbands and accessories you want to use for the improvisation are close at hand. Set some mutually agreed parameters regarding potential styling.*
- *Each pick your Effort Archetype.*
- *Begin the improvisation with the hairdresser welcoming the client to the salon.*
- *Remember you are bound by your Archetype's Effort Code. Notice if there are times when the Archetype is being compromised because you are dropping out of the Effort Quality, or not being precise with the Elements (WTS).*
- *Make sure all your movement is motivated by thought or feeling. Don't add in additional movement just to demonstrate that the Effort is present.*
- *Remember, listening is vital to the success of the improvisation and it is also an action. Check that you are listening in the Effort of your Archetype.*
- *Make sure that you are not suppressing Unconscious Gestures.[8]*
- *Make sure that you are really doing the Physical Action of hairdressing (i.e. changing the style of the hair). As the hairdresser, take your time to interact in detail with the*

---

[6] If you'd like to remind yourself about Responsive Physical Action, see pp. 113–114.
[7] If you'd like to remind yourself about Passive Physical Action, see p. 112.
[8] For more detail on Unconscious Gestures, see 'Working with Gestures', p. 260.

objects. Know which bits of the object and the action it requires you like, and which you don't.

- *Keep control of how you use the conversation. Don't talk for the sake of talking.* The conversation shouldn't become a runaway train that takes over; but neither should it dry up completely because it is a forum for the situation to develop and where emotions can emerge.

- *Discover how communication works in your Effort Archetype.* You can talk to each other via the mirror, communicating with yourself at the same time as communicating with your partner. The client can also be watching themselves in the mirror as the haircut takes place. As the hairdresser, if your Effort is Direct you might need to drop down to the level of the chair to get Direct eye contact with your client.

- *Be true to the improvisation; remember to play the high stakes of the situation. Make it real for yourselves.*

- *You may find that you need to allow yourself to do less, and internalize the Effort more.* The only Agenda for the improvisation is that you express everything using your Archetype's one Effort, not that you have to keep moving all the time or produce large-scale or extraneous action.

- *Towards the end of your improvisation, take a moment to admire the end result (the created hairstyle).*

- *Take some time to analyse and reflect.*

Once you have explored this improvisation, you can create other contexts and scenarios that also allow you to experiment in your Effort Archetype with different types of Responsive and Passive Physical Action. Examples might include: being at the ice cream parlour; being at the dentist; making and writing a card for someone important, then standing at the post box deciding whether to post it; etc.

A Journey of Feeling: At the Doctor's

The doctor's waiting room is a place where feelings run high. The patient is in a vulnerable place, and there is a particular emotional resonance around illness because it brings to mind our human frailty. In this improvisation, the created stakes are the highest possible because the patients in the waiting room are expecting vital test results during their upcoming appointment. It doesn't matter exactly what the test is for (though you may wish to decide this detail for yourself), but what is important is that the results will be life-changing.

In this improvisation, you focus on feeling and are led by that. Of course, your thoughts are ever-present but in this scenario you are in a situation where your feelings are running away with you. Even though your feelings are dominating, this does not necessarily mean that they are fully on show. You are sitting in a real-world situation with people around you, so you are socially obliged to do your best to hide what you feel. You can work in an internalized mode even when extreme feelings are dominating your current experience. Maintain the atmosphere of a doctor's waiting room: if you are improvising in a group, don't turn it into a place to strike up relationships. This is the exploration of a mostly personal scenario.

A receptionist can provide a counterpoint to the patient(s). They are the only person in the improvisation who is led by thought, as they are not emotionally involved but are doing their job and dealing with administrative tasks. The role of the receptionist helps create the normality of the world: they are living their everyday reality against which the patients' tapestry of emotions plays out. The receptionist has the power to help or obstruct the patients; to influence the feelings that the patients are experiencing by bringing in or removing conflict.

Video Resource

Effort Archetypes Improvisation: At the Doctor's
https://vimeo.com/251618326

- This is an improvisation for the individual actor, or a group of up to eight actors.
- For a group: *set up a patients' waiting room with a row of chairs and a separate desk for the doctor's receptionist, on which are some pens, paper and a telephone.*
- *Pick your Effort Archetype.*
- *Begin with the patient(s) already in the waiting room.*
- *The receptionist deals with paperwork and phone calls whilst the patient waits. The receptionist may ask the patient to fill out some paperwork.*
- *After a while, the receptionist receives a call from the doctor asking them to send the patient through. They call out the patient's name and guide them towards the door of the doctor's surgery. The patient briefly leaves the improvisation.*
- *Whilst the actor playing the patient is outside the improvisation they decide whether they want the doctor to have delivered them good or bad news regarding their vital test results.*
- *The patient then re-enters the waiting room in either a state of elation or despair. Explore how the Archetype can express extreme emotions without shifting out of their given Effort.*
- *The receptionist asks them to wait again briefly, and then fill out some paperwork before they leave.*
- *Take some time to analyse and reflect.*

Once you have explored this improvisation, you can create other contexts and scenarios that also allow you to experiment with a Journey of Feeling in your Effort Archetype. Examples might include: being told you've been given an official warning by your line-manager; opening driving test results in front of your partner; reading a break-up text on a train; etc.

Figure 7.1 Effort Archetype Improvisations (Top Left: *Thrusting* | Top Right: *Floating* | Bottom: *Slashing*).

A Journey of Thought: On an Intellectual Quiz Show

This improvisation gives you the opportunity to practise thinking in an Effort by placing you in a situation where emotion won't help you. In an intellectual Quiz context, precedence is given to thought, as you focus with precision on scanning your brain for answers to questions. The time pressure and competitive context raise the stakes, so that thinking becomes the key priority over and above anything else. Emotions don't come into play as you concentrate solely on thinking.

When you are playing the Quiz, you have to search your brain for answers using your Archetype's Effort. At first, you'll find that your own Effort for thinking will come into play because the habit of using it to seek answers is so ingrained. Try not to let that happen. Stay with the Effort Code (WTS) and gradually you will be able to transform the Effort Quality of your thinking patterns into that of your Archetype.

Find out how you can use your Archetype's Effort to embody experiences for which you would normally use a different Effort. How, for example, do you give a confident, correct answer as Mr. Float, or experience uncertainty and inability to answer questions as Ms. Thrust? Strong/Heavy Weight can have a tendency to lead to emotions. However, this is not a given – it is very possible to use these Efforts for a thought-led character. It can help to think of your Archetype as someone who has 'weighty' thoughts. To do this you need to connect the Strong/Heavy Weight to the thinking itself (rather than allowing the Weight to arrive only with the emotions associated with the thinking).

You can do this improvisation at home, exploring your Archetype listening (and responding out loud) to a real radio Quiz; or you can imagine yourself on a TV Quiz show. Both of these environments encourage you to spatialize your act of thinking (not letting your eye-line drop or retreating into yourself as you think).[9]

- This is an improvisation for the individual actor, or for a group of up to eight actors.

- For the individual: *listen to a radio or TV Quiz show and imagine you are on one of the teams.*

- For a group: *set up a Quiz show improvisation. If you are working with a Buddy, you can each be an individual contestant and take it in turns to ask the questions. If you are in a larger group, set up two teams. Either pre-set your own Quiz questions, or use question cards from any board games you might have.*[10]

- *Pick your Effort Archetype.*

- *Make sure thought is leading as you play. Feelings cannot come in, as all your energy is involved in concentrated thinking.*

- *Search your brain using the Effort of your Archetype. Locate the place of thought.* Dominant body parts will be the head, face, mouth and hands.

- *The whole body should express the Effort Archetype (e.g. your sitting posture; your interaction with the chair, table, buzzer).*

---

[9] This is good practice for the actor: sharing your landscape of thought and feeling through physical expression even when the Efforts are internalized is a vital skill for all camera-work. The skilled actor can make tiny movements just as articulate as big movements, and can make stillness an action that is just as embodied as large-scale movement.

[10] Sample questions can also be found at www.labaneffortsinaction.com

- *Don't change your Effort; stay in your Archetype. Trust your Archetype's Effort: it's the way you think and that's what got you on the Quiz show in the first place.*

- *Let the use of language help you: how do you articulate your answers? Do you prefer consonants or vowels?* Depending on your Effort Archetype, you might enunciate words differently, or choose certain words over others.

- *Take some time to analyse and reflect.*

Once you have explored this improvisation, you can create other contexts and scenarios that also allow you to experiment with a Journey of Thought in your Effort Archetype. Examples might include: sitting an exam; preparing a pitch to win a project; working out a seating plan for a big event; etc.

Passive Action: Sunbathing

In Passive Action, the interior movement of thoughts and feelings lives through the body, even if you are seemingly 'doing' very little. Your Effort Archetype determines how you sit, lie down, do minimal movements – even how you breathe.

- *Pick your Effort Archetype.*

- *Settle yourself into a sunbathing position. Let your given Effort affect how you choose to lie down.*

- *Take time to allow yourself to settle into Passive Action; find the sensation of this simple way of being.*

- *Make sure you do not allow other Efforts to seep into your expression; stay in your Archetype.*

- *Intersperse your sunbathing with other Passive Actions such as sleeping, reading and waiting.*

- *Take some time to analyse and reflect.*

Reading Out-loud

Your Effort Archetype affects how you meet and receive what is written on the page. When reading aloud, you experience the meeting point between your Archetype's Effort and the writer's particular style (the form and use of language; stylistic choices relating to the era in which it was written; etc.). This is similar to the experience of Responsive Physical Action.[11]

- *Pick your Effort Archetype.*

---

[11] Cf. 'Responsive Physical Action: Having a Drink', p. 113.

- *Choose a book (fiction works well). Open it at any page and read from it out-loud.* This is not for an audience: you read aloud simply so that you can hear your choices for yourself.

- *Make sure you do not allow other Efforts to seep into your expression; stay in your Archetype.*

- *Take some time to analyse and reflect.*

APPLYING THE EIGHT EFFORT ARCHETYPES

Devising Character Material

Articulation of Personality on Paper

Writing is a very tangible action – thoughts and feelings are clearly manifested through the visible marks left on the page. Your Effort Archetype affects how and what you write, as you put your thoughts and feelings into action through doodling, writing or drawing.

- *Pick your Effort Archetype.*

- *Select the paper and pen that suits your Archetype. Do they use a fountain pen, biro, large marker pen, or delicate pencil?* If you are unused to writing by hand, use your computer to write an email as a first exploration.

- *Play with how you pick up and hold the pen. Discover how this Archetype puts pen to paper.*

- *Allow your mind to wander and begin to doodle. Let the style and form of the doodle reflect your Archetype's given Effort.*

- *Find your signature as dictated by your Archetype's given Effort. What does the signature look like?*

- *Now, use the pen and paper to express whatever your Archetype wants. This might be drawing a picture, writing a poem, making a list, etc. It could be to communicate with someone else (a letter or note) or it could be a solitary activity. Discover how the chosen activity expresses the personality of your Archetype.*

- *Take some time to analyse and reflect.*

Manifestation of Self: At the Office

The way in which we create and inhabit any environments over which we have ownership manifests our Effort Affinities (e.g. our choice of furniture and how it is arranged; whether it is sparse or cluttered; organized or chaotic; cosily decorated or kept minimal and bare).

An office cubicle has a basic configuration, as well as some freedom of choice for alteration according to your Archetype's personal inclinations. The office cubicle would have a table, chair and waste-paper bin, but it is the choice of the Archetype whether these are neatly placed and aligned with each other, or whether the bin is overflowing and the chair is placed at an angle that is just right for putting your feet up on the desk.[12] During this improvisation, you engage in a range of typical activities done in an administrative office job. For this, you need to set up a basic office environment. You don't need a lot: table/chair (if you can get a spinning office chair with wheels, this offers a lot of potential opportunities)/phone/papers/pens/a computer keyboard/waste-paper bin.

Your Effort Archetype will dictate both how you balance the tasks you choose to do and the way in which you carry them out. For example, Mr. Dab might love the action of typing, as it fits so neatly with his natural Affinity, whereas Mr. Float might enjoy speaking endlessly on the phone, as he coils the wire around his hands and spins himself round and round in the office chair; Ms. Slash might love tearing up notes and throwing them messily towards the bin, whereas Ms. Press might spend a long time making sure a pile of papers is exactly aligned with the edge of the table.

This improvisation centres around the potentially conflicted interaction between the Effort Archetype and their context. Their job might make requirements of them which the Archetype finds hard to meet: perhaps, for example, Mr. Float struggles to answer a series of demanding phone calls which require looking through a pile of papers for immediate answers. At times, your job will require Responsive Physical Action that does not align with your Affinity: Ms. Glide may have to staple a number of papers together requiring a series of short, sharp actions as she uses the stapler, or Mr. Thrust may carefully have to use a cloth to clean his computer screen. Make sure that you know what company the Archetype is employed by: perhaps Ms. Wring loves her job working at a company that manufactures coils of rope, or maybe she perseveres at a company that makes rulers.

The Archetype must believe that they are functional, and that the way they organize their environment and do their job is the best (only) way to do it. The conflict between the Archetype and their context provides the dramatic potential, but the Archetype themselves does not admit their failings. If the actor knowingly plays the ways in which the Archetype fails in the world, then they are telling us that the Archetype they are playing is negative or weak. In fact, each Effort Archetype has their own unique way of interacting with the world, and both succeeds and fails. By celebrating the Archetype, the actor begins to unlock what each Effort Archetype has to offer.

Video Resource

Effort Archetypes Improvisation: At the Office
https://vimeo.com/251509916

- *Pick your Effort Archetype.*
- *Before you begin, lay the office out the way your Effort Archetype would choose to have it arranged.*

---

[12] For more insight into the potential of interaction with objects and surroundings, see Hagen and Frankel, *Respect for Acting*, particularly the 'Object Exercises'.

- *Exist in the office as your Archetype.* You can begin the improvisation already in your office: you are just in the middle of your routine, and it's a familiar environment which you inhabit for many hours every day.

- *Discover how the way in which you interact with objects tells us something about who you are.* Actions should include: walking and thinking, sitting at your desk, looking out of the window, typing, sharpening a pencil, searching through a card index, making a call, writing a memo, drinking coffee, doodling, accounting.

- *Make sure that you move through a range of thoughts and feelings in the improvisation.*

- *Take some time to analyse and reflect.*

Manifestation of Relationship: Siblings/Parent–Child

Two people playing the same Effort Archetype will have a shared movement 'DNA'. The Effort Code (WTS) of each person's movement is identical and so their physical expression is very similar, just as it often is with relations who share close biological DNA. This can be used to create relationships between Archetypes (e.g. the Dab Sisters, the Wring Brothers, the Flick Siblings). Shared Elements can give a sense of collective identity because shared movement tendencies will lead to a similar outlook. This can be explored through simple Physical Actions with both actors playing the same Effort Archetype. During your improvisation, each Element will become clearer in its significance for you as a related pair: the Wring Brothers, for example, might both understand Indirect through a sense of nesting, so they hug pillows, nurse cups of coffee or curl into comfy spaces.

- This is an improvisation for two actors.

- *Before you begin, set up an environment in which you can do simple everyday Physical Actions, such as: getting ready to go out for a walk, preparing and eating a snack, waiting for someone to arrive, etc.*

- *Pick your Effort Archetype (the same one for both actors).*

- *Begin by briefly re-discovering the Effort Archetype independently of one another.*

- *Now work together. First, simply spend time together in your shared environment without communicating with each other.*

- *Progress to doing an activity together.* Don't do too much: use as little communication between you as possible and keep the activity based around simple actions (e.g. walking, sitting, thinking, doodling).

- *Start to pick up from each other the movement tendencies that you share because of playing the same Archetype.* This silent 'pick up' of information will not take too long.

- *Keep your focus on just living in your shared environment together and being involved in the same understated activity.* The relationship between you is one that could be that of grown-up twins or siblings.

- *Notice any sense of collective identity that arises from the Elements you share. Play with how sharing an Element affects the way you do an activity together.* You might, for example, discover that Light Weight means you share a delicate caring touch as you fold clothes.
- *Explore highlighting each of the Elements of your shared Effort Archetype.*
- *Take some time to analyse and reflect.*

You can also explore a relationship that is once removed (e.g. parent–child, cousins) by playing in the Archetypes of two 'neighbouring' Efforts.[13] A Wringing and a Floating Archetype, for example, will have the shared 'DNA' of Indirect Space and Sustained Time, but differ in Weight.

- *Repeat the exploration as outlined above, but this time pick the Effort Archetypes of two neighbouring Efforts.*
- *Which movement tendencies are the same as your partner, and which differ?*
- *Notice any sense of collective identity that arises from the Elements you share. Then pay attention to how the Element which you don't share affects the way you do an activity together.*
- *Take some time to analyse and reflect.*

Manifestation of Partnership: Pair Bonds

We form relationships according to how another person's Effort expression is similar or different to our own. The actor can use an understanding of the Efforts to portray this underlying interrelationship of qualities in all its richness: the ways it can cause us to form or break relationships, and how it can reinforce or overturn our habits. The archetypes of Ms. Float and Ms. Wring, for example, may appear to be very different types of people who would have little in common. However, they share the same Elements of both Sustained Time and Indirect Space, and differ only in Weight. This helps explain how people understand and empathize with each other, even though they might appear to have no obvious connection at first glance. Often, relationships occur between people because of their partially overlapping Effort Affinities.

When two different Effort Archetypes form a pair-bond (e.g. a romantic partnership), each Archetype comes into stark relief through being placed in contrast with their partner. In this improvisation, a pair is placed in front of an imagined studio audience to be interviewed on national television about their relationship. Their responses will point to the way in which their Efforts interact: answering questions gives an opportunity for each Effort Archetype to celebrate what they love about their partner, and therefore about their partner's particular Effort. Perhaps Ms. Press and Ms. Wring love each other because of their shared Strong/Heavy Weight and Sustained Time, perceiving each other

---

[13] Two Efforts which differ in only one Element (WTS). See Table 3: Neighbouring Efforts, p. 192

as equally steadfast and reliable; or perhaps, conversely, Ms. Press is in a relationship with Mr. Dab because she feels his Light Weight and Sudden Time make him carefree, something she feels she is missing in her own personality. This improvisation allows you to discover how the Efforts of each person work in symbiosis with each other.

Of course, relationships can be built around both similarity and difference as a cause of attraction, conflict, or both. There is a great deal of potential within this improvisation not only to celebrate what is good about the relationship, but for the conflict in the relationship to emerge through the subtext of the answers, or to spill over. Perhaps it becomes apparent in the relationship between Mr. Glide and Mr. Flick that Mr. Glide loves the spontaneous changeability he finds in Mr. Flick's Indirect Suddenness, but finds his chaotic lack of ability to stick to one plan incredibly frustrating; and that Mr. Flick loves Mr. Glide's focus and ability to carry something out, but also finds him overly controlling and boring in his Sustained Directness. To locate the conflict in the relationship, you can ask yourself what these partners regularly bicker or argue about.

This is also an opportunity to find out how different Effort Archetypes relate to each other physically. Perhaps Mr. Wring likes to curl himself around his partner Ms. Thrust, and finds security in the straight lines of Ms. Thrust's body; or perhaps Mr. Float really likes to hold hands for a long period of time with his partner Ms. Slash, but she doesn't enjoy the Sustained softness of the physical intimacy, so often moves a bit away from him to guard her Personal Space.

Video Resource

Effort Archetypes Improvisation: Pair Bonds and Relatives
https://vimeo.com/251618485

- For this improvisation, you need at least one other actor. If you are in a larger group, you may wish to have an interviewer who asks the questions and interacts with the imagined studio audience, or if you are working with your Buddy you can take it in turns to ask each other the questions.
- *Set up two chairs side-by-side facing the imagined studio audience and cameras.*
- *Pre-prepare some questions for the interview in which you have been invited to share what makes your relationship such a success* (e.g. What do you love most about them? How would you describe them in just three words, etc.).[14]
- *Pick your Effort Archetype.*
- *Sit side-by-side and begin the interview.*
- *Explore how you and your partner sit. Are you in close physical proximity? Are you touching, or is there distance between you?*

---

[14] Sample questions can also be found at www.labaneffortsinaction.com

- *Explore how you and your partner communicate physically. Do you make regular eye contact? Do you mirror each other's body language, or share Gestures? Do you have patterns of physical behaviour, such as one putting an arm around the other and the other pulling away from, or softening into, the physical contact?*
- *Take some time to analyse and reflect.*

Manifestation of Group Identity: Politicians

When a group of the same Effort Archetype gathers together, they create an amplified version of the individual Archetype. A political party is an ideal example of this: the instinctive traits, beliefs, strategies and articulation of the Archetype are reinforced and intensified.

Setting a political agenda allows you to explore how this Effort Archetype would choose to organize the world around them. Writing a manifesto enables you to find the way in which habitually thinking and feeling through the prism of one Effort affects what you believe. The manifesto is written led by thought, without allowing emotion to step in: this is a clear and calculated experience of the Effort maximizing its potential as it sells itself to the world.

The Effort Archetype becomes manifest in both the form and content of their political speech – their policies reflect their movement Affinities, as does their choice of language and style: a Sudden Effort Archetype such as MP Thrust might make policies based on hard and fast short-term change, whereas a Sustained Effort Archetype such as MP Float might argue for long-term measures to address a problem gradually. Working out the words your Archetype uses will deepen your understanding of how they think and how this forms their party's identity. It is useful to pay particular attention to the verbs (action words) they use. MP Thrust might deliver a speech made of punchy, short pronouncements; MP Float might use longer words and more meandering sentence structures.

Video Resource

Effort Archetypes Improvisation: Politicians
https://vimeo.com/251618878

- This is an improvisation for the individual actor, or for a group of up to eight actors.
- *Pick your Effort Archetype.*
- *Imagine yourself as the chosen representative of a political party (e.g. MP Thrust for the Thrust Party).*
- *Come up with a number of policies which your Effort Archetype believes in deeply.* These might cover typical political topics such as Healthcare, Education, Foreign Policy, etc.

- *Write a short speech/manifesto outlining the policies of your Effort Archetype's political party, and stating your case as to why your party should be elected.* Remember to find a way of articulating your policies using the language and mode of expression that your Effort Archetype would use. You can use the standard tactics of politicians, such as choosing to speak negatively of other political parties in order to sell your own.

- *Identify what your party political slogan would be, and really aim to sell your political beliefs: how can you write a speech that will appeal to everyone and bring them over to your way of thinking and being?*

- *Once you are satisfied with your manifesto, deliver it as your Archetype to an imagined camera (or real camera for playback).* If you are in a group, the different Effort Archetypes can pit themselves against each other, each delivering their speech one after the other.

- *Take some time to analyse and reflect.*

OBSERVING THE EIGHT EFFORT ARCHETYPES

Of course, no human being operates in exactly the same way as an Effort Archetype: we utilize a shifting mixture of layered Effort Qualities as we move through life. However, it is possible to identify people who have a dominant Effort, or who have moments where one Effort dominates within certain contexts or situations.

Start to observe people in the world around you. Look for moments where you can briefly identify a dominant Effort emerging. Feed the knowledge you gain from observation back into your Effort Archetype improvisations. In this way, you can start to perceive how the Effort Archetypes live in the world as parts of each person. The Effort Archetypes provide a foundation on which you can build ways of using the Efforts for creating character.

CHAPTER 8
THE EFFORT WEAVE

WHAT IS AN EFFORT WEAVE?

An **Effort Weave**[1] is a way of exploring how to change from one Effort to another. Simple shifts between Efforts occur by changing one Element of Weight, Time, or Space. For example, if you are Floating and you alter Weight from Light to Strong/Heavy your movement will change into Wringing. Each Effort remains distinct but by switching Elements you can weave from one Effort to the next, creating a journey through all eight in turn. Laban likens moving from Effort to Effort to 'the grading one into another of the colours in a rainbow'.[2]

Discovering the Inter-relationship of the Efforts

By switching between the Efforts, you can begin to deepen your understanding of the relationships between the individual Effort Qualities – their similarities and differences. Laban believes that 'the awakening of the understanding and feel of these connections' is 'fundamental' to learning how to embody the Efforts.[3] You experience each Effort more fully once there is a change to the other, through the contrast between the two. The moment of change – the transition – is the moment of drama.

Starting to move from one Effort to another clarifies their individual characteristics. A Weave can be seen as forcing the 'family' of Efforts to co-habit, thereby highlighting how they relate: one might dominate another, or two might reside next to each other in harmony. This could be compared to the complex weave of a piece of music: it is possible to pick out the juxtaposition of one instrument's pitch, tone and timbre with another's, and ask what the relationships are between these varying qualities of sound.

Laban placed the Efforts on a cubic diagram. In this way, he created a spatialized diagram of the way in which the Efforts relate to each other. For some, referring to this

---

[1] Laban spoke of explorations that moved from one Effort to another but he did not use this specific term. It was coined in the studio to describe the experience of transitioning between the Efforts in this way. There is a sense of 'weaving' from one Effort to the next. The inter-relationship of the two Efforts creates moments of transition in which the visibility of some movement 'threads' appear and disappear.

[2] Laban, *The Mastery of Movement*, p. 113.

[3] Laban and Lawrence, *Effort*, p. 33.

diagram can be a helpful way to understand and remember the interrelationships between all the Efforts, and how to move between them.[4]

EFFORT WEAVE PREPARATION

Re-experiencing Each of the Eight Efforts
Briefly remind yourself of each Effort before starting to move between them in an Effort Weave. This will give you an opportunity to see where you are at in relation to each Effort and place them all on an equal footing.

- *Spend five minutes re-visiting each individual Effort. Use this time to embody the Effort in full-body mode motivated by thoughts and feelings.[5] Make sure you spend the same amount of time on each Effort. Aim to re-access the movement of the Effort Quality itself, not the remembered 'shape' of the Effort.*

Discovering the Relationship between 'Neighbouring' Efforts
Efforts which share two Elements can be viewed as 'neighbouring Efforts' because you only have to alter one Element to move between them.[6] *Table 3* lists all the different neighbouring Efforts.

Table 3: Neighbouring Efforts

Neighbouring Efforts which differ in **WEIGHT** [Light – Strong/Heavy]	Neighbouring Efforts which differ in **TIME** [Sudden – Sustained]	Neighbouring Efforts which differ in **SPACE** [Direct – Indirect]
Dabbing - Thrusting	Dabbing - Gliding	Dabbing - Flicking
Floating - Wringing	Floating - Flicking	Floating - Gliding
Flicking - Slashing	Thrusting - Pressing	Thrusting - Slashing
Gliding - Pressing	Wringing - Slashing	Wringing - Pressing

Neighbouring Efforts often pose similar technical challenges because of their shared Elements. Moving between Efforts can allow you to transfer knowledge and understanding about one Effort to help face the similar challenges posed by its neighbouring Effort.

---

[4] Cf. Figure A3: The Cube with Efforts, p. 268.
[5] This is the same mode that you enter into during Phase 2 of a Journey Improvisation. You are amoeba-like but with the addition of human condition (i.e. presence of thoughts and feelings). See 'Phase 2: Adding Human Condition', p. 110.
[6] This means they are 'neighbours' in their placement on the Cube diagram created by Laban. See 'The Cube with Efforts', p. 268.

- *Choose a pair of neighbouring Efforts from Table 3.*
- *Choose one of the Efforts and begin an improvisation in full-body mode motivated by thoughts and feelings.*
- *After a little time, change the Element which takes you from this Effort to its neighbouring Effort.*
- *Carry on improvising in the second Effort.*
- *A little time later, switch the Element back again so that you return to the initial Effort.*
- *In this way, keep moving back and forth between the pair of neighbouring Efforts. Remember: two of the Elements remain exactly the same, and it is only the third which changes.*
- *Explore how one Effort can serve the other, and vice versa; notice how each one informs the other.*
- *One at a time, explore all the different pairs of neighbouring Efforts found in Table 3.*
- *After each exploration, take some time to analyse and reflect.*

BASIC PHILOSOPHIES

Some **Basic Philosophies** inform all Effort Weaves. Before you do an Effort Weave, read through the Basic Philosophies outlined below. It may be helpful to re-visit these from time to time as you progress through different types of Effort Weave.

//Journey through it
An Effort Weave is an improvisation not a technical exercise. It should be experienced as one journey that moves you through many different experiences, transitioning from one to the next. Make sure you don't break up the Weave: get on the 'train' and don't get off until you reach the end of the journey. The only prescribed action is to move through each given Effort in turn. Other than this, you can do anything. Give yourself permission to play with thoughts and feelings as you move from one Effort to another. Go to the extremes. Have fun. Let the experience of the Weave tell you something about the human condition.

//Work with both focus and ease
Focus is required to move through the pattern of the Efforts with precision. Make sure you do not allow additional unwanted tension to creep into the body. Work with ease, and allow your body to enjoy each transition from one Effort to another as the Weave evolves. All you need to do is play and explore. Moving through an Effort Weave will become much easier once you have experienced it a few times.

//Keep each Effort distinct

As you move from one Effort to another, there is a moment of transition. Do not get stuck in this moment and accidentally 'blend' the two Efforts. Keep one Effort distinct from the other. When switching from one Effort to the next, the Efforts should be juxtaposed not felt as a halfway point between the two.

//Treat each Effort as equal

The Efforts are all equal. Be aware of any tendency to spend more time with your favourites. Instead, allow every Effort its full process of exploration within the Weave.

//Avoid phrases and patterns

There can be a temptation to plan transitions, or to get stuck in familiar movements. Try to avoid phrasing or patterning movements and then going into the next Effort only at the end of the phrase. A shift from one Effort to another can happen at any point. Keep in the present tense, and allow the movement to evolve.

//Value the transitions

Invest in the transition between one Effort and the next. This is where discoveries are made, so don't rush them or skip key stages. Each transition progresses through four stages:
  - Stage One: You express one Effort only.
  - Stage Two: A neighbouring Effort appears in the body very briefly, and then disappears.
  - Stage Three: The same neighbouring Effort reappears. It stays for longer this time and the two Efforts co-exist in the body.
  - Stage Four: The invading Effort 'wins'. It becomes the new sole Effort as the initial Effort disappears.

//Use thoughts and feelings

A Basic Effort Weave uses full-body movement but it is not an abstract dance. As you become proficient at shifting through the Efforts, there can be a temptation to become overly lyrical. Keep in mind that this is an actor's improvisation motivated by thought and feeling. One way to make sure that thought and feeling are always present as you improvise is to include occasional gestural movement throughout the Weave.

//Experience each improvisation anew

Each time you do an Effort Weave it is an opportunity to make new discoveries. Just as each Effort has an infinite range of possible movements, the relationship between one Effort and the next can be different each time you experience it. Work with a mindset of exploration and previously unnoticed movements and resonances will emerge in each new Weave. A moment of reflection after each Weave will allow you to note down and bank any golden moments.

BASIC EFFORT WEAVE

A **Basic Effort Weave** is an exploration in which you move through each of the eight Efforts in turn. It is done using full-body movement, motivated by thoughts and feelings. It does not place the Weave in a context or internalize the Effort (except at the very end). It allows you to focus on precise embodiment of each Effort in turn. The movement should use the whole body – each and every muscle, the skeleton, organs and surfaces – as well as locating the Effort in your pattern of thoughts and feelings. It will help you learn how to switch cleanly between Efforts, and to experience transitions from one Effort to another in every body part. It is a good idea to ease into the improvisation through one of the Light Efforts, so the Weave below begins with Floating.

Video Resource

Basic Effort Weave
https://vimeo.com/251506266

- *Use the following framework of instructions to guide you through a Basic Effort Weave improvisation.*[7]

Audio Resource

Basic Effort Weave
https://vimeo.com/251652803

Effort Weave with Music

Once you have experienced a Basic Effort Weave, it can be a valuable experience to do another one with music playing as you move. You will be in a relationship with the music but this is not the same as 'fitting' the movement to the music.[8]

- *Re-visit the Basic Effort Weave improvisation, but now play music while you move through the Weave.* Try to play a piece of music that offers a spectrum of qualities, so that you can experience a shifting sensation of your movement either being in harmony or in conflict with the music.

---

[7] Alternatively, this guidance is also available as a written Framework of Instructions at www.labaneffortsinaction.com
[8] For more information, see 'Using Music', p. 89.

- *You may wish to do this a number of times, discovering how different musical choices affect your experience of each unique journey through the Effort Weave.*
- *After each exploration, take some time to analyse and reflect.*

Once you have discovered how to work with music during a Basic Effort Weave, it is possible to work with music or in silence for any Effort Weave.

Discovering and Guiding Your Own Effort Weaves

There are 144 possible sequences for a Basic Effort Weave that moves through the eight Efforts simply by shifting one Element at a time.[9] If you do a Weave in which you re-visit some Efforts more than once, or reverse some transitions, then there are an infinite number of ways in which you can construct an Effort Weave. It is now possible for you to construct and guide your own Effort Weaves; or you can simply start moving and see what Weave you create by chance.

At first, you may find it helpful to write down the Efforts through which you will move in your Weave; or you can make an audio recording in which you read out your pre-selected Efforts. Later, you will find you are gradually able to identify the Effort Weave in your head as you work.

- *Identify a Basic Effort Weave which travels through each of the eight Efforts in turn. Looking at the diagram of the Cube with Efforts can help visualize new sequences.*[10]
- *Following verbal guidance (either from a Buddy or a recording), move through your chosen Effort Weave.*
- *After your Effort Weave, take some time to analyse and reflect.*

After you have explored a few Basic Effort Weaves in this way, experiment with moving through a Weave without prompting. Once you do not have external guidance, it can be hard to move through all eight Efforts without becoming preoccupied by which of the Efforts you have not yet journeyed through. So allow this Effort Weave to take you through more than just the eight Efforts, with some being re-visited, and some transitions being reversed. This will release you to follow the journey of the Weave as it emerges in the moment.

- *Choose an Effort in which to begin your Weave. Set a time-limit for the Weave. You may wish to set a timer.*
- *Move freely through the Effort Weave, allowing the improvisation to take you through a series of shifts from one Effort to another.*
- *Allow the journey of the Weave to unfold; enjoy moving in the present moment.*
- *After your Effort Weave, take some time to analyse and reflect.*

---

[9] A complete list of all the possible options for a Basic Effort Weave can be found at www.labaneffortsinaction.com
[10] Cf. Figure A.3: The Cube with Efforts, p. 268; or refer to the list of options for a Basic Effort Weave at www.labaneffortsinaction.com

INTERNALIZED EFFORT WEAVES

In the same way that you embodied each individual Effort in an internalized mode, it is possible to do an internalized Effort Weave.[11] Although our everyday experience is that we are both thinking and feeling simultaneously, it is possible to identify a sensation of being led by one or the other – of one being dominant at any given time. An internalized Effort Weave might be led by thought or led by feeling; or it might switch between the two. When you are working with thoughts, it can be useful to improvise using 'thoughts-out-loud'.[12] When working with feelings, exclamations can be helpful.[13] It is important to remember that Gestures play a key role in allowing the movement to remain expressive when working in an internalized mode.[14]

Effort Weave on Thought
Our thoughts have a pattern of movement expression that can also be altered and transformed. The Effort Quality of your thoughts affects your body movements, and vice versa. The content of your thoughts is related to the Effort Quality in which you think

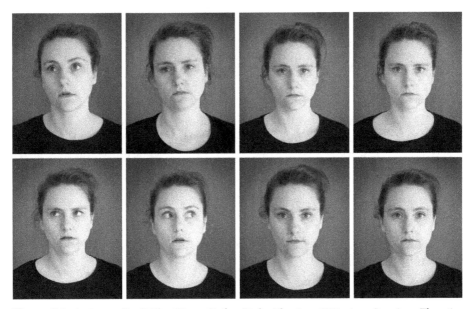

Figure 8.1 An Internalized Effort Weave (Left to Right: *Floating – Wringing – Pressing – Thrusting – Slashing – Flicking – Dabbing – Gliding*).

---

[11] If you wish to remind yourself about Internalized Efforts, see 'Internalized', p. 111.
[12] Cf. 'Thoughts-out-loud', p. 262.
[13] Cf. 'Exclamations', p. 262.
[14] Cf. 'Working with Gestures', p. 260.

them. So you may find that thinking in a particular Effort alters what you are thinking; or that what you are thinking triggers a change in Effort Quality. As you weave through each Effort, your Affinity may mean that you find it easier to think in some Efforts than in others.

- *Start by sitting on a chair. Choose a simple subject that you are going to think about during this Effort Weave. Hold this as the subject in your mind.* It should be something that is easy to think about, and about which you can have many thoughts (e.g. an imminent event, a problem, an issue).

- *Choose an Effort in which to begin.*

- *Allow a thought about your subject to emerge and begin to articulate your thoughts-out-loud in your chosen Effort. Throughout the rest of your exploration, switch between short periods of thoughts-out-loud and periods during which you allow your thoughts to be back inside your head.*

- *Begin to weave through different internalized Efforts. Allow shifts in thought to lead you from one Effort to the next. Make sure you are allowing expressive Gestures to occur.*

- *Your thoughts might change quite fast: you don't have to stay with one thought for a long time. Let the progression of your thoughts take you somewhere.*

- *Make sure that you don't just stick to the Efforts that feel more 'natural' for you when thinking.*

- *Keep it real: use real thoughts as a resource (not pretend thoughts), and as much as possible just stick to thinking without doing anything else.* You remain sitting in the chair – passive – but there is intense movement activity in one body part: your brain.

- *Don't work too hard – you're just having a little think.* You don't need to display the thoughts: if you're experiencing them, an outside observer will perceive them in your overall physical expression and through your gestural movement.

- *Make sure that you keep your focus on thinking articulate thoughts about the chosen topic. When a feeling intrudes, use the word 'interesting' as your response to keep it at bay.*

- *After your Effort Weave, take some time to analyse and reflect.*

- *Now, try the same exploration but while you consider a mental puzzle (i.e. take yourself on a more complicated thought process while you move through the Effort Weave).*

Effort Weave on Feeling

Your feelings also have a pattern of movement expression that can be altered and transformed. Our feelings are related to the Effort in which we feel them. Changes in feeling can trigger a shift in Effort; and vice versa. As you weave through each Effort, your Affinity may mean that you find it easier to feel in some Efforts than in others.

- *Re-visit the exploration above, but this time choose a subject that can offer you a mix of feelings.* Almost any subject can work if you approach it broadly. The topic of 'fish', for example, can provoke feelings with regards to it as a food, the political/ecological implications of eating it, fish as pets, and so on.

- *Allow a feeling about your subject to emerge and develop. Make sure your movement is connected to your breath. From time to time, you may wish to use exclamations as you journey through your Weave.*

- *Begin to weave through different internalized Efforts, as shifts in feeling lead you to change from one Effort to the next. Make sure you are allowing expressive Gestures to occur.*

- *Make sure that each shift in feeling is connected to a precise change in Effort.*

- *Use a broad range of positive and negative feelings, and take them as far as you want to.*

- *Your feelings might change quite fast: you don't have to stay with one feeling for a long time. Let the progression of your feelings take you somewhere.*

- *Make sure you don't just stick to the Efforts that feel more 'natural' for you when feeling.*

- *After your Effort Weave, take some time to analyse and reflect.*

Effort Weave on Thought and Feeling

You may have an Affinity to being led more often by thought or led more often by feeling. However, we all experience both sensations and switch between the two. This exploration allows you to experience these switches between thought and feeling as you move through an internalized Effort Weave.

- *Choose a Passive Action (e.g. doodling, reading, sunbathing, doing a jigsaw puzzle or embroidery).*

- *Begin to weave through different internalized Efforts, allowing yourself to change between being led by thought and led by feeling. Let the changes in thought and feeling shift you from one Effort to the next. Make sure you are allowing expressive Gestures to occur.*

- *Make sure that you are always aware of whether you are being led by thought or feeling, and what Effort you are in at any point during the Weave.*

- *After your Effort Weave, take some time to analyse and reflect.*

EFFORT WEAVES WITH AN AGENDA

You can now set an Agenda that affects the expression of your Effort Weave. Each Weave below could be done using full-body movement or in an internalized mode. You might choose to explore an Effort Weave:

- *in one body part; or shifting between different body parts*
- *using gestural movement*[15]
- *in the core body; or in the peripheral body*
- *on breath*
- *on contracting (Gathering) or expanding (Scattering) or actions*
- *at high level or low level*
- *sitting on a chair; lying on the floor, etc.*

Sample Agenda: Effort Weave during Physical Action[16]

- *Choose a simple physical action (e.g. walking).*

- *Start your Effort Weave. Move through the Efforts while still doing your chosen action. Don't let the Weave affect its purpose. Walking, for example, should not change to running or standing.*

- *Try this with a few different simple physical actions.*

- *Once you have done an Effort Weave during several simple physical actions, choose a more complex physical action. This can include actions you encounter each day (e.g. brushing your teeth, typing an email, washing dishes).*

- *Thoughts and feelings will pop in and out, but don't let them take over. Keep your focus on maintaining your physical action.*

---

[15] For more information on gestural movement, see 'Working with Gestures', p. 260.
[16] For more examples of an Effort Weave with an Agenda visit www.labaneffortsinaction.com

CHAPTER 9
EFFORT DUOS

WHAT IS AN EFFORT DUO?

An **Effort Duo**[1] is two different Efforts that are expressed through the body at the same time. The placement of two Efforts in the body creates conflict. So working with an Effort Duo moves the actor away from the simpler, single drive of the Archetypes into something more sophisticated – and, once internalized, more recognizably 'real' or 'human'.

The actor works from an understanding that every human knows what it is to be in a state of conflict and struggle. We experience conflict all the time in our feelings and our thoughts; within our bodies and our minds; with the outside world; or all of these together. The use of Effort Duos gives you a tangible way to work with the expression of conflict.

There are several ways in which the function of each of the two Efforts can be described. One of the ways in which Laban described two simultaneously expressed Efforts was as a 'disguising' Effort and a 'revealing' Effort.[2] We feel the need or desire to hide our internal drives, and try to do this by disguising the expression of our thoughts or, more often, feelings. An Effort Duo can be said to be expressing the 'conflict between a character's inner attitude and [their] outer demeanour'.[3] This could also be articulated as in *Table 4*.

One way or another of describing the function of the two Efforts might work better for different actors. Different descriptions might also be useful depending on the work

Table 4: Placement of Effort Duo

Effort A	Effort B
Thought	Feeling
Outer	Inner
External	Internal
Revealed	Hidden
Social Mask	Self
Facade	Reality
Etc.	Etc.

---

[1] This term did not originate from Laban. It was coined in the studio to describe this process for actors to work with two co-existing Efforts to express thought and feeling.

[2] Laban, *The Mastery of Movement*, p. 106.

[3] Laban, *The Mastery of Movement*, p. 106.

you are exploring. To begin with, many actors find it easier to conceive of an inner Effort and an outer Effort, as this helps them locate the two Efforts in the body at the same time.

However, conceptualizing the two Efforts as thought and feeling becomes important. This is because many of the other descriptions rely on a divide between something hidden and something revealed, suggesting that one Effort is always more visibly dominant to the outside world. If thought and feeling are placed on two Efforts, this gives the possibility for either Effort to become more or less visible to the world (depending on whether the character is currently allowing a greater expression of thought or feeling). This gives the actor more to play with.

When two Efforts co-exist in the body, they do not merge. Each separate Element of the two Efforts is at play, without blending. It is like two individual people living in the same house who don't necessarily co-habit easily. Each Effort is confronted by the other all the time, as they work to interrelate in a constantly shifting power dynamic. This is both inherently dramatic and recognizably human, as we are constantly balancing our conflicting Effort drives, to varying degrees of success.

Video Resource

Effort Duos
https://vimeo.com/251619191

The Fifty-Six Characters

The Efforts give us eight ways of describing the basic movement qualities in the world. Once you know how to combine two of these Efforts in an Effort Duo, you will instantly have access to fifty-six different character types (i.e. ways of being). These basic combinations form a blueprint for you as an actor to transform far beyond your own habitual movement Affinities (see *Table 5*).

DISCOVERING EFFORT DUOS

Preparation

Warm-up: Two Simultaneous Actions

To begin with, it can feel daunting or overwhelming to express two different Efforts at the same time. It can feel like the classic example of an 'impossible' physical duo: rubbing your head while patting your stomach. There is a simple well-known acting game that asks you to name a different action from the one you are actually doing (i.e. to do two things at once by adding an additional thought task to a physical action). If you are too tense when you play the game, it becomes impossible to do. However, if you let the physical action drop

Table 5: The Fifty-Six Characters

THOUGHT	FEELING	THOUGHT	FEELING
Dabbing	Wringing	Wringing	Dabbing
Thrusting	Floating	Floating	Thrusting
Pressing	Flicking	Flicking	Pressing
Gliding	Slashing	Slashing	Gliding
Slashing	Dabbing	Dabbing	Slashing
Flicking	Thrusting	Thrusting	Flicking
Floating	Pressing	Pressing	Floating
Wringing	Gliding	Gliding	Wringing
Dabbing	Floating	Floating	Dabbing
Thrusting	Wringing	Wringing	Thrusting
Pressing	Slashing	Slashing	Pressing
Gliding	Flicking	Flicking	Gliding
Flicking	Dabbing	Dabbing	Flicking
Slashing	Thrusting	Thrusting	Slashing
Wringing	Pressing	Pressing	Wringing
Floating	Gliding	Gliding	Floating
Dabbing	Thrusting	Thrusting	Dabbing
Thrusting	Pressing	Pressing	Thrusting
Pressing	Gliding	Gliding	Pressing
Gliding	Dabbing	Dabbing	Gliding
Flicking	Slashing	Slashing	Flicking
Slashing	Wringing	Wringing	Slashing
Wringing	Floating	Floating	Wringing
Floating	Flicking	Flicking	Floating
Dabbing	Pressing	Pressing	Dabbing
Thrusting	Gliding	Gliding	Thrusting
Flicking	Wringing	Wringing	Flicking
Slashing	Floating	Floating	Slashing

into body memory so you carry on doing it without thinking, it frees your brain up for the new task of thinking of a different action. This provides a simple training for allowing your body to carry on with an action without you having consciously to mind it. The actions can be anything from simple everyday actions (e.g. 'drinking a glass of water', 'jumping up and down', 'tying my shoelace') to outrageous flights of fancy (e.g. 'grooming my pet dragon', 'pushing a cow up a hill', 'eating my hat'). Any objects that are part of the stated action can be mimed; you cannot plan your response in advance; and the action you say mustn't be similar to, or inspired by, the actual action you are doing.

- This is an exercise for two actors.
- *Actor A does an action.*
- *Actor B asks A: 'what are you doing?'*
- *Actor A continues with their action and at the same time replies, stating a different action from the one they're actually doing.*
- *Actor A stops their action, while Actor B begins doing the action Actor A has just said they were doing.*
- *Actor A then asks Actor B: 'what are you doing?'*
- *Actor B continues with the action and at the same time replies, stating a different action from the one they're actually doing.*
- *Actor B stops their action, while Actor A begins doing the action Actor B has just said they were doing.*
- *And so on.*

Ways In

Interrupted Effort Weave

An interrupted Effort Weave allows you to experience shifting from one Effort to a non-neighbouring Effort. This opens a door to exploring how different pairs of non-neighbouring Efforts relate to each other.

- *Move through a Basic Effort Weave in full-body mode motivated by thoughts and feelings.*[4]
- *Allow an Effort to 'interrupt' the Effort Weave: instead of transitioning to a neighbouring Effort, shift to one that differs in two or all three Elements. The new Effort will simply cut in and take over immediately.*
- *Continue to move through a Basic Effort Weave, freely transitioning from one Effort to a neighbouring Effort.*

---

[4] This is the same mode that you enter into during Phase 2 of a Journey Improvisation. You are amoeba-like but with the addition of human condition (i.e. presence of thoughts and feelings). See 'Phase 2: Adding Human Condition', p. 110.

- *Allow another non-neighbouring Effort to interrupt the Weave.*

- *Carry on exploring moving through an Effort Weave with periodic interruptions from non-neighbouring Efforts.*

- *After your Effort Weave, take some time to analyse and reflect.*

Pausing in an Effort Weave Transition

This exploration examines the specifics of two Efforts while removing them from the other six, as if placing them under a microscope. Focusing on two Efforts deepens your understanding of the relationship between them, and increases your sense of their connectedness.

- *Move through a Basic Effort Weave in full-body mode motivated by thoughts and feelings.*

- *Pick two Efforts to work with and start to transition between just these Efforts, moving from one Effort to the other, and back again.* You can shift back and forth between them quickly, or play with staying in each Effort for longer.

- *Now, rather than switching wholly from one Effort to the other, allow a moment of overlap: a moment where both Efforts are being expressed in the body at the same time.* Keep in mind that this does not mean that they blend together. Each continues to be expressed precisely with all three of its Elements.

- *Begin to allow this moment of overlap in the transition to last a little longer, so that you extend the experience of expressing the two Efforts at the same time.*

- *Don't impose anything. Simply enjoy the images, metaphors and narrative moments that emerge naturally.*

- *Now, move through an Interrupted Effort Weave in full-body mode motivated by thoughts and feelings.*

- *Pick two Efforts from a moment of interruption in the Effort Weave (i.e. two Efforts that are different in two or all three of their Elements).*

- *As before, experiment with shifting back and forth between them, allowing a moment of overlap to occur.*

- *Take some time to analyse and reflect.*

EMBODYING EFFORT DUOS

Locating Co-existing Efforts

In an Effort Duo, the two Efforts co-exist in the body and you let them fight each other. One Effort will express thought, and the other Effort will express feeling. If you find it more accessible to think of an inner Effort and an outer Effort, then start by working with this idea (i.e. one Effort you don't mind presenting to the world, and one which you wish to keep hidden). Once you have experienced how to locate two co-existing Efforts, you will then be able to repeat the exploration with the two Efforts expressing thought and feeling.

When working with two Efforts, one will dominate at any given time: one is 'major' and the other is 'minor'. However, there should be a fluid interplay in this relationship. The Efforts will switch between being dominant (major) and subservient (minor) depending on the ebb and flow of the improvisation. When the two Efforts are expressing thought and feeling, this means that sometimes thought will be leading and sometimes feeling. If you are working with the two Efforts as inner and outer, it means that sometimes the inner will be successfully hidden, and sometimes it will emerge to become visible.

- *Choose two Efforts that are opposites (i.e. all three Elements are different).*
- *Place thought on one Effort, and feeling on the other.*
- *Move in the space, experimenting with how the Efforts interrelate. Work in full-body mode motivated by thoughts and feelings.*
- *Find the relationship between the two Efforts. They can co-exist.* It is normal for us to express more than one Effort – we do it all the time, so it's easier than you think. You will need to trust your body.
- *Use sounds to remind you of what you're doing: exclamations, thoughts-out-loud, etc.*[5]
- *Remember: this is not an equal relationship. At any given time, one Effort will be dominant (major) and one subservient (minor). Articulate and enjoy the interchange between the two Efforts: how they meet; what the conflict is between them; how they might switch from minor to major, and back again.*
- *Don't make a plan. Let the Effort Duo take you.* If you think you know what you are going to offer, then you diminish it: it becomes boundaried by your expectations and you shut down its potential.
- *There's no need to overwork: don't be afraid to have a simple experience.* If it is clear, even a simple experience will speak to us. The interplay of one Effort with another is found in small moments of closing in, shifting, sinking, expanding, etc. The story of life doesn't always emerge through large-scale action. Human experience also lives in the simplicity of the everyday.
- *As soon as you feel clear in expressing the Effort Duo, internalize it and carry on moving in the space.*
- *Don't forget to use Gestures. Allow them to help you find an expression of the Effort Duo.* Gestures will help you understand yourself by telling you what you are thinking and feeling.
- *Play with switching between full-body and internalized, particularly if you feel your Efforts are becoming imprecise when internalized.*

---

[5] Cf. 'Exclamations', p. 262; 'Thoughts-out-loud', p. 262.

- *Pause for a moment of reflection. Note any elements of either Effort that are unclear or imprecise.*
- *Repeat the same process working with a new Effort Duo made up of Efforts that are different to each other in two Elements.*
- *Once you are confident of the process, try working with a new Effort Duo made up of neighbouring Efforts.*[6]

Figure 9.1 Top: Effort Duo (*Wringing* and *Floating*) | Bottom: Internalized Effort Duo (*Wringing* and *Dabbing*).

---

[6] For a list of all the neighbouring Efforts, see Table 3: Neighbouring Efforts, p. 192.

Exploring a Major–Minor Switch

Using Anxiety

There are some experiences in life where we become more consciously aware of two separate drives battling each other – one that is a deliberately presented front and one that we wish to hide. For most people, the experience of anxiety in a social context brings about this conflicted sensation. The anxiety bubbles away inside. Yet we actively work at our outer presentation of self to suppress and hide the fact that something is making us anxious. Playing with the sensation of rising anxiety enables you to experience the shifts between a dominant (major) and a suppressed (minor) Effort. You experience the suppressed Effort fighting to take over dominance, and how it occasionally emerges into visibility. This switch might be gradual as it slowly and uncontrollably grows, or it might be immediate. You have probably discovered how to express thought and feeling through an Effort Duo in the last exploration, but if you haven't this will clarify it for you.

- *Pick an Effort Duo in which you wish to work.*

- *Identify one Effort as an inner (the anxiety) and one as an outer (the façade).* You can also think of the anxiety (fear) as the feeling Effort that is rising and your façade as the thought Effort (thoughts which are trying to keep your feelings at bay).

- *Warm-up your chosen Effort Duo with a few minutes of free play in the space: embody the Effort Duo in full-body mode motivated by thoughts and feelings.*

- *Internalize the Effort Duo.*

- *Imagine you are at a party where you don't know anyone well: perhaps at the end of a conference, or a wedding disco.* Make the stakes high so that you feel the pressure to hide your anxiety – to perform 'well' according to social convention.

- *Use thoughts-out-loud. Start with the outer Effort as the major (i.e. the Effort which has clear dominance). What are the thoughts that are successfully controlling the feelings? Voice these out loud ('you're fine, don't worry about it, no-one saw, you've got this', etc.). Find the ways in which your intellect is fighting to stop your feelings from happening, meaning your thoughts are working overtime.*

- *Now allow the inner Effort – the feeling of anxiety – to rise uncontrollably until it switches from being the minor to being the major (i.e. assumes dominance). You can use sounding and exclamations ('oh, no, I don't, I can't', etc.).*

- *Reverse the switch: let your thoughts become dominant once again, hiding your feelings.*

- *Continue to switch back and forth, alternating between which Effort is dominant and which is suppressed. Feel the conflict between the two Efforts in each moment: will you combat your rising anxiety with calming thoughts? Or will the anxiety overwhelm you?*

- *Experiment with volume control.* Perhaps when the inner Effort emerges with the rising anxiety it is also less internalized, and so has both an increasing dominance and an increase in scale towards full-body expression.

- *Allow thought to be dominant as you hide your anxiety to say 'hi' to someone, introduce yourself and ask their name. Keep it simple and true.* You can either do this by imagining meeting someone and practising what you would say or, if you are working with a Buddy, you could engage in an interaction.

- *As soon as you turn away from them, switch so that feeling is dominant as you are swamped by the memory of this interaction ('oh no, why did I, that was, argh, I'm so', etc.).*

- *Keep playing with how social interaction forces the change between thought or feeling being the major (dominant; visible) Effort.*

- *Take some time to analyse and reflect.*

Using Flirtation

Another common experience where we become more consciously aware of two separate drives battling each other is when we are attracted to someone. This creates vulnerability due to fear of rejection, or of letting someone know they have a power over you. So it is often the social norm to hide the attraction; to 'play it cool'. In this case, the outcome of the conflict between thought and feeling is what we call flirting – where someone hides their attraction behind a deliberate façade of something else, and actively plays with the amount of inner feeling they allow the other person to perceive.

- *Repeat the steps of the exploration outlined above. However, this time allow the inner Effort to be a sense of increasing attraction. Place one Effort as an inner (the attraction) and the other as an outer (the façade).* You can also think of the attraction as the feeling Effort that is developing and threatens to tip into lust; and your façade as the thought Effort (thoughts which are trying to keep your socially inappropriate feelings at bay).

Using Other Struggles

You can also use other struggles to explore the interplay of your thoughts and feelings. Set out without knowing whether thought or feeling will end up winning. Neither you nor an audience know what the outcome will be, so you are offering something enjoyable: the drama of you trying to deal with yourself. This has both comic and tragic potential, and it is a game the actor can really enjoy playing.

- *Use the same model of exploration as you did with Anxiety and Flirtation to explore different struggles, such as:*
  - *playful (feeling) vs. 'no, that's inappropriate' (thought)*
  - *excited (feeling) vs. 'must stay focused' (thought)*
  - *hungry (feeling) vs. 'on a diet' (thought)*
  - *scared (feeling) vs. 'don't be so silly' (thought)*
    etc.

EFFORT EQUATION

What is an Effort Equation?

An **Effort Equation**[7] is a way for the actor to work with an Effort Duo to capture the essence of a person/character. It could be written like this:

Effort Duo + Physical Action = Expression of Character

In an Effort Duo, thought and Feeling are each expressed on a different Effort. So the equation could also read:

Effort [Thought] + Effort [Feeling] + Physical Action = Expression of Character

We are all the sum of much more than two Efforts. However, as we have already discovered, we each have a strong Affinity to a few habitual Efforts. It is these that make you so recognizably 'you' to other people. By discovering just two key Efforts for a character, you have a Code that can become the essence of their movement expression – the character's movement 'DNA'.

Our interface with the world during physical action causes us to modify our Efforts to meet the inherent requirements of particular tasks.[8] So, moments of additional Efforts will naturally occur as the actor meets the demands of certain actions. When an actor working with an Effort Duo meets the world through physical action, we perceive somebody who is utilizing the Efforts with the level of complexity and conflict that occurs in everyday life. So working with an Effort Duo creates an expression of character which is recognizably individual and also seems 'real' to the audience.

This is a highly practical way of playing with key movement choices when you are developing a character. You can instantly set an Effort Equation for your character as you play on your feet in the room. Any or all parts of the Equation can then be easily altered as you explore what works best for the character you are creating.

Once you have worked on a particular Effort Equation, it remains within your body memory: just as a guitarist learns to play certain chords without conscious thought, if you've worked with an Effort Equation, then it's a part of your understanding forever. It will be available for you to recall at will.

---

[7] This term did not originate from Laban. It was coined in the studio to describe this process for actors to work with Effort Duos in the creation of character.
[8] Cf. 'Responsive Physical Action', p. 113.

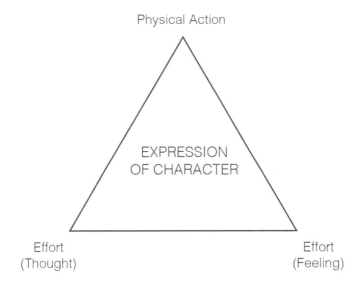

Physical Action

EXPRESSION
OF CHARACTER

Effort
(Thought)

Effort
(Feeling)

Figure 9.2 Visualizing an Effort Equation.

Identifying Your Effort Map

The aim of this exploration is to identify the habitual Efforts that dominate your physical expression, and which other people would perceive as recognizably 'you': your **Effort Map**. This is the Effort Duo to which you have the strongest Affinity and so use most regularly. It is important to remind yourself at this point that all the Efforts are equal: equally beautiful, equally expressive, equally capable of meaning or being anything. There is no one Effort Map that is 'better' than another. Too often we try to conform or wish to be other than we are, when in fact each unique, individual Effort Map should be celebrated. You are a specialist of your Effort Map, so it is something powerful that you can offer as an actor. Also, awareness of your own Effort Map empowers you to analyse and shift your expressive choices, so that you can transform fully into any number of other characters.

- *Choose whether you are feeling-led or thought-led.* Of course, we all have both thoughts and feelings but which for you, in the broadest sense, is most dominant? What is your instinctive answer to the question: do you think your way through life, or do you feel your way through life?

- *If you chose thought, start by identifying the Effort you use most for thinking. If you chose feeling, start by identifying the Effort you use most for feeling.* This is the first half of your Effort Map. It may help to think back to which Efforts you discovered you had a strong Affinity with when you first encountered each Effort.

- *Now, identify which other Effort you use most regularly.* This is the second half of your Effort Map. It will be the Effort you use for thinking or feeling (depending on which you have not yet identified).

- *You now have a potential Effort Map to try out: an Effort Duo with thought placed on one Effort and feeling on the other. Work practically to try out this Effort Duo: move in the space in full-body mode motivated by thoughts and feelings.*

- *Internalize these Efforts. Ask yourself: does this feel like a very familiar relationship of thought and feeling?*

- *Take some moments where you return to being yourself and are not actively using the Effort Duo. Ask yourself: does it feel like a significant change? If so, perhaps you have not yet identified your Effort Map correctly.*

- *Keep experimenting and fine-tuning until you feel you have discovered the right Duo.* You may have to change one of the Efforts within the Duo; switch which Effort is expressing thought and which is expressing feeling; or choose a different Effort Duo entirely. Look for the underlying thought and feeling Efforts. You may be misled by a seeming external appearance of a particular Effort, but this is likely to be the result of seeing a mix of Elements from both Efforts.

- *In your Effort Duo, move through a short sequence of Fundamental Physical Actions (e.g. walk to a chair, sit down, look around the room).* If these are the Efforts you've been doing all of your life it will feel natural, and you will know you've found your Effort Map.

- *Observe a family member and work out their Effort Map.* Often, our Effort Map shares similarities with those of our family members. You may use the same Efforts as them, or neighbouring Efforts that share many Elements.

- *Observe your familiar environments. Your Effort Map may have Elements imposed from the outside world (e.g. someone who has been trained in military school for many years may have a learnt Directness in their Effort Map).*

- *Persevere.* It may take you holding the question with you for some days or weeks, and exploring over time. Eventually you will land upon which Effort Duo feels 'right' in your body. This is your Effort Map.

Understanding Your Own Effort Equation

Once you have identified your Effort Map, you can use this Effort Duo during Responsive Physical Action to come to a full understanding of your own personal Effort Equation. This will tell you something about the essence of your unique movement expression.

- *Start by embodying your discovered Effort Map (internalized Effort Duo).*

- *Now begin to do some simple activities that demand Responsive Physical Action (e.g. opening a bottle of water and taking a sip, opening a door and walking through it, putting your shoes on, etc.).*

- *Take a moment to notice how your Effort Duo shifts slightly in response to the demands of each particular action.*

Understanding Your Habitual Action

The habitual Efforts we use for thought and feeling dictate how we express ourselves through physical action. Thus, we do all physical actions in a certain idiosyncratic way. The actions we find easy/satisfying because of our Effort Map we will do more readily; and those that we find harder/less satisfying we will tend to avoid. So we also favour some particular physical actions over others. The actions we choose to do most regularly, together with how we choose to do all actions, make up our pattern of Habitual Action.

- *Start by embodying your discovered Effort Map (internalized Effort Duo).*
- *Begin to engage in a range of Fundamental Physical Actions (eg. running, walking, sitting, lying, etc.).*
- *As you embody your Effort Duo, notice how it guides your interface with the world. Use simple questions to examine your physical action:*
  - *How do I tend to journey through the space: fast walk? meander? run? etc.*
  - *How do I sit: on a chair? on the floor? etc.*
- *Begin to do some simple activities that demand Responsive Physical Action (e.g. opening a bottle of water and taking a sip; opening a door and walking through it; putting your shoes on; etc.).*
- *Notice how your Effort Map affects the way you do these actions.*
- *Create a 'cartoon strip' of yourself: a short sequence of everyday movements which capture something of your Habitual Action. It should include both Fundamental and Responsive Physical Action, and be no more than about five movements long.*

CREATING EFFORT EQUATIONS

Using Improvisation

Using a Scenario

You can now re-visit many of the familiar scenarios which you used for working with Effort Archetypes, but working with internalized Effort Duos instead. Improvisations you can return to include:

- *A Journey of Feeling: At the Doctor's*
- *A Journey of Thought: On an Intellectual Quiz Show*
- *Passive Action: Sunbathing*
- *Articulation of Personality on Paper*
- *Manifestation of Self: At the Office*
- *Manifestation of Relationship: Siblings/Parent–Child*
- *Manifestation of Partnership: Pair Bonds*

> ## Video Resource
>
> *Effort Duos Improvisation: At the Office*
> https://vimeo.com/251619952

- *Choose an Effort Duo, placing thought on one Effort and feeling on the other.*
- *Warm up your chosen Effort Duo for about five minutes prior to the improvisation, moving in full-body mode motivated by thoughts and feelings. Then internalize the Efforts.* This will allow you to discover the relationship between the two Efforts, and express each individual Effort with precision.
- *Make sure you know which Effort is major and which is minor at any given point. Find the ways in which the dominant Effort switches between thought and feeling as the improvisation progresses.*
- *If you are improvising in a pair, notice how the similarity/difference between you and your partner's Effort Duo affects your interactions.*
- *Take some time to analyse and reflect.* N.B. When observing, it can be harder to identify an Effort Duo than an Effort Archetype. This is because you can be misled by the merged outcome of the two Efforts in an actor's body. If you are finding it hard to perceive a clear Effort Duo, look out for moments when the actor is wholly thought-led or wholly feeling-led. This will allow you to see a single Effort that makes up one half of the Duo.

Using a Physical Score

The actor will sometimes be in a situation in which their spatial choices or actions are dictated to them. This can lead to a debilitating sense of confusion or restriction. Yet it is possible to find the freedom to express character within a set Physical Score. By moving through the given actions in your chosen Effort Duo, you can find your character's way of inhabiting the movement. The Effort Equation of your character will emerge as thinking, feeling and physical action occur.

- *Create a simple Physical Score of about five actions which includes Fundamental, Passive and Responsive Physical Actions (e.g. walk across the room, sit, drink some water, sharpen a pencil, write your signature, look out of the window).*
- *First do the Physical Score as yourself.*
- *Choose an Effort Duo, placing thought on one Effort and feeling on the other.*
- *Warm-up your chosen Effort Duo for about five minutes prior to the improvisation, moving in full-body mode motivated by thoughts and feelings. Then internalize the Efforts.*
- *Using your internalized Effort Duo, play through the Physical Score a few times.*

- *Improvise a short scene, into which you interweave your Physical Score. Create a few lines of dialogue which you deliver as you move through the Physical Score. This should all be done in your Effort Duo.*

- *Take a moment to analyse and reflect.*

- *Then, repeat all the steps above with a new Effort Duo. Feel the difference from your previous Effort Duo.* The choice of Effort Duo affects the improvisation by altering the timing, delivery and meaning of both the Physical Score and the lines of dialogue.

- *Once again, analyse and reflect: what changed when you altered the Effort Duo? How different were the physical actions? Were there different key moments?*

- *Keep playing with different Effort Duos using the same Physical Score.*

In the Real World

It can be useful to explore a character's Effort Equation in real-life situations. The real world demands you 'fit in'. So you are challenged to make sure you have fully internalized the Effort Duo in order to pass as 'normal'. There may be no particularly identifiable external 'movement' when you are, for example, sitting at a bus stop. Yet the Effort Equation will still be present in your overall physical expression, creating an identifiable character who has their own way of holding themselves, breathing, thinking, feeling and responding to the world.

- *Choose an Effort Duo that you want to play with for a longer time.*

- *Prepare your chosen Effort Duo by improvising in your work-space in full-body mode motivated by thoughts and feelings. Make sure you include Sounding. Then internalize the Efforts and speak some thoughts-out-loud.*

- *Take a brief foray into the real world in this Effort Duo. Give yourself a motivation for heading outside: perhaps you want to sit in the sunshine, or get some fresh air, or want to pop to the shops to get something.*

- *Make sure you stay in the character of your Effort Duo the whole time and don't allow yourself to drop out of it.*

- *You'll need to fit into society, so seek how you can embody this internalized Effort Duo as 'naturalistically' as possible. Make sure that all your movement is motivated by your thoughts and feelings – that nothing is detached or disconnected.*

- *If you speak, remember your vocal quality will also be affected by your Effort Duo.*

- *Notice how your Effort Duo affects your way of being in the world.*

- *When you return to your work-space, take some time to analyse and reflect.*

PART E
APPLYING THE EFFORTS

CHAPTER 10
ADVANCED EXPLORATIONS

You now have a deep embodied understanding of the Efforts. This means you can work with them to express whatever you need or desire. These advanced explorations unlock text and character by applying many of the Effort skills you have already learnt (Effort Weaves, Effort Duos, Effort Equations, etc.). There will be aspects of each exploration which can be adapted and applied to different rehearsal processes. Keep your explorations playful: the Efforts are not a technique you can get 'right' or 'wrong'. Some explorations will unlock something for you and some may not. You will discover a personal way of working with the Efforts that meets different needs according to context. This approach will empower you by giving you the confidence and ability to unlock a richer palette of physical expression during any kind of work.

UNITING EFFORTS AND TEXT

This exploration allows you to **experiment with speaking text on each Effort** and during transitions from one Effort to another. It is playful and free. By placing text on an Effort Weave, you can discover how the text and the Effort interact, informing one another and unlocking meaning.

- *Choose a speech (monologue) that you know well.*
- *Before you start: write down some Efforts to move through in a Basic Effort Weave so that you can refer to it as you work[1] (or record them to play back).*
- *Guide yourself through a Basic Effort Weave as you speak your chosen text aloud. Move in full-body mode motivated by thoughts and feelings.* If speaking and moving together seems too much, remember that you are used to Sounding the Effort.
- *Do not worry about actively trying to communicate the 'meaning' of the words.* You are simply allowing the words to speak on the Effort and seeing what connections between the Effort and the text happen to occur.
- *Make sure that you allow Gestures to emerge whilst avoiding the trap of forcing them.* Gestures help illuminate the meaning of the text but forcing them can lead to indicating on every word, particularly with the Sudden Efforts.

---

[1] Cf. 'Basic Effort Weave', p. 195.

- *Notice any moments where speaking the text on a particular Effort opens up the potential of the words.* Moving through the Efforts can give you a heightened awareness of the possibilities that lie within the text.

- *Repeat the exploration but now make different choices about when to shift to the next Effort in your Weave. Work instinctively, allowing the progression of the text to guide your choice to change Effort.*

- *Repeat the text again but this time on an internalized Effort Weave. You might be sitting, standing or walking. Remember to include Gestures.*

- *Take some time to analyse and reflect.*

'GIVING BIRTH': EMBODIED STORYTELLING

In some situations, we employ more than our usual number of Efforts to meet the circumstances of what is happening. A character moves far beyond their usual Affinity when they are in an extraordinary situation which confronts them with pressurized demands: their habitual use of two or three main Efforts becomes a quick-shifting cycle through many (or all) of the Efforts. When you **apply an Effort Weave to action**, you can explore situations in which the use of Efforts becomes hyper-fluid in this way. Narrative is created by the shifting of Efforts in response to the unfolding scenario.

In this scenario, you are completely involved in responding to your body during a life-changing event. The process of labour offers a huge range of physical experiences as you track through many thoughts, feelings and sensations (e.g. acute changes in pain level). So you are asked to shift rapidly through all eight Efforts during this exploration. These shifts create a Weave that is extreme, yet logical. This is an improvisation for all actors to do, including those who identify as male. Giving birth can be a metaphor – you can 'birth' an idea. So it is a powerful experience that all actors need to be able to express.

Video Resource

Applying the Efforts: Giving Birth
https://vimeo.com/251631834

- This is an exploration for an individual actor; or for two actors, with one playing the role of the birthing partner.
- *Start with a brief full-body Interrupted Effort Weave as a warm-up.*[2]

---

[2] Cf 'Interrupted Effort Weave', p. 204.

- *Begin the improvisation: you are in the later stages of labour, leading up to the birth.* You don't need to improvise the actual arrival of the baby.

- *During the improvisation, shift through different Efforts (as you would in an Interrupted Effort Weave). Include all eight Efforts.* If you consciously choose to express a given Effort, it will find a place in the story. Choosing to Dab may lead to panting; choosing to Press may lead to expressing the pain of harnessing a contraction; choosing to Float might express being weak and scared; etc.

- *Repeat the improvisation several times, until you can allow the Effort Weave to carry you.*

- *Now, create an exactly repeatable structure within which you can fine-tune your choices. Write the plot-line down, along with the narrative of changing Efforts. Ask:*
  - *When do the Efforts shift?*
  - *When does the Effort change to a Neighbouring Effort, and when is it 'interrupted' by an Effort which is different in two or more Elements?*
  - *What are the Efforts expressing?*
  - *Where are the Efforts located in the body?*

- *If you have a birthing partner, allow the improvisation to reveal the relationship between you.*

- *Run through the scene several times.*

The experience of being in labour can now be used as a way of bringing text to life ('birthing' it). This can liberate the whole body to express the text, and create an Effort narrative that unfolds as the speech progresses towards its conclusion.

- *Choose a speech (monologue) that emerges from a need to be spoken to someone (i.e. not a reflective piece or poem), and is leading to an outcome or aiming to reach a decision.*

- *Return to your improvised labour scene. Move through it whilst speaking the text: keep to the Physical Score of the labour scenario, including your chosen Efforts and your movements for giving birth. Retain your heightened state.*

- *When you feel the movement and the text working together, enjoy playing with the sense that you are 'giving birth' to the speech.* The times when the text is in conflict with the Physical Score also offer an opportunity to sharpen what you are saying.

- *Now, take this one step further: as you progress through the speech, imagine you are giving birth to the objective of your argument (e.g. the mobilization of an army; a seizing of power; the making of lots of money; etc.).*

Once you have explored this improvisation, you can create other scenarios that allow you to experiment with an Effort narrative. Examples might include: trying to stay awake when you haven't slept for several days; defusing a bomb; facing a firing squad; catching a very big fish; etc.

CREATING A PRECISE PHYSICAL SCORE

You can use the Efforts to make detailed choices about the Physical Score in a text fragment or scene. This exploration examines how to use the Efforts together with the text to **create a precise Physical Score**. It should express acting choices (intentions, aims, etc.) not replace them.

- *Choose a short speech (monologue) that you know well.*

- *Read the text aloud a number of times.* Keep the reading as simple as possible to allow the meaning to emerge.

- *As you read, note any key changes in thought or feeling. Mark these changes in the text.* Try to be precise about when the impulse for thought or feeling changes for the character (as opposed to when the result of that change is articulated in the text).

- *Allocate each change a corresponding shift in Effort Quality (i.e. each time the thought or feeling changes there is a corresponding change of Effort). Place all eight Efforts within the text.*

- *Work practically: speak the text aloud as you move in full-body mode motivated by thoughts and feelings. Shift between your chosen Efforts at the places you have identified.*

- *Work through the text again, but this time with the Efforts internalized.*

- *Focus on action within the scene and set a simple Physical Score.* This could include Fundamental Action (walking, sitting, standing, etc.); Responsive Physical Action (handling objects, doing tasks, etc.); and Passive Action (thinking, reading, doodling, etc.). For example: you stand up, you place your hand on the table, you leave.

- *Work through the text again. This time, move through both your chosen Efforts and your Physical Score.*

- *Notice how the changes in Effort affect your progression through your Physical Score.* It may be that you are remaining in one action through one or more changes in Effort; or that the action and the Effort change at the same time.

- *Play with different variations.* The meaning will change according to whether it feels as though the action is supporting, opposing, or overriding the text.
  - *Try doing one action from your Physical Score throughout the text. Notice how the changes in Effort affect the expression of the action.*
  - *Try changing action every time you shift Effort. Notice how you can emphasize a change in thought or feeling by a simultaneous change in both Effort and action.*

Figure 10.1 Top: Giving Birth | Bottom: Cloning.

'CLONING': DISCOVERING CHARACTERS

'Cloning' uses another person's Effort expression as a starting point for character transformation. The other person's movement provides a template which you work to alter your own way of being. You create a simple yet specific Effort Map of the observed person. By pinpointing the way in which someone else places thought and feeling on two Efforts, you can then translate the same observed Effort Duo into your own body. This allows you to embody an 'essence' of another person's movement patterns.

Identifying a dominant Effort Duo is a tool to capture a flavour of someone's personality, and **create a movement 'DNA' for a character**. It does not imply that the 'cloned' person only ever uses this particular Effort Duo.[3] It is simply a way of pinpointing two Efforts which, when used exclusively, read as identifiably 'them' to the outside eye.

Once the process is familiar, you can draw from observation of anyone, anywhere. Each new person you 'clone' will give you a basic movement DNA for a different character. This is an efficient way of analysing and retaining the information you gain through observation. You will be able to recall people by their Effort Equation, in the same way you might by looking at a photo of them. There are fifty-six possible Effort Duos, so repeating this process over time allows you to build an expansive bank of possibilities to draw on for creating character.[4]

Video Resource

Applying the Efforts: Cloning
https://vimeo.com/251632021

- This is an exploration for two actors.
- Actor A (whose movement is to be cloned): *create a 'cartoon strip' of yourself.* This is a short sequence of everyday movements which captures something of your habitual movement patterns. It should be no more than about five movements long, and made up of Fundamental Physical Actions and Gestures. You must be able to repeat it exactly.
- Actor A: *present your 'cartoon strip'.*
- Actor B: *observe Actor A and ask what were the main actions? Were there any immediately identifiable Efforts or Elements?*
- Actor A: *teach the sequence to Actor B.*
- *Discuss together the actions in the sequence.* Examine where weight is distributed in the body and the Lightness/Heaviness of the movements; the timing of each

---

[3] Cf. 'What is an Effort Equation?', p. 210.
[4] Cf. Table 5: 'The Fifty-Six Characters', p. 203.

movement and of the sequence; the shaping of the body and its relationship to the Planes. You don't need to take too long over this.

- *Now, identify Actor A's Effort Map: which Effort is being used for thought and which for feeling? Make sure you try out different possibilities: experimenting physically will provide clearer answers than simply talking about it.* Actor B can ask Actor A to inhabit the two Efforts you choose for thought and feeling as they do the sequence of actions. If the chosen Effort Duo is right, it will feel natural to them and look natural to you – the 'cartoon strip' will be the same.

- *Once you have successfully identified the Effort Map, practise moving through the 'cartoon strip' side by side. Then record the sequence for video playback, or do it together in front of an Outside Eye.*

- *Use analysis and feedback to identify where your use of Efforts is still not quite the same. Look for accuracy in the Effort Map, and use the language of the Efforts to offer feedback in terms of the Elements (WTS).* This is not about mimicry. The form of the movements Actor B is doing may be accurate but they also need to embody the Effort Map that informs the movement quality.

- *Now, once again film yourselves as you move through the 'cartoon strip' at the same time as each other. This time do not stop at the end of the known sequence. Instead, both carry on spontaneously existing in the space and see what moves naturally occur next.* Actor B should continue embodying the Effort Map and Actor A simply continues to be true to themselves. Make sure that neither of you are over-working or straying into parody. The Effort Map will continue in both bodies without either of you having to predict, manufacture or enforce it. You will discover that often in the moments after the sequence, the moves that occur are the same for both actors. They are now expressing themselves in the same way because they are working from the same Effort Map.

- *Perhaps have a little conversation with each other.* The Effort Map will also be expressed in the vocal quality of both actors.

- *Take a moment to watch the footage and observe what you have just experienced from an outside perspective.*

- *Now, Actor B performs the 'cartoon strip' alone. Again, carry on beyond the known sequence and continue to exist in the space.* Actor B is now able to transform into the cloned study without needing them in the space as a reference. They are now a character true to, but independent of, the original.

- *Swap roles and repeat the whole exploration.*

Once you have mastered this process, it is possible to do it without needing to work directly with the person you have chosen to study.

- *Think of someone you know well, perhaps a family member or close friend. Create a 'cartoon strip' of them, using their most familiar movements.*

- *Use your 'cartoon strip' to identify their Effort Map: experiment practically to identify which Efforts they use for thinking and feeling. You can then work with this as the basis for a character.*

- *Once you are familiar with identifying an Effort Map, follow this process with an unfamiliar subject. Observe someone you do not know and remember some of the key movements that they are doing as you watch. Then use this to create the 'cartoon strip'. This will give you the material you need to identify the Efforts they are using.* Over time, you will be able to identify a person's Effort Map much more quickly. You will become increasingly fluent in perceiving the Efforts being used by the people around you.

'GALLERY-GLIDE': UNLOCKING TEXT

Glide helps the actor **find a mode in which 'less is more' when working on text**. This exploration unlocks the meaning of the text, without actively playing character or nuances of interpretation. You simply allow the words to travel on a Glide into the space.

Glide is used as a calm and cool exterior.[5] If the Efforts were compared to different colours, Gliding would be white. It is rich in its simplicity; both spacious and full. It allows the actor to cultivate a presence that is open, expansive and released with a sense of ease and efficiency. This relates closely to the physical state that is often described as 'Neutral'.[6]

Working with an embodied Glide, you will discover more about allowing the text to speak for itself. The Effort carries the inherent power of the words, offering you the chance to find out what you need to do to supplement the text – which is probably very little. Actors can find themselves squeezing or pushing emotions, or adding a multitude of small actions. The Glide allows you to discover how to simply channel the text, using only whatever action is needed to deliver the words.

Preparation

- *Choose a speech (monologue) which emerges from a need to be spoken to someone (i.e. not a reflective piece or poem), and that has an emotional journey.* Use something you know well and which you can deliver by heart. Two paragraphs are enough. Classical text will serve this exercise well – particularly Shakespeare.

- *As a warm-up, do a short Gliding improvisation in full-body mode motivated by thoughts and feelings. Use this to remind yourself of the sensation of an expansive Glide.*

---

[5] Of course, the Glide can express anything. So this is one specific way of working with an aspect of Glide.
[6] For more on Neutral, see Ewan and Green, *Actor Movement*, pp. 63–88.

In the Gallery: On the Wall

- *Place a block or sturdy table that is easy and safe for you to stand on up against the wall. Climb onto this higher-level surface. Stand with your back lightly touching the wall.*

- *Allow your relationship to Space to feed you: notice your new perspective (you are now inhabiting the space that is usually above your head). Look out and down and see all the space into which you can expand. Feel how the touch of the wall gives you an awareness of your back-space but relinquishes you from the responsibility to fill it.* Being against the wall gives you a heightened awareness of the space to the sides/above/below by removing the sense of the space behind.

- *Imagine that you are a painting hanging in a magnificent gallery. Using Glide, embody the flat width of the painting by spreading your arms wide along the wall into a full wingspan.*

- *Let go any sense of the 'barrier' at the edge of your skin. Experience yourself as part of something else – part of the painting, part of the gallery.* We tend to think of ourselves and others as having an outline around us; having a person-shaped boundary. This can be dissolved through imagination.

- *Allow yourself to be fed by the heightened sensation of two-dimensional width. Extend along the wall into your side space; lengthen the back of your neck against the wall, sensing how your lungs can expand outwards.*

- *You can Glide your arms upwards and downwards on the wall at full extension to express the whole size and scope of the painting.* From hand to hand the span of our arms is generally the same as our height. So, when you embody this painting, you are both literally and imaginatively as wide as you are tall.

- *How does your painting look in your mind's eye? What are the colours and shapes? What is the material and style of the frame that contains them?* The answers to these questions will be informed by your chosen text. The painting is a visual manifestation of the character and their words. Do not simply see the character as a figure within the painting. The character is the whole painting: all the colours and all the textures, including the frame.

- *Remember: the Glide travels along Direct lines in the body which extend outwards into Space. As you Glide, experience a sense of joining imagined pre-existing lines.*[7]

- *Allow yourself to work with Sounding in the Glide.* The sound may be minimal but don't hold your breath or let it go quiet.

- *Don't zone out.* The Glide demands constant engaged commitment, so doing less is still very active.

---

[7] Cf. 'The Dimensional Cross', p. 36; 'The Planes', p. 36.

In the Gallery: Onto the Floor

- *You are the painting (standing on a higher surface, Gliding). Imagine the art gallery at the end of a long, busy day: all the people who've been walking past you are now leaving; the caretaker slams and locks the door; it is quiet and the whole gallery-space is all yours.*
- *Begin to discover small moments where your Gliding takes you into three-dimensional movement (e.g. moving your arms forward in front of you). Use the expansion of the Glide to carry your energy out into the whole of the space.*
- *Allow your Gliding movements to bring you safely from your higher-level surface down to the floor.*
- *As you move to the centre of the floor, bring your sensation of Space with you. Remain connected to the space in front, above and below you; as well as experiencing the additional connection to the space behind you (now you are no longer against the wall).*
- *Trust that you are the vehicle for the story of the painting. Feel you are holding responsibility for that energy, that life, and are connecting to the world with ease.*
- *Keep returning to the higher surface to re-find the Glide. Briefly use being against the wall to re-gain a connection to the space and to your breath.* When you first move into the centre of the floor, you will probably only be able to maintain a truly expansive Glide for a short time. However, once you've felt this sensation, you can develop it. After a few attempts, you will find the length of time you can maintain the expansive Glide increases.

Into Gliding with Text

- *Return to standing on the higher surface. Use the Glide to extend your arms outwards into a full wingspan. Connect to the Space.*
- *Speak your text. You might speak it through two or three times. Feel how the words hold their own meaning and need to be spoken. Let their sound out into the world; allow them to do their job. The words are part of the 'painting'. You are the vehicle and the text passes through you: just open the channel so the words spill out.* The action of speaking is not passive. In this Glide, it is Direct – pinpointed – and the words travel clearly into the space; they echo around the gallery.
- *Remember: all you can do is Glide, you don't have any other options.*
- *Allow the space around you to carry all the thoughts and feelings expressed by the words you are saying.*
- *When you've been fed by the high-level Space, allow your Gliding movements to bring you safely from your higher-level surface down to the floor. Maintain your sense of expansive Space as you move down into the room.*

- *Continue to speak the text. Trust that the Glide can carry the action: Lightness doesn't mean any lack of clarity in the text; you can be crystal-clear without using Heavy Weight.* On text, the voice becomes a mirror to the body. For example, if there is a Press in the voice on the emotional words, then you know you are not accepting or realizing the power of the Glide.

- *Don't become passive or static.* Direct is always moving towards a known end-point.

- *Enjoy the moments where the text happens to synchronize with your actions and Gestures.* Movements forwards/backwards/sideways/up/down are all particular acts of storytelling. You will feel this if, for example, you happen to be moving upwards as an uplifting thought is occurring in the text.

- *Don't allow your brain to switch off.* Just because you are allowing the Glide to be the vehicle for the words, it doesn't mean that the words become disconnected from the thoughts, feelings and images which they contain and express.

- *Remember: if you lose the precision of the expansive Glide, you can return to standing on the higher surface to re-find it.*

- *Once you have completed your exploration of the text, finish back on the higher surface as your painting. Take a moment to feel how the text and all that it contains now lives in the space around you and in the space of the room. As you imagine that day is arriving and the caretaker is opening back up, feel the whole space as the painting of your text.*

- *Take some time to analyse and reflect.*

MANIFESTING THOUGHTS AND FEELINGS: SUBTEXT IN ACTION

Text emerges out of a character's internal world of thoughts and feelings. So you can discover a character's hidden or suppressed motivations by careful examination of the words they speak. This is often referred to as the subtext: that which is driving the spoken words of the character but is not explicitly stated.

It is now familiar to you that thought and feeling can be expressed on a chosen Effort Duo; and that this can lead to specific choices about which physical actions to do, and how they are carried out. In this way, the actor is able to **manifest the thoughts and feelings of a character through physical action**. These inner drives of the character – the subtext – are communicated through the actor's every move (how they sit down, drink from a glass, position a chair, etc.). Thoughts, feelings, and the changes between them are identified through analysis of the text. This means that physical action becomes an immediate expression of the subtext contained in the words on the page.

- *Choose a short piece of text you know well (monologue).*

- *Choose an Effort Duo that you wish to explore. Place thought on one Effort and feeling on the other.*

- *Warm up your chosen Effort Duo for five minutes: improvise in full-body mode motivated by thoughts and feelings. Notice the interplay between the two Efforts.*

- *Internalize the Effort Duo and sense where it now resides in the body.*

- *Break from conscious exploration of the Effort Duo for a minute or two.*

- *Now, visit the text in a liberated way as if you're working on it at home, or in a private space. Don't face an imagined audience or go into a performative body. Speak the text out-loud without consciously expressing the Efforts. Trust that your body has a memory of them: if it's relevant in the moment of saying the text, the appropriate Effort Quality will emerge. Observe how your expression of the text is informed by the preparatory physical work.*

- *Say the text again while changing position, moving, and/or picking up and putting down objects. Observe how your chosen Effort Duo informs your physical action. This focus on physical action also forces you into relying on body memory for maintaining the Effort Duo in your body.*

- *Notice: how do your instinctive changes in physical action reflect the shifting thoughts and feelings in the text?*

- *Choose a moment where you have found an eloquent shift: a moment when your physical action reflects a change in the dominant Effort, as thought shifts to feeling, or feeling shifts to thought. Work with this moment to explore its full potential. Make it precise so that you can repeat it truthfully each time you do it.*

- *You can repeat this process using the same piece of text with a new Effort Duo to discover the diverse possibilities that emerge with each different Effort Equation.*

'BOTTLING': MAPPING BOTTLED EMOTIONS

'Bottling' allows you to move the feelings running through a piece of text in a committed and tangible way. It is called 'Bottling' because it lets you **explore a character's 'bottled' emotions**: the feelings that they habitually suppress. We all have experience of censoring ourselves – keeping our 'demons' hidden from the outside world because we fear they have the power to destroy us. This exploration lets you uncover the 'unacceptable', unseen, internal reality that drives the 'acceptable', visible, outer expression.[8]

This exploration relies on the idea of a performing (public) space. The actor changes between facing towards and away from an imaginary audience. When facing the front, the actor is the character in the world and speaking the text. The character presents the person

---

[8] The 'demon' is not necessarily something which is in and of itself bad or negative. It could be excitement, happiness, or some other articulation of love. It is a 'demon' because it has power over you – because allowing it to be seen would threaten something you care about, such as your status, reputation, relationships, etc.

they wish to be, by using an outer Effort that hides and suppresses what is going on inside. When facing away from the front, they become invisible to the rest of the world. This allows all the character's raw feelings out to play: the actor uses full-body movement in a chosen inner Effort to become the feelings that are usually kept locked up inside.

When they return to facing the front, this inner Effort must be 'bottled' back inside; hidden behind the façade of the outer Effort. The outer and inner Effort come into conflict, as the outer Effort is used to keep the inner Effort concealed.[9] This conflict plays out during delivery of the text. The bottled-up emotional life of the character lives in the body, whilst the words grapple to make sense of what the character is experiencing. The character does their utmost to keep their internal emotional life hidden, but nonetheless it will emerge in glimpses. It will seep out in Gestures and in moments where they can no longer maintain their guard. The audience finds this conflict satisfying because they recognize it as inherently human.

To begin with, it is useful to use Glide as the outer Effort. The Glide enables you to present a seemingly calm, gathered, socially acceptable exterior when facing the front (public space). You also already have an embodied knowledge of expressing text on a Glide from the *Gallery-Glide* exploration.[10]

'Bottling' can be done with many different types of text but at first it is good to work with Shakespeare. His writing can be trusted to offer authentic patterns of human behaviour governed by thought and feeling. This helps with pinpointing the moments where particular emotions come into play. There is also plenty of variety of Efforts amongst the characters.

'Bottling' is designed to be used as pre-rehearsal preparation for characters that have meaty, emotional monologues. As such, it could be done as part of your warm-up during the early stages of a rehearsal process. This work does not interfere with other acting processes. Bottling does not seek to dictate *what* the meaning of the text is via, for example, the prescription of intentions or actions. Rather, it explores *how* the Efforts might be used as a physical vehicle to convey the textual content once it has been identified. Use of the Efforts in this way helps the actor move from an intellectual understanding of the text, to a live physical expression of it.[11] It also enables you to use your physical resources to bring the emotional landscape of the text to life, without the necessity for large-scale physical action: the whole body can be used for nuanced physical expression even if you are seemingly just 'standing still'. Try the process to learn how it works, so that it is a tool you have already mastered once you come to use it for work on a specific play.

---

[9] For this exploration, it is usually easier for the actor to think of the two Efforts as 'inner' and 'outer', so that is how they will be referred to in this outline. However, it is also possible to frame the Efforts as feeling and thought – the text being viewed as an intellectual articulation (thought) arising out of, and simultaneously masking, the emotional experience that is occurring (feeling).

[10] N.B. '"Gallery-Glide": Unlocking Text' (p. 226) unlocks the text itself with simplicity. Whereas 'Bottling' is an exploration of how the emotional life of the character can inform and drive the expression of the text. You may want to work with the same text as you used for *Gallery-Glide* to experience how doing this exploration builds on the foundation of the previous process.

[11] Cf. 'The Efforts and Acting Systems', p. 11.

Video Resource

Applying the Efforts: Bottling
https://vimeo.com/251632628

Identifying Feelings/Emotions

- *Choose a speech (monologue) which emerges from a need to be spoken to someone (i.e. not a reflective piece or poem), and that has an emotional journey.* Use something you know well and which you can deliver by heart. Two paragraphs are enough. If this is your first time working with Bottling, then it should ideally be from Shakespeare (but not a sonnet).

- *Read through the speech and identify possible internal emotions (feelings) that the character is experiencing from the clues offered by the text.*[12] *In order accurately to identify the feelings, ask yourself: what is it that the character is suppressing? What do they not want to be seen by the world? What are they hiding?* You are seeking to identify the internal driving emotion (experienced as 'feelings'): it may be, for example, that what you perceive immediately in the text is anger, yet when you analyse it more closely you realize that what is driving the anger is fear. In this case, fear is the internal emotion and anger is the coping strategy used to hide the fear. The less socially acceptable emotion is hidden under the one the character feels more able to show.

- *Give each feeling a concrete name (e.g. happiness, anger, grief, fear, hope, relief, acceptance, determination, hopelessness, etc.).*[13] *Then choose one of them with which to work first.*

- *Select an Effort with which to express the feeling you have identified.* It may seem straightforward to identify the Effort you wish to use. However, if you find yourself uncertain, try breaking it down into its Elements (WTS): ask yourself is it a Light

---

[12] The word 'emotion' is, at heart, an action word: it is derived from the Latin *emovere* (to disturb, agitate or perturb). Emotions are rooted in instinct and seem to be fairly universal, although they engender strong and complicated responses that are personal. These personal responses are referred to as feelings. Experts have differing opinions on the definition, range and mechanism of emotions and feelings. Four basic emotions are generally identified: happiness, anger, grief and fear. For the purposes of working on this exploration, this list can be widened to include a broad range of both emotions and feelings. For more on emotions and feelings, see Damasio, *The Feeling of What Happens*.

[13] N.B. Frustration is not an emotion. The expression of 'frustration' can demand substantial energy and feel tangible, powerful and overwhelming to an actor. You might therefore think of it and treat it as an emotion, but it is not. Frustration is the barrier between emotions and the world. Frustration can only exist for the actor if you know what it is that you are frustrating – what it is that is being blocked or thwarted. You need to look behind, beneath or inside it in order to perceive it doing its job of holding back emotions/feelings. In other words, frustration should neither be perceived nor 'done' as a feeling in itself. Once the feelings or emotions have been discovered, there is then something to frustrate.

or Strong/Heavy Effort? Sudden or Sustained? Direct or Indirect? In this way, you can guide yourself into making a decision.

The Bottling Mechanism

- *Set up your work-space with the idea of an audience, so that you can face front (public space) or back (private space).* If you are filming yourself or have a Buddy observing, then this should be done from the front.

- *Facing the front, find an internalized Glide so that you appear to be simply 'standing still'.*

- *Once you have spent a few moments in this Glide, turn to face away from the front. Immediately enter into a full-body (amoebic-like) expression of the Effort that you have chosen for your first feeling, including Sounding. You are no longer a person but a physical expression of the feeling itself.* For example, instead of being a Wring amoeba, you are 'the hurt'; or instead of being a Slash amoeba, you are 'the fear'; etc.

- *Allow yourself to really go for it – you are letting one of this character's 'demons' out to play. Let the Effort expression of the internal emotion reveal its power in you; vibrant and dynamic.* You can be wherever the Effort takes you (on the floor, upside down, all over the place) as long as you never face the front. Make sure you keep the Effort accurate to its three Elements (WTS): to be powerful, it must also be precise.

- *Let the Effort take hold.* The more you invest in expressing the Effort while you are turned away, the easier it is to 'bottle it' when you return to facing the front. We are often afraid of our inner selves. So you will know you have released yourself fully to become an expression of the powerful inner emotion when your movement provokes a sense of 'aahh, that's a bit scary'.

- *Once you have reached full embodiment of the Effort, 'bottle' it and turn to face the front. Return to a human form, as you hide the feeling inside and resume the outer Effort of Glide over the top of your inner Effort.* If it helps, visualize the bottling: imagine you are a bottle that has a small open neck, so that all the movement rushes in through the top of your head and down into your belly. This bottling moment happens in a quick beat, without either indulging in the moment or rushing through it.

- *Feel how the two Efforts at play in your body interact with each other: how you are actively using the Glide to hide the demon. Locate the conflict within yourself.* You now have an internalized version of an Effort Duo. Your chosen inner Effort is hidden under the outer Effort of Glide. You seem to be, once more, a human being standing still on Glide but there is a conflict in play.

- *Chose another of the feelings you have identified in your text and repeat this process.* Once you feel you have a good understanding of the Bottling Mechanism and have experienced hiding a few different Efforts under a Glide, then you are ready to move on to the next stage of the exploration outlined below.

Locating a Moment

In this stage, you pinpoint the moment when one of the feelings you have identified begins. It is quite often mid-sentence, just before its overt appearance in the text. Actors often start the emotion too late: they start it when the world sees it (i.e. when the text makes it apparent) but it is likely to have begun earlier than that. The shift in feeling is often what leads to the need to speak the words; and the next feeling is already starting as we are still articulating the words that emerged from the feeling before.

- *Return to examining the text. Seek where the first of the feelings you have already identified begins. Pinpoint an exact moment and mark it in the text with a line and the named feeling. Ask yourself: where does the feeling start to germinate? When does the impulse related to that feeling occur? What is the exact word, or even syllable, where it kicks in? The more exact you are, the easier it is. Note that this trigger point is never at the end of a sentence: we don't have nicely dove-tailed thoughts and feelings.*

- *Make sure you identify just one feeling – the first one to occur.* Work from the understanding that different feelings can never happen at the same time: although it can appear that a character is experiencing many feelings at the same time, this is the result of a quick succession of shifts from one feeling to another.

- *Commit to a choice even if you are uncertain of where the feeling begins.* You will only know if it is the right choice after you have committed yourself to it and tried it out through the process outlined below.

- *Select an inner Effort for this feeling, so you now know where the feeling begins and the Effort on which it will be expressed.*

Introducing Text

- *Facing the front, start your text on a Glide. Be clear and committed.*

- *When you get to the moment you marked in the text, turn away from the front. Immediately enter into a full-body (amoebic-like) expression of the inner Effort you chose for this feeling, including Sounding. Remember: you are no longer a person, but a physical expression of the feeling itself.*

- *Embody the inner Effort for just a few moments, then 'bottle' it and turn to face the front.*

- *Straight away – not rushed but with no hesitation – return to speaking the text on your outer Effort (Glide). Use the Glide to prevent the inner Effort (hidden feeling) from emerging. It should seem as if you've turned away from a freeze frame to release your inner self in a different time and space, before returning to the same place you left and hitting play. Go straight back into the text at the place you left off.*

- *Let the text channel the full effect of the inner–outer Effort conflict, rather than playing your interpretation of the words. Let go of any sense that you have to 'do' something with the text. Allow the words to do the work for you: let them do their job of working to civilize and make sense of what you are feeling inside. Make sure you feel the need to tell someone the text, a desire to make them understand.*

Transposing the Inner Effort

When learning 'Bottling', it is worth taking the time to play with the same moment using a different choice of inner Effort. The internal feeling you have identified remains the same; it is just expressed through the vehicle of a different Effort. It can be useful to do this because your first choice of inner Effort may have reflected a leaning towards your own Affinity. By experimenting, you may find that a different inner Effort choice can work equally well, or perhaps even better, to express the feeling.

- *Choose a different inner Effort and repeat the steps for 'Introducing Text' above.*

Mapping the Inner Efforts

- *Once you are satisfied with your exploration of the first moment, find where the next feeling in the text begins to make itself known.*
- *Repeat the steps of the process:*
  - *name the feeling*
  - *choose an Effort for it*
  - *face towards the back to embody it*
  - *'Bottle' it and turn to face the front.*
- *Continue through the text in this way, mapping all the different feelings that occur throughout the progression of the speech.*
- *Once you have mapped all the inner Efforts in this way, do the whole speech through without breaking to face the back.* You will find that an echo of all the different inner Efforts remains, without you having consciously to do anything – they will have become mapped into the text, and you can trust your body memory to recall them. The text will do its work and tiny moments of each 'bottled' Effort will surface when the feeling is experienced. These are moments that reveal compelling glimmers of the suppressed interior.

Transposing the Outer Effort

Once you have explored 'Bottling' on a Glide, you can repeat the whole process with a different outer Effort. While one character (or one style of acting) may employ Glide as a hiding mechanism, another character may feel the need to use a different Effort. Every person has different social expectations placed upon them according to gender, race, sexuality, environment, occupation, etc. This affects how they present themselves to the world. For example, someone might feel it is more socially acceptable, advantageous or safe to appear less powerful than they are. So perhaps they use a Light, Indirect outer Effort such as Float or Flick. Someone else may use a Strong outer Effort to convey power, or a Direct Effort to convey organization, etc.

- *Choose an outer Effort by asking yourself: how does my character wish to be seen in the world? How does my character believe they need to be seen in the world? What is the exterior they choose to hide their feelings behind?*
- *Once you have chosen an outer Effort, discover what it is to deliver the text on that Effort.*
- *Then repeat the steps of the 'Bottling' exploration using your newly chosen outer Effort instead of Glide.*
- *Do not over-exaggerate the outer Effort. Simply use it as a mechanism to hide or suppress what is going on inside.*

Using Other Text

Like Shakespeare, the Greek tragedies offer emotional intensity and so can be good to use for work on 'Bottling'. So far, the process has focused on delivery of the text during which the identified feelings have a chance to emerge spontaneously through Gestures. However, you can also experiment with allowing more of the internal emotional landscape to be visible, in an acting style that leans more towards what we might call 'expressionism' rather than 'naturalism'. You might play with identifying one or even two places in the text where it feels right to allow the inner Effort to rise more fully – or entirely – to the surface before being suppressed once again.

CHAPTER 11
EFFORTS IN REHEARSAL

There are an infinity of ways in which the Efforts can be used to inform any creative, rehearsal or performance process. This chapter offers examples of key explorations that can help the actor. These give you a starting point for playing with the Efforts at a sophisticated level. They are designed to be applied directly to working on character, including text work. You might find it useful to play with them to find out how they work before applying them to a specific rehearsal process.

During a rehearsal process, the work of the actor falls into two categories: the work done inside the rehearsal room with the rest of the company, and the work done outside of the rehearsal room (both before and during the process). The work done outside the rehearsal room includes research, exploration, and preparation for character, ongoing reflection, and the graft needed to gain ownership of text – including learning lines and integrating a deep understanding of patterns of subtext, events, etc. Inside the rehearsal room, the actor must offer themselves to the collaborative process of the ensemble, following the lead of the director. The director will have their own process, which may not include explicit reference to working with the Efforts. So much of an actor's work with the Efforts will be during their own independent work outside the rehearsal room. This will inform their process and deepen their embodied understanding of text and character. They can then engage in any rehearsal room process, safe in the knowledge that their work will be well-founded, articulate and physically expressive.

PREPARATION

Using Effort Weaves for Warm-up[1]

Moving through an Effort Weave requires technical precision and offers new potential for expression every time – so it can help keep the repeated process of daily warm-up both alive and disciplined. It helps you feel (re)charged and ready to work from a place of clarity, control and ease. Each Effort Weave is different: it will adapt itself to your needs on a particular day of rehearsal or to what is required when playing a specific character.

---

[1] Ideally, an Effort Weave would serve as part of a thorough, wide-ranging warm-up. However, it can in itself constitute a warm-up if the situation requires it. Remember though: if this is the case, it is vital to start with an extended time in a Light Effort, which can ease the body safely into the improvisation. It is best to begin with either Dabbing or Floating.

Doing an Effort Weave in warm-up allows you to **re-access your movement 'bank' ready for you to draw on throughout a rehearsal**. It becomes a tool which helps you find subtle clues, hints and suggestions to aid you in your process. After an Effort Weave, the movement continues to exist in the body and will emerge as instinctive connections and responses to situations or people. Having these options readily accessible within the creative process helps broaden the choices available to you in the moments when you are experimenting with developing a character's movement. You do not have to think about Efforts in the moment of exploration but might reflect afterwards about what Effort Codes you ended up drawing on to bring clarity to your choices. Using Effort Weaves as a regular part of your practice will mean movement options live within your body and can be more readily drawn upon when building a character.

Undertaking an Effort Weave can also prepare you for physical expression of intense emotion in rehearsal, without you needing to drain your own emotional resources. If you build regular Effort Weaves into your pre-rehearsal preparation, then over time they will become more and more efficient. The optimum time-frame for doing an Effort Weave is between fifteen to twenty minutes. The aim is to take time to channel the Efforts freely, enabling you to make discoveries and reconnect to your body. However, even a very short Effort Weave can function as a trigger to bring you to a place of readiness, where it is easy to access physical expression. You will know that at any given moment you can immediately draw on the Efforts as a vehicle to access and express emotional intensity.

Speed Version

Once the process of an Effort Weave has become habitual, you may choose to do a Speed Weave. This takes you through all eight Efforts in a short time. It can be done in as little as twenty seconds. By now, the Efforts reside easily in your body and so a Speed Weave will trigger your body memory to access a vast bank of movement expression. The Speed Weave can also allow you to focus on a tighter interplay between the Efforts, as it transitions rapidly from Effort to Effort and may move back and forth between two Efforts a number of times.

- *Use the prompts in the following audio to guide you through some Speed Weaves:*

Audio Resource

Speed Weaves
https://vimeo.com/251653121

- *Create your own Speed Weave which will last from one to five minutes. Set a timer, giving yourself a little more time if you do not yet feel familiar with doing a Speed Weave.*
- *Try this with different time limits to become accustomed to moving through an Effort Weave at different speeds.*

Secret Warm-up

As an actor, you are sometimes placed in a situation where there is little time or space for warm-up at all. This might happen when you are attending a briefing, a casting or are under constraint on a film set; or when the environment itself prevents you being able to undertake a full physical warm-up. In these circumstances, an Effort Weave can be a useful tool as it can be done secretly, and you will still gain some benefit of warming up and preparing your physical expression. An internalized Effort Weave, or an Effort Weave localized in a body part (e.g. Gestures of the hand), can be done almost anywhere. An Effort Weave on thought or feeling, for example, could be done somewhere as public and busy as a tube train or bus without anyone noticing anything out of the ordinary.

Video Resource

Secret Effort Weave
https://vimeo.com/251506763

- *Use the prompts in the following audio to guide you through a Secret Effort Weave:*

Audio Resource

Secret Effort Weave
https://vimeo.com/251653549

- *Practise moving through a secret Effort Weave (internalized movement) in a public place. You might try this on thought or feeling (or switching between the two); on breath; or in one small body part such as the fingers or toes.*
- *Try this in a number of places and contexts until you are confident that you can do an Effort Weave whenever and wherever you require.*

During Other Exercises

Sometimes you will be in a situation where you are not responsible for your own preparation but are part of a led warm-up. You can use an understanding of the Efforts to make technical exercises more articulate and warm up your physical expression. Tuning into your expression is the same as tuning an instrument to re-find the quality and tone of the notes you know how to make. It's not enough just to get the blood circulating.

When doing physical exercises, identify the Efforts being used and then employ them consciously with precision. For example, you may choose to do an exercise such as a roll-down using a small Effort Weave moment in which you switch from Gliding as you roll down to Pressing as you roll back up again; or to switch from Flicking to Slashing during an exercise that involves swings. No-one else will necessarily know that you are also using these exercises to warm-up the quality of your movement. In fact, everything you do can be used in this way – even everyday actions. Simply noticing, for example, that you are running your hand across your cheek and then retracing it as a Glide; or Pressing your back into the chair as you are sitting. Even recalling your yawn as a Wring, or your blinking as a Dab, is enough to re-access your bank of movement expression.

Efforts Suggesting Exercises

When you are leading yourself through a warm-up, you can **let the Efforts suggest particular exercises to you**. A moment of Flicking might, for example, suggest an exercise involving swings; or a moment of Gliding might suggest an exercise involving a roll-down. Allow expressing the Efforts to lead you into exercises that you already have within your wider bank of movement knowledge.

Video Resource

Using the Efforts to Warm Up
https://vimeo.com/251507200

Applied Effort Weaves

An Effort Weave can be deliberately tailored and applied to help you **access the physical life of any play or film** on which you are currently working. Examples include:

- *Effort Weave with a Code (e.g. drunk, old age, period etiquette; etc.)*[2]
- *Effort Weave using a set of Gestures (e.g. flirting, anxious, scared; etc.)*
- *Effort Weave in a given context (e.g. at home, during a battle; etc.)*
- *Effort Weave during a set of actions (e.g. making a meal, getting dressed, having sex, giving birth; etc.)*[3]
- *Effort Weave of a specific obstacle encountered by your character (e.g. whether to stay or to go; etc.).*

CREATING CHARACTER

'Tasting' the Efforts

When you are in the process of developing a character, it can be helpful to 'taste' the Efforts. The 'tasting' of Efforts means that you are allowing yourself to do small

---

[2] Cf. 'Effort as Code', p. 106.
[3] Cf. ''Giving Birth': Embodied Storytelling', p. 220; Video Resource: 'Applying the Efforts: Giving Birth', p. 284.

experiments with different Efforts, in order to **let your body discover what fits the character**. To do this you need to be in a state of relaxed awareness. This allows you to make all of yourself available, so transformation can occur throughout the self. Don't underestimate what everyday movement can express about the human condition. Playing with the Efforts while maintaining this sensitized awareness will provoke shifts in your ways of thinking, feeling and being that can inform the creation of character. These explorations can be part of your pre-rehearsal preparation or your independent work outside the rehearsal room.

Small Shifts from Self

- *Briefly check-in with yourself: sit comfortably and bring your attention to yourself and to the world around you, without losing any of the naturalness of being you. One at a time bring your awareness to:*
  - *your thoughts*
  - *your feelings*
  - *your breath*
  - *your breath in relation to your thoughts and feelings*
  - *the room*
  - *the room in relation to your gaze*
  - *the atmosphere (the temperature and feel of the air)*
  - *the outside (if there is a window).*

  Track through these a few times without changing anything or imposing an Agenda.
- *Allow a 'taste' (small moment) of an Effort to enter your body.* For example, a moment of Press in the abdomen that affects what you are feeling and alters your breath as it squeezes your insides; or a moment of Dab in your forehead that affects your thoughts as it lifts and lightens the eyebrows, etc.
- *Identify a thought of your own, or a Gesture you can repeat without losing its meaning. Easily and simply track through different Efforts on this same thought or Gesture.*
- *Now simply allow a moment of Effort expression to cause a shift in your thoughts and feelings: don't add things or make anything up.* You are aiming at transforming from yourself but the visible changes will only be slight. At any stage of this exploration, you should be able to exist in a real situation without any hint of it becoming a caricature, or cartoon.
- *Keep returning to an awareness of yourself, so that you remain engaged and are working with ease. If you lose your connection to self, briefly return to doing a simple check-in (as described in the first step above).*
- *Bank any moments which work well, or seem to hold some helpful clues about the character you are creating.*

On Fundamental Action

- *With your character in mind, carry on 'tasting' different Efforts but now use these moments of different Efforts to explore various Fundamental Actions (e.g. walking, sitting, standing, running, etc.).* If, for example, you are playing with the action of sitting, explore moments of different Efforts and how they affect your positioning on the chair. If you are exploring the action of walking, explore how they influence where you lead from, the size of step, the swinging of your arms, etc.

- *Play with just one Fundamental Action at a time. Explore it in isolation. Do not construct anything but simply discover if certain Efforts fit well and take you closer to your character.*

- *Then explore transitional moments between different Fundamental Actions (e.g. sitting down, standing up, etc.).*

- *Play with one Action (or transitional moment) at a time. Explore it in isolation.*

- *Remember: you can always return to the very first step (a simple check-in) if you feel you have become disconnected from self.*

- *Bank any moments which work well, or seem to hold some helpful clues about the character you are creating.*

In Response to Your Environment

- *Carry on 'tasting' different Efforts on Fundamental Actions, but now introduce an active awareness of the environment around you.* Discovering small moments where certain Efforts fit or juxtapose with the environment can help define the character you are exploring.

- *Find something in the room which echoes something of the Efforts and what they express for this character.* If, for example, you have discovered a moment of controlled calm as Gliding, then this might lead you to align yourself to the back of a sofa with its long, soft, horizontal line.

- *Allow yourself to move and interact with your environment.* For example, in the Gliding moment described above, you might move to the sofa and sit on it with an awareness of its lines, reclining lengthways, or with your arm across the back.

- *Now, become aware of something in the room which forms a juxtaposition or contrast to the Efforts and what they express for this character.* For example, in this Gliding moment you might notice that a noisy hubbub outside the window is in contrast to the Light Sustain which you are currently experiencing as controlled calm.

- *Explore what your character might change in the environment around you.* For example, you might move from the sofa to shut the window and block out the noise.

- *Notice which parts of your environment try to make you conform to them, and which allow you to be 'yourself'. So, in this example, the soft, spongy quality of the* sofa will try to persuade you to be more circular and invite you to give in to gravity. The straight, flat plane of the window through which you can see a clear blue sky, in contrast, will affirm this moment of controlled calm as Gliding.

- *Remember: you can return to the very first step (a simple check-in with yourself) at any time you feel you are losing your sense of ease or your attention is wandering.*

On a Revealing Action

- *Carry on 'tasting' different Efforts, but now use these moments of different Efforts to explore a revealing action. A good action to begin with is a laugh.* Your character's laugh is an action that reveals something about them. It is always helpful to explore how a character laughs, even if your character does not actually laugh in the play/film.

- *Explore expressing a laugh moving through different Efforts (without over-exerting). You can do this by trying out one Effort at a time, as well as by using a mini Speed Weave.*[4]

- *Discover what fits with the character you are creating.*

- *You might decide to pause and play with a laugh when you encounter something that you think fits. Don't let it become disconnected: check in with yourself to ensure you are not over-working and becoming extreme, or forcing something 'comical'. Your own laugh and the eventual laugh you create for the character should be as real as each other.*

- *Play with all sorts of laughs and discover your character's range: full-belly laugh, a guffaw, a silent laugh, fits of the giggles, etc.*

- *Now, experiment with expressing other actions that reveal character while 'tasting' a variety of Efforts. Discover:*
  - *how your character writes their signature*
  - *how they eat*
  - *how they greet someone*
  - *how they put on their shoes,*
    etc.

- *Don't overwork or force anything. Take your time. Simply explore the actions with the Efforts while keeping the character you are creating in mind.*

- *You can return to the very first step (a simple check-in with yourself) any time you feel you are losing your sense of ease or working too hard.*

---

[4] Cf. 'Using Effort Weaves: Speed Version', p. 238.

With Other Agendas

- *There is no limit to how you can use 'tasting' the Efforts: you will find that other games and explorations will occur to you as you play. Set your own Agenda according to what is most interesting to you. You may, for example, wish to play with Responsive Physical Action; a Physical Score; with text; etc.*
- *As you use 'tasting' the Efforts with each different Agenda, remember:*
  - *Allow yourself simply to play whilst keeping the character you are creating in mind.*
  - *Bank any moments which work well or seem to hold some helpful clues about the character you are creating, but don't overwork or force anything.*
  - *You can always return to the very first step (a simple check-in) if you feel you have become disconnected from self.*

Playing Body Types

There is an Affinity between certain Efforts and each of the three body components: bone, flesh and muscle.[5] Examining these Affinities can help you discover more about how to move in a bony, fleshy or muscly way. If you think about the Elements of a given Effort, it will give you clues as to its Affinity. Pressing, for example, is an expression of Strong/Heavy Weight that is both Sustained and Direct. This requires significant muscular engagement. So Pressing has an Affinity to muscly.

By exploring the relationship between body components and the Efforts, you can **discover how to play characters of different body types**. If, for example, you are an actor who is bony or fleshy in body-type (or has a self-perception of yourself as bony or fleshy), you might choose to work with Pressing in order to express the story of a character who is muscly.[6]

- *Choose an action, (e.g. putting on your coat).*
- *Move from an awareness of your bones, and as much as possible move only your bones and joints.*
- *Now, explore moving using all three body components (bones, flesh and muscle) but imagining that they are all bones.*
- *Moving in this way, express each of the Efforts in turn.*
- *Discover which Efforts you experience as suitable for moving in a 'bony' way.*
- *Now, do the same exploration with 'fleshy', and then 'muscly'.*
- *Explore how working with a chosen Effort can help you play a character of a particular body type.*

---

[5] Cf. 'Body Components: Bony, muscly, fleshy', p. 47.

[6] Remember, Affinity refers to an instinctive connection but it is not a hard and fast rule. An actor can exploit an Affinity to tell a particular story, by, for example, working with natural Affinity and using Dabbing to express the story of a bony person. Yet, this does not mean that a bony person cannot work against Affinity and express other Efforts, such as Wringing or Pressing. For more information, see 'Affinity', p. 94.

Playing Personality Traits

A description of a character can include useful adjectives that describe their key personality traits. You can use adjectives to **explore how a character expresses key personality traits through a dominant Effort**. Adjectives can describe a character's behaviour in a given moment or context (e.g. 'he was flirtatious when he met her'; 'she was flirtatious at the party'). They can also describe ingrained behaviours that have become part of a character's personality (e.g. 'he/she is flirtatious').

- *Choose an adjective which gives a clue as to the personality of a character.*
- *Identify how the chosen adjective can relate to a particular Effort.* An obvious match for flirtatious would be Flicking, for example, because it Lightly throws itself about. You might decide to explore: flirtatious as Flicking; demure as Gliding; crazed as Slashing; ashamed as Wringing, etc.
- *Explore your pairing in different ways: Full-body movement motivated by thoughts and feelings; internalized; in one body part; just using breath; doing a physical action; with a Physical Score[7]; with text; etc.*
- *Once you have explored some matches which seem easy or obvious, play with less obvious choices, such as: flirtatious as Pressing; demure as Wringing; crazed as Floating; ashamed as Thrusting, etc.* Noting the role of one Element in particular can help you find an initial connection between the adjective and the Effort. When expressing 'crazed' as Floating, for example, Indirect can become the expression of unpredictability; or when expressing 'flirtatious' as Pressing, Direct can become the expression of pinpointed focus on the object of desire.
- *If you are identifying adjectives for a specific character that you are creating, you can deepen your exploration by using additional information. You could, for example, include a simple context from the world of the play and allow that to inform your improvisation.*

Re-visiting Comfort/Trap

It is familiar to you that an Effort Code (WTS) can be emotionally experienced as either a 'comfort' or a 'trap'.[8] Re-visit and play with this concept when you are developing a character for a play/film. You can seek for clues in the script which lead you to **discover the character's Effort Affinities and how they influence and affect their idea of self**, and their way of being in the world.

---

[7] A set sequence of actions that is known and repeatable.
[8] Cf. 'Effort Archetype Experienced as Trap and Comfort', p. 110.

THE WORLD OF THE PLAY

Manifesting Self

You have previously discovered that a character's Effort expression can be manifested through the way they establish and interact with the spaces over which they have ownership.[9] When developing a character for a play or film, it can be useful to re-visit an adapted version of the *At the Office* exploration. **Explore existing in whatever space belongs to your character** (e.g. the academic's reading room; the athlete's home gym; the teenager's bedroom, etc.). The choice of this space may be either given or implied in the script, and sometimes you may even get access to do this on set. However, it is useful to do the exploration whether or not the story explicitly shows the character in that space. You can also do a similar improvisation exploring environments which the character has to exist within but does not own or control.

Manifesting Relationship

Similarity

You have previously discovered two key ways to **work with the Efforts to tell the story of relationships between characters** (familial relationships and pair bonds).[10] When working on a project, you may not be with other actors who share your process. Yet you can still work with the Efforts to create character relationships. It is possible to adapt the principles of this work and use it responsively by relating yourself to others (i.e. you perceive and respond to the other actor's conscious or unconscious physical choices). Perhaps, for example, you are playing characters who are siblings and you notice that the other actor has discovered a particular way of jutting their chin which expresses anger on Thrust. You do not necessarily need to copy the exact Gesture but can instead translate the use of Thrust into your own body and make it part of your character's Effort expression (or even just translate one or two of its Elements).

Difference

Just as an awareness of another actor's Effort expression can enable you to tell the story of similarity or sameness, they can also allow you to make choices that speak of difference or opposition. This can help you **retain your unique expression**. Actors who are working closely together can end up accidentally picking up each other's expressive habits. This sometimes results in the rhythm of their performances unintentionally becoming the same. Being aware of the other actor's Effort expression will prevent you from inadvertently mirroring and reproducing physical choices that are not right for your character.

---

[9] Cf. 'Manifestation of Self: At the Office', p. 184.
[10] Cf. 'Manifestation of Relationship: Sibling/Parent–Child', p. 186; 'Cloning', p. 224; 'Manifestation of Partnership: Pair Bonds', p. 187.

Specialist Physical Action

As is now familiar to you, some actions demand particular Efforts in order to be carried out successfully.[11] When someone uses the Efforts that perfectly match the strict demands of a given physical action, they are able to execute the action with a high level of efficiency and skill. So we perceive them as being a 'specialist' in that action. Most people are specialists in one physical action or another, and it tends to feed into their choice of job, occupation, hobby, etc. So their **Specialist Physical Action** also defines their identity. Someone who can, for example, perfectly match the Effort demands of a golf swing will be a specialist in golf, and so will be perceived as a 'golfer' by both themselves and others. Someone may be able to meet the Effort demands of a given action because it naturally fits with their instinctive use of Efforts, or because they have learned to meet its specific demands. Usually, it is a mixture of the two. You can work with the Efforts to **master your character's Specialist Physical Action** (which may be either given or implied by the text).

Breaking Down a Physical Action

You may be playing a part which demands you to master a particular physical action (e.g. a chef preparing food, a musician playing the piano, etc.). Breaking down the action into its component parts allows you to understand the exact form of the action. By understanding in detail the Efforts which an action requires, you can become a specialist in any action. It's not about discovering the way the character does the action but about the Efforts the physical action itself demands. Imagine a human machine designed solely for the purpose of executing this physical action in the most efficient possible way: what Efforts would be involved? Answering this question allows you to fine-tune the precise detail of an action (or a Physical Score composed of several actions) so that it can be repeated exactly each and every time you do it.

- *You can choose an everyday action to explore the process of mastering a Specialist Physical Action. You might choose to: make a cup of tea, wrap a present, fold a sheet, etc.*

- *Do the whole action. Then, if it is quite complex pick just one part of it.* For example, you may wish to choose drinking from the cup of tea (rather than all the actions involved in making the tea).

- *Break this part down into smaller sections of action.* Drinking from the cup of tea can be broken into: look at the cup / move your arm towards the cup / grasp the handle / pick the cup up / etc.

- *Choose one of these smaller sections of action. Break this down into three parts by identifying the beginning, middle, and end of the movement. Identify which Effort is*

---

[11] Cf. 'Responsive Physical Action', p. 113.

needed for each part of the action. Be precise in your analysis. Only look at the movement that the task demands (not how you, or a character, would prefer to do the movement). The whole action of sewing, for example, might appear at a glance to be a Glide. Yet you can break down the action of sewing a stitch to discover that it contains: Dab, Dab (the needle piercing in and out the cloth) / Flick (the hand moving to take the needle and leave the cloth) / Float (the cotton travelling through the cloth).

- *Notice the precise point of change from one Effort to another. Pay attention to exactly what changes in these moments: does it change from Sudden to Sustained? Or does it gain Strength? Become Indirect? Etc.*

- *Notice the rhythm of the action. Use an understanding of the precise rhythm to help you move playfully through the action and clarify the progression of Efforts.*

Relationship of Character to Specialist Physical Action

When someone is engaged in a Physical Action which they have mastered, there are times when all of them is involved in it, and times when parts of them are not. Usually, the more they have mastered the skill, the more able they are to utilize only the parts of their body that need to be involved in the action, whilst the rest of their body expresses other things. A bartender, for example, may be able to mix a complicated cocktail and also hold a conversation, or glance at a TV. The way in which they mix the drink is dictated by meeting the Effort demands of this Specialist Physical Action, but the way they converse or glance at the TV will be expressive of their usual Effort Map. The information contained in the Effort expression which takes place around the Specialist Physical Action gives essential clues as to the character – it conveys the parts of them which will not be compromised by the demands of the task and that therefore speak most loudly of that character's personality. Once you have mastered a Specialist Physical Action, you can then ask: what is the character's relationship to this action? You can explore the small ways in which your character's idiosyncrasies emerge whilst doing the action, without throwing away mastery of the action itself.

- *Choose a physical action to master, as suggested by a script. Use the steps outlined in the stage above to break it down and become skilled at it.*

- *To check that you have mastered your chosen action, do it blindfolded (as long as this is safe with your task).*

- *Carry out the action once more but now identify which parts of your body are involved and which are not. Notice: are the body parts which are not directly involved free to move or being held still?*

- *Discover which body parts you can move in isolation without interfering with the execution of the action. Try out some random movements with these body parts.* You might, for example, play with twitching your eyebrow as you wrap a present, or tapping your foot as you iron clothes etc.

- *Now you have discovered which body parts are free for expression of character, play with doing your action:*
  - *whilst doing other actions at the same time (e.g. talking, laughing, crying, singing, looking somewhere else, etc.)*
  - *with different mindsets or emotional journeys.*

- *Make sure that you never compromise the action.* A surgeon doesn't cut up their patient because they are angry; a chef doesn't spill the sauce because they are having a conversation at the same time as stirring a pot.

- *Now, take time to explore the actions that come before and after you execute the Specialist Physical Action you have now mastered.* How, for example, does a calligrapher pick up the pen before they write, or put it down afterwards? These 'tops' and 'tails' are valuable: they are moments which speak of the character's relationship to their Specialist Physical Action. They are the point at which the character's Effort map meets/leaves the Effort demands of the task. Often, it is these moments which are shown in screen performances to tell the story rather than the action itself.

- *Place your Specialist Physical Action back within the context of the dialogue, by delivering the text whilst you simultaneously execute the action.*

Relationship of Character to Specialism

The way a character such as a butler, a vicar or an astronaut exists within the score of physical actions demanded by their specialism tells us about their character. For example, an actor playing a business executive might convey specialism in closing a deal through a habitual use of Direct Efforts (Thrust, Dab, Glide, and Press).

However, character will not only be revealed in the contexts where the actor is using perfectly matched Efforts to demonstrate a specialism. The richest moments can be when the character is in a context where their specialism is not what is being required of them: perhaps the business executive is in a situation that requires circles (Indirect) such as hula-hooping at the office party, or braiding their young child's hair. Satisfying dramatic conflict occurs as the character's usual way of operating in the world is challenged by actions which are outside of their specialism. You may want to set up an improvisation for yourself which explores this.

Key Action

Your character is likely to have one action which is identifiably 'them': a **Key Action**. This can be any kind of action (Fundamental Action; Passive Action; Responsive Physical Action; Specialist Physical Action). If a character's profession is identified, this can often be a useful clue as to what their Key Action might be. Often, this action will be included in a play/film because it says something important about the character: it defines them.

Whether it is included or not, it is useful to **identify and experiment with your character's Key Action** because it will unlock so much about them.

You will find that the Efforts the character uses for their Key Action translate easily to other actions, because they define how the character approaches action in general. A surgeon's Key Action, for example, is likely be related to operating on someone. The same Efforts with which they prepare a syringe would inform the meticulous way in which they refill an ink pen; or the same Efforts with which they wield a scalpel would inform a precision and efficiency in the way they prepare a sandwich.

- *First, identify your character's Key Action from any clues in the script.*
- *Carry out the Specialist Physical Action exploration: break the action down and discover which Efforts it demands. Discover the relationship of the character to the action.*[12]
- *Choose another everyday action which your character does within the play/film. Transpose the way in which they approach their Key Action to this everyday action.*

Uncovering Action

The actor can gain a lot of information not only from any written description of the character, but also through the ways in which action is written into the fabric of the script. Clues about the physical expression of a character emerge through the way in which the writer has formed the text: the choice of actions; how they are woven into the story; which actions are demanded by the world of the play (the context/environment in which the characters exist); etc. This is an exploration which lets the actor **discover more about the character by uncovering and meeting the action of the play/film**.

- *Go through the script and pick out all the overtly physical moments it contains.* List all the visible actions to which the text refers, including Fundamental Actions such as walking, sitting, etc. and Passive Actions such as waiting, thinking, etc.
- *Highlight any actions that stand out.* Perhaps there are some actions that your character does many times; actions that are very specific to the world of the play; or actions that change the whole course of the narrative. Can you identify any Specialist Physical Actions, or your character's Key Action?
- *Play with each of these actions in turn while embodying the Effort Map of your character.*[13] *Notice the way in which your character meets the action that belongs to the world of the play.*

---

[12] Cf. 'Specialist Physical Action', p. 247.
[13] Cf. 'Effort Map', p. 211.

ADVANCED OBSERVATION

You now have an actor's knowledge and understanding of both the Efforts and of the Motion Factors. Working with the Elements in each Effort has fine-tuned your understanding of Weight, Time, and Space. They will now be undeniably present for you in all movement. This makes them perfect as a lens through which to look when you are observing the world. The Efforts and their Motion Factors are a resource which can prompt and frame your observations. You can carry WTS with you as a checklist both in daily life and in the studio, drawing on them as vital observational cues.[14]

Observation gives you the information you need to feed the creation of character during a rehearsal process. There are many ways to **work with the Efforts to deepen your ability for Observation and Translation**. These include: Regaining Trust in Your Instinct | Practising 'Active' Observation of WTS | Observing and Analysing the Whole Picture | Keeping the Efforts Alive | Perceiving the Efforts in Other Art Forms.

Regaining Trust in Your Instinct

Often, when new knowledge is acquired it disrupts your original understanding. The new knowledge needs to be integrated into a more balanced actor mindset.[15] It is important to **allow your work with the Efforts to become more instinctive** and invite parts of your past knowledge back. A mix of planned and 'on the go' observation exercises can be used to focus on letting your instinct lead you. Through this you can test out your ownership of the work and locate the placement of your new skill within the bigger picture of 'you' as an actor. You will discover that you can trust the new knowledge to be present, and so have faith that it will be an instinctive part of your work in the future.

- *Sit and observe but without actively employing the Efforts. Aim towards allowing your full self to be present as you observe.* Remember: observing is more than simply seeing. It engages all your senses.

- *Just follow your curiosity without searching or working at it. Watch for however long it takes until something catches your eye, something interests you or affects you in some other way.* Your interest will have emerged because, without realizing, you have already begun to understand something of what you are seeing.

- *Collect and identify pockets of information. Can you identify movements that are part of the natural world? (e.g. a squirrel waving its tail; a leaf dropping down from a tree; the glinting of sunlight on water; etc.); movements that are part of the man-made world? (e.g. a door opening; an escalator rising upwards; a mobile phone*

---

[14] Breath is integral to life and often goes unobserved. You may wish to add a 'B' for breath to your mental checklist (BWTS) so that you develop a habit of noting it during all observation.

[15] This is not the same as going back to a previous mindset. It is simply progressing to not consciously working/over-working the new 'toy' (skillset).

vibrating; etc.); movements where the man-made world interacts with the natural world? (e.g. a boat moving along a river; a dog pulling on its lead; a turbine turning in the wind; etc.).

- *Observe someone's movement. Take in the environment as well: locate its role in the movement you observe in the person.*
- *Keep to this way of observing.*
- *Now, invite your new skill back in.*
- *As before, simply and gently enliven your curiosity by allowing something to catch your eye, or invade your consciousness.*
- *As your instinct leads your observation, allow yourself to drop in questions using WTS as prompts.*
- *Ask yourself: how is Weight being expressed in this movement? Time? Space? Can you see any ways in which Weight, Time and Space are combining to create recognizable Efforts?*
- *Aim towards allowing your previous knowledge to sit together with your newly developed understanding of WTS and the Efforts.*

Practising 'Active' Observation of WTS

Observation can be active without it feeling like work. This exploration asks you to observe without putting in place a time-frame, or adding any other parameters or goals. It allows you to **identify an expression of an Effort Quality and make it available for later use**.

- *Look out of the window or, if you are outside, find somewhere to sit and choose a direction in which to look. You may be able to see people from where you are sitting. If you can't see any people that is fine. Your observation can be fed by anything that moves.*
- *Simply sit, aware of the life of things around you.*
- *Let something catch your eye.*
- *Connect with a particular Element (WTS) of its movement; or an Effort Quality of the movement that particularly stands out to you.*
- *Take on the movement and let it inform your next action (e.g. how you shift in your chair, pick something up, turn your head, or other gestural movement). This will allow you to bank the observed Effort expression.*

Observing and Analysing the Whole Picture

Generally, when we observe people we only consciously notice what is out of the ordinary. For example, if you are watching someone walk down the street, you might articulate something to yourself about their personality, mood or style choices. However, you probably don't consciously articulate (even to yourself) your immediate assumptions about their age, gender, social status, relationship status, what they do for a living, etc. There is a long list of things that you will have instantly assumed from details of their physical expression. You unconsciously perceive the bigger picture: in your mind, these are 'givens' that you have observed without even realizing. Now that you have a precise lens through which to view the world, **use the Efforts consciously to observe and analyse the whole picture**, including these assumptions.

- *Sit and observe someone's movement.*
- *Consciously articulate to yourself something that you have made an assumption about without even realizing (e.g. age, gender, etc.).*
- *Ask yourself "how do I 'know' this about this person?" Use the prompt of WTS to help you articulate what you are observing.*
- *See how much you can get from one observation of one person.*
- *Observe using your actor's mindset, employing the Motion Factors as your lens and collecting the movement information that conveys meaning.*
- *Only read the movement of the person. Don't get side-tracked, for example, by the clothes they are wearing or the narrative they are engaged in. Look past these and focus on their physical expression. This keeps it about key information and liberates you to translate their movement into your own body in a different context.*
- *Include observation of them when they are still. Observe their body 'shape' (habitual posture).*
- *Ask yourself: how does the shape of their body tell you how they tend to express themselves? Their body has been partly shaped by their past movement and is moulded by their ongoing use of Effort. The still body is readable as 'frozen' Effort manifestations.*[16]
- *Check the conclusions you arrive at against what you learn from seeing them move. Notice any discrepancies.*

Keeping the Efforts Alive

When you regularly speak and hear a language, you very rarely need to think about the language itself. It is alive for you through your day-to-day usage. Like all languages, the Efforts need to be kept alive as part of your essential self. To do this, use them in connection with your curiosity: **make observation and translation an active part of your life**, whether you are currently working on a specific project or not. You have the potential to translate all things into character. The great game (and important practice)

---

[16] Laban, *The Mastery of Movement*, p. 11.

of people-watching is always available to you, so you can take pleasure in being an actor every day. Nothing is wasted. An articulate observation that you store in your body will be called up later when something you are working on connects to its meaning.

Perceiving the Efforts in Other Art Forms

The Efforts can also be identified in other forms of expression. You can **describe your experience of a painting, piece of music or architectural space using the Motion Factors or the Efforts**: for example, a Mondrian painting such as *Composition with Yellow, Blue and Red* might be described as Pressing because the colour is bold (Strong), but the lines are straight (Direct) and unending (Sustained). The Effort you perceive is subjective: someone else might experience the Mondrian as Gliding not Pressing, because they feel the white squares give a sensation of Light not Strong. It does not matter that there is not one definitive answer: the variation of response is because viewing the external art form is a moment of interface between your Effort expression and the Efforts expressed in the art form.

Using the language of the Efforts to analyse other forms helps deepen our understanding of the ways in which external stimuli affect the movement of our thoughts and feelings. Transference of different movement qualities is part of what allows art works to give us a powerful, visceral insight into the range of human experience, both familiar and unfamiliar. Engaging with works of art takes us outside ourselves to experience the world as other people with different Affinities experience it.

- *Identify a selection of art works in different forms that you perceive as expressing each different Effort.*

- *Notice which art works you like best, and which you find less appealing. Do the works in each category tend to share any particular Elements or Efforts? Consider how your preferences for particular works of art might reflect your own Affinities.*

- *Look back through the same range of art works but this time through the lens of each Effort (i.e. embodying each different Effort in turn). How does this alter the effect the art works have on you? How have your responses to the different works changed?*

FINAL REFLECTIONS

This is really the beginning, not the end. The Efforts are yours, and you can apply them in whatever way you wish, in any given context. All these explorations have been simply that: structures within which you could familiarize yourself with the Efforts and discover their potential. You are now able to set the parameters of your ongoing explorations yourself.

Your body is newly articulate and will remain so. The Efforts use language to identify ways of moving in the world. They themselves become an applied language through which you can transform your physical expression. You now own this 'language' of the Efforts. Perhaps you have become so fluent that you feel as if you have always known it. You keep the language alive by using it regularly: working with the Efforts during your warm-ups, independent work, and in different creative processes; by allowing it to inform your view of the world, and feed your practice of Observation and Translation.

Any time you want to sharpen your expression of the Efforts, you can revisit a playful, full-body improvisation. Your body will remember the eloquence of the Efforts and re-find what it is to be truly Light or Strong/Heavy; Sudden or Sustained; Direct or Indirect. These eight Efforts will always provide a gateway into new ways of being. If you allow them to take you on a journey, they will transform you. In turn, you and your work will transform others. This is a journey of transformation that will last for as long as you choose to be an actor; for as long as you seek to embody the story of life.

APPENDICES

APPENDIX A: NOTES ON PROCESS

The Role of Flow

Flow is the fourth Motion Factor. **Flow** is a continuum between two Elements: **Bound** and **Free**. To understand these two contrasting Elements, it may be helpful to think about movement as expressing either 'a liberating or withholding attitude towards Flow'.[1]

Examining the role of Flow is useful because shifts in Flow help to control movement. The actor must be able to control their movement so that it is both safe and articulate, whilst also making sure their physical expression is not overly controlled (Bound) in a way that prevents free communication with an audience.

//Flow affects Flux
Everything is always in flux.[2] Objects or people may appear to be still but 'in reality continuous exchange and movement are taking place. Not for a moment do they come to a complete standstill, since matter itself is a compound of vibrations'.[3] However, Flux can be controlled to a greater or lesser extent. If the Motion Factor of Flow is Bound, then there is a 'readiness to stop flux', bringing about the 'sensation of pausing'.[4] In contrast, if the Motion Factor of Flow is Free, then movement has 'released flux' bringing about the 'sensation of fluid [fluidity]'.[5] Movement hasn't ceased in the stillness of a pause, it is just that 'the sensation of fluency, the feeling of being carried on . . . is controlled to the utmost'.[6]

//Flow is an important component of Counter-tension
When an action requires internal resistance, we instinctively engage our muscles in such a way as to provide Counter-tension to the main drive of the action.[7] Simultaneously, our Flow of energy alters so that it 'seems to stream backwards . . . in a contrary direction to that of the action'.[8] This subtle control of Flow is an unconscious response carried out by our body without us even realizing it.

---

[1] Laban, *The Mastery of Movement*, p. 69.
[2] Laban describes flux as 'the normal continuation of movement' like that of 'a flowing stream' (Laban, *The Mastery of Movement*, p. 50).
[3] Laban, *Choreutics*, p. 4.
[4] Laban, *The Mastery of Movement*, p. 76.
[5] Laban, *The Mastery of Movement*, p. 76.
[6] Laban, *The Mastery of Movement*, p. 76.
[7] Cf. 'Counter-tension', p. 40.
[8] Laban, *The Mastery of Movement*, p. 76.

//Shifts in Flow are inherently linked to physical control

As Laban states: 'it is obvious that it is risky to use Free Flow in actions which demand extreme precision or caution'. Some movements require 'restraint of Flow so that the movement can be stopped at any moment', whereas others can safely be allowed to be 'energetically released'.[9] We naturally employ a more Bound flow whenever we need an 'inner preparedness to stop the action at any given moment'.[10]

//Flow is related to expenditure of physical energy

Throughout our lives, we unconsciously control the amount of physical energy we expend. When the body needs to conserve energy, Flow becomes more Bound. So Flow becomes progressively more Bound as we become older. This is because we not only have less physical energy but are also more experienced at being ourselves and intuitively select when to use or conserve energy. Young children will tend to have a Free Flow of energy, whilst elderly people's energy tends to become increasingly Bound. A similar instinctive conservation of energy can be seen in someone who is recovering from illness: they will temporarily bind their Flow to conserve energy. Someone who suffers from chronic illness is likely to have developed an ingrained physical habit of Bound energy Flow. Bound Flow can be imagined as energy trapped inside the body, as if the body were wrapped in a layer of invisible 'cling-film'; while youthful Free Flow allows energy to travel out through every pore of the body like a water sprinkler.

//Free or Bound Flow can be expressed in any scale of action

Free Flow tends to enable larger, less restrained movements, whilst Bound Flow tends to restrict and reduce movement. Yet it is possible to alter the degree of Flow in any action. When standing still, flux is more or less arrested (it can never be fully stopped). This would most naturally correspond with Bound Flow, which helps control the movement into stillness. However, if you were to imagine energy freely flowing outwards or inwards between your body and the Space surrounding you, Free Flow would be expressed even in the action of standing still. Although the action itself would not change – you remain sitting or standing 'still' – an identifiable shift in the quality of your physical expression occurs. This may be a familiar experience for you from spiritual practices such as meditation or prayer that cultivate stillness of the body whilst using breath and imagination to foster a sense of freely flowing energy.

//Free Flow is vital for connection and communication

The actor needs to be able to access and maintain a Free Flow of energy. Being able to embody freely flowing energy, even in stillness or small-scale action, is a vital part of being able to connect with an audience. Often, when we speak of an actor having 'presence', we are unconsciously responding to their ability to let their liberated Flow of energy reach us, thereby fostering interaction, communication and relationship. This means that one of the actor's key concerns regarding Flow is learning to release overly

---

[9] Laban, *The Mastery of Movement*, p. 18.
[10] Laban, *The Mastery of Movement*, p. 76.

Bound Flow that is controlling movement to the detriment of physical expressivity. Discovering and maintaining this ability is a fundamental practice for actors of all ages.

Self-reflection

Buddying

A **Buddy** is someone engaged in a practical process alongside you. Working with a Buddy, you are able to rely on the support and guidance offered by another (who will, of course, have an empathetic perspective as they themselves are doing the same work).

'Buddy' in this context does not mean the same as 'friend'. It draws on the way the term 'Buddy' is used in deep-sea diving: a partner who accompanies you into challenging environments and has responsibility for looking after your safety (and you theirs). Turning the buddying task into friendly 'caring' is unhelpful. Your emotional and physical safety as you work are the absolute priority for your Buddy, and this will be best protected if they are alert, objective and detached – professional. In this mode, you will each be able to work with integrity, give useful feedback, and help foster the other's development.

Feedback

Actor Movement is centred around exploring, playing and discovering, so there is no right or wrong. There is only fitting / helpful / useful / safe for the task at hand; or not. The key function of **feedback** is to allow the actor to develop and progress with the work.

Your feedback should be clearly delivered and contain observations without apology or emotional slant. Keep it precise and don't over-explain. Too much elaboration can make observations less clear. When feedback becomes lengthy and repetitive, it slows the progression of the work. It can be useful to ask yourself simple questions to help clarify and refine your feedback: 'What did I see? What stood out to me? What provoked a response in me?', etc. Questions like these feed a habitual attitude of open curiosity.

Your phrasing should reflect that feedback is from your subjective perspective: 'my experience was'; 'for me'; 'my body responded by'; etc. Feedback is not teaching, directing or psycho-analysis. It does not involve telling or showing someone how it 'should' be done, what they were not doing, or how to make something 'work'. Make sure that you respond with detailed reflection, rather than a quality judgement (i.e. a criticism or a compliment). To do this, it can also be useful to use questions such as 'how did that arm movement feel this time?' Useful feedback will always leave scope for further exploration and development. You should certainly never dismiss or make light of someone's personal acting choices.

Observing and feeding back is not just a cerebral process. The body remains engaged throughout. Watch with your whole self, including maintaining an awareness of how your own body is responding. It is also useful to notice what your body is doing when giving and/or receiving feedback. Is your body giving a message that supports or contradicts your spoken words? Keeping yourself open to the alternative perspectives of others allows you to accept feedback without needing to agree/disagree, or hold on to it unnecessarily. Feedback belongs to the moment, which always moves on swiftly.

All of these pointers also apply if you are giving yourself feedback after reviewing video footage. We are often harder on ourselves than we are on others. When you are reviewing and internally commenting on your own work, always watch with an Agenda in mind and try to adopt the same interest and patience you would have with a partner. Consciously verbalize the feedback you are giving to yourself by writing brief notes. Use precisely the same ways of articulating feedback that are outlined above for use with a partner.

Whether working individually or with a partner, it can be useful to retain a brief written record of your reflective feedback throughout your process. This allows you to understand your progress through the work.

Control

Lack of **control** should be an illusion: the actor who has not located where the control in a situation is held – who is truly physically 'out of control' – becomes a danger to themselves and to others. Once an actor understands the placement of control, then they can offer an expression of something risky without it actually being dangerous.

When someone feels 'out of control', it may be because someone else has the control, and the handover of that control has either been done unconsciously or without the right amount of consent or trust. Imagine an actor who is to 'fly' through the air by using a harness attached to a wire. The actor needs to use the harness, so they have to hand over some control – but it should always be with precise knowledge of exactly how much control they are relinquishing and to what/whom.

Developing a habit of stopping to locate the control in any situation is a vital part of the actor's process. This step is important for both physical and emotional safety, whether the actor is in an overtly 'risky' situation (such as being flown) or one where the risk may be less obvious but is nonetheless still present.

Working with Gestures

Speaking technically for notating movement, Laban defines a **Gesture** as a non-weight-bearing movement of a part of the body. However, when we speak colloquially of Gestures, we tend to mean a movement that is conveying information, ideas, opinions or emotions to other people. Gestures are expressive rather than functional.

If you were asked to do a Gesture, you would probably do a movement actively intended to communicate to other people (e.g. a thumbs up, a raised solidarity fist, a swear sign). Laban named these 'conventional Gestures'. They are related to thought as they replace words and phrases to speed up communication: a wave can mean 'hello'; nodding the head can mean 'yes'.

This type of conscious Gesture is often culturally specific: a side-to-side shake of the head in the UK means 'no', but a similar movement in India means 'yes'. They also come in and out of fashion. To convey 'take a picture' in the nineties, you would probably have created a camera shape with two hands up by your eyes, making a button-pressing motion. Nowadays, you would be much more likely to use a Gesture related to how we take pictures on a smartphone.

These conscious Gestures are not the only form of Gesture. Gestures include movements that are done less intentionally: crossing your arms across your body when feeling defensive; jiggling your legs when feeling anxious; shifting your weight forward on the feet when your interest in something increases. Unconscious Gestures arise out of shifts in thinking and feeling and are more universal. When we try to suppress what we are thinking or feeling, unconscious Gestures will emerge because 'the inner movements of thinking and feeling are mirrored in [someone's] eyes and in the expression of [their] face and hands'.[11] We may even mask one Gesture with another: a desire to flip someone a swear sign might get translated into a fierce scratch of the head with an accompanying exhalation of breath.

We are very sensitive to reading the unconscious Gestures of other people. This means they are particularly catching: if someone scratches their face whilst engaged in empathetic conversation, the other person will likely mirror their Gesture and also touch their face. We use gestural movement to communicate with ourselves as well as others, so unconscious Gestures happen even when we are alone. Analysts who dissect body language rely a lot on observation of unconscious Gestures because these give away what is going on inside and something of who we are.

Laban referred to unconscious gestural movements as 'shadow movements'. He described them as 'tiny muscular movements … which have none other than expressive value … [they] often accompany movements of the purposeful action like a shadow – hence the term'.[12] Physical expression during improvisation is likely to contain a mixture of both conscious and unconscious Gestures simultaneously. So it is easier for the actor simply to refer to 'Gestures' (rather than shadow movements) knowing that this umbrella term also includes all the small, expressive movements which emerge out of thought and feeling.

When you are exploring the Efforts, you should be working with the broadest possible understanding of what a Gesture is or might be. This will ensure you are allowing your inner life to emerge in your gestural movement, and are accessing a full range of physical expression. As Laban states, 'many of a person's most characteristic movements are those which he does unconsciously and which precede, accompany or shadow his deliberate actions'.[13] Expression of thoughts and feelings through unconscious gestural movement is vital to the creation of character.[14]

---

[11] Laban, *The Mastery of Movement*, p. 90.
[12] Laban, *The Mastery of Movement*, p. 11.
[13] Laban, *The Mastery of Movement*, p. 104.
[14] Laban identified four phases which precede physical actions: attention, intention, decision, precision. These phases sometimes occur one after the other in sequence, but they can also happen simultaneously, in a different sequence, or independently of each other. These phases 'become visible in small expressive bodily movements' (i.e. Gestures). You may find playing with these four phases of 'mental effort' useful in identifying some of the ways in which even the slightest shifts in thinking and feeling emerge in unconscious gestural movement.

Working with Vocalization

Thoughts-out-loud

Using **thoughts-out-loud** is a way of vocalizing your stream of consciousness during improvisation. It is a tool which enables you to bring your focus to the movement of your thoughts.

Thoughts-out-loud are an attempt at thinking in the present tense. They should not sound like a lucid performance of a monologue. It is simply as if the outside world can suddenly hear the internal thoughts of the character. As much as possible, they should reflect recognizable thought patterns. You do not have to use full sentences, or articulate fully formed or complete thoughts. You can use sentence fragments and switch between thoughts according to where the flow of thoughts takes you, or how the context to which you are responding shifts your thinking.

The way someone thinks is reflected in both the form and content of their thoughts: what kind of words are used; how quickly or slowly they move from one thought to another; whether they circle back round to thoughts or move from one to another in a linear progression; etc.

Exclamations

Exclamations are verbal responses. They tend to emerge unexpectedly in response to external stimuli and convey our present-tense feelings. They may be words or sounds, or a mixture of the two. 'Ouch', 'oh', and 'ahhah' are all examples of exclamations.

Although an exclamation is generally voiced out loud, it can also be part of our internal stream of consciousness. As an actor, it can be helpful to work with both spoken and unspoken exclamations, depending on the context of the improvisation.

Using Music

Movement and **music** are often seen as belonging together. This is because dance is so often inspired by and choreographed to music – dance steps tend to follow the music. Yet movement has its own structure and meaning. Music can be an overpowering stimulus which 'tells' the actor what to do. Silence brings space for the actor to listen to their body. Actor Movement explorations are most often done without music. So, to use music is always a conscious choice.

Playing music as you move can provide a stimulus which opens up new movement responses. It provokes different thoughts or feelings, and becomes another character for you to respond to. Different types of music inspire different responses. You may find certain types of music elicit a certain 'programmed' response from you (e.g. a particular form of dance you have learnt in the past). This is not helpful, so work with music that doesn't immediately take you to a place of habit but allows you to move in an exploratory way.

The actor should be able to work with music in a way which enables them to appreciate the power of it without being carried along by it. An actor can allow themselves to be in relationship with music without choreographing their movement to it. Music has its own journey that can be moved 'with' or moved 'against': sometimes the music will feel as if it 'fits' with your movement, and sometimes it won't. Both of these experiences are useful and give you something as an actor. One offers harmony and intensification; the other juxtaposition and conflict.

Although you may feel that there are times when you are working 'with' the music and times when you are working 'against' it, make sure you never ignore the music completely. Even if the music does not fit with your movement quality, it is present. You can exist in conflict with your context, but you cannot ignore it: sometimes in life you may experience great loss on a beautiful sunny day, yet the day is still sunny. You can ignore the music no more than you can shift the weather to suit you, or ignore another actor coming on stage just because you feel it doesn't fit for your character at that moment.

It is also important that you do not make the mistake of thinking that musical accompaniment will do the job of expressing or communicating for you. Make sure your movement is as alive, precise and expressive when you are working with music as when you are working in silence.

The Game of Life

When engaged in a creative process, the actor must view everything as part of the **Game of Life**: they must be able to play with and explore everything, even things which are dark and distressing. Process occurs in the studio, and the studio is a work-space which is separate from the rest of your life. Placing a boundary between the two and not bringing your own life into the studio, or vice versa, keeps you safe. By understanding what it means to be in character, you are able to play all parts of the Game of Life without it affecting your everyday existence.

The actor must find enjoyment during every part of the process. 'Enjoyment' does not mean an easy or simplistic happiness. A true process will never be easy. It means locating the pleasure which occurs for the actor during a process in which they can to get to grips with something; to interrogate and own it. During process, enjoyment may be located in many things such as new experiences, awareness of learning, facing challenges, stubbornness, physical exertion, constructive conflict, sheer hard work, etc. As long as the actor can locate enjoyment, they can know they are truly engaged with the process and are carrying out the actor's job (i.e. playing the Game of Life).

Relating to Constraints

When you first begin to learn something, there are often **constraints** which need to be put in place so that the task can be approached in its simplest form. This helps you to understand with clarity, and learn efficiently. These constraints are often referred to as 'rules'. However, once you are familiar with a skill, it becomes apparent that these 'rules' are simply guidelines. A world-class specialist is unlikely to execute a physical action in the technically 'correct' way that beginners will be taught. Experts in many different fields, such as musicians and athletes, will modify their approach according to increasingly sophisticated and specific aims.

This is the same with the Efforts. None of the constraints articulated in the book are 'rules'. They are guidelines to help your learning process, but should be played with over time. Once you are deeply familiar with the Efforts, you will discover that there are ways to play with the guidelines you adhered to when first learning, and you can expand the boundaries of what an expression of each Effort means for you. For example, the actor is encouraged to discover Direct without use of diagonals – they tend to draw the learner towards Lability, and so are harder to relate to than the horizontal and vertical lines of the Dimensional Cross and the Planes. However, using diagonals with Direct movement is possible. Many birds, for example, move their heads using a Dabbing action but moving through diagonals and stopping on an angle.

APPENDIX B: A NOTE ON WORD CHOICES

Use of 'Sequential'

Laban referred to movement as being either 'Simultaneous' or 'Successive'. The word 'simultaneous' has remained in common usage, so the term is easily understood by everyone. However, actors often find the term 'Successive' less easy to understand, as we now rarely refer to one thing as 'succeeding' another. For most people, the word carries the unhelpful echo of 'successful', rather than the meaning of 'following' or 'coming after'. The term 'Sequential' is therefore used instead, as it has a clearer connotation of movements happening one after another in sequence.

Use of 'Strong/Heavy'

As a term, 'Strong/Heavy' is a little unwieldy, but it enables a precise understanding of both aspects of this Element: 'Heavy', which linguistically seems the natural opposite of 'Light' and implies releasing to go with gravity; and 'Strong', which is a manifestation of Weight when significant force is used and can be an act of resistance to gravity. It also enables us to refer with precision to the sensations of both 'Heaviness' and 'Strength'.

Laban also referred to the two Elements of Weight as 'Gentle' and 'Firm'. For most people, the common usage of these words evokes an emotional attitude towards something or someone (we speak of being 'firm' with someone to set boundaries to their behaviour, or being 'gentle' with someone who is emotionally vulnerable). So Strong/Heavy is used throughout, as most actors find this an easier term to relate to during practical work. However, 'Firm' can be useful as a composite term that encompasses both 'Strong' and 'Heavy'. It may be useful to keep the alternative term 'Firm' in mind, or to use a mixture of the two.

Use of 'Sudden'

Laban also referred to this Element as 'Quick'. However, as both Elements of Time can be maintained at a range of speeds from fast to slow, the term 'Quick' is lacking in a range of interpretations: it takes the actor to an objective understanding of the movement in terms of 'clock-time', rather than to a subjective experience of a particular quality of Time. The terms 'Sudden' and 'Sustained' guide the actor towards an expression of Time which incorporates both an objective and subjective perception.

Use of 'Indirect'

Laban also referred to this Element as 'Flexible'. However, in most movement practices the word 'flexible' now has a very specific connotation of being able to bend or stretch without difficulty. It can also carry an inherent value judgement (flexible equals good), as many dance and gymnastic practices aspire fiercely towards greater flexibility. For many actors, the word is overloaded with too many such connotations and they find connecting to it troublesome.

Indirect is by no means a perfect substitute because it is a negative version of Direct rather than its own unique descriptor. It is vital that the actor relates to Indirect as an Element in its own right, and not simply as 'not Direct'. Direct and Indirect have the same status, and each offers something unique. The term 'Indirect' is used throughout, as most actors find this the easiest term to relate to during practical work. However, it may be useful to keep the alternative term 'Flexible' in mind, or to use a mixture of the two.

Use of 'Affinity'

It is possible to identify inherent connections or attractions between different movement structures. There is, for example, an Affinity (natural correlation or pairing) between Heavy Weight and moving downwards, and Light Weight and moving upwards.[15] This does not mean that you cannot move upwards with Heavy Weight, or downwards with Light Weight, but these combinations are less readily available.

A similar sense of instinctive preference for – or natural connection to – certain types of movement over others can be identified in each individual person. Laban is clear that our use of Effort is 'a question of individual temperament',[16] and that people each have differing 'personal Effort characteristics'.[17] He tends to employ the word 'habit' ('favourite

---

[15] For more on the relationship between the Elements (WTS) and the six key directions, see Laban, *Choreutics*, p. 31.
[16] Laban, *Choreutics*, p. 111.
[17] Laban, *The Mastery of Movement*, p. 10.

habits of Effort').[18] However, the word 'Affinity' is useful to the actor because it encompasses inherent tendencies towards certain qualities of movement, as well as those that arise from learned habits – both of which affect our individual, customary use of certain Efforts.

Use of 'Thrusting'

Thrusting is sometimes referred to as 'Punching'. This can be misleading. A punch is a well-known Gesture of the arm and hand. So use of the term Punching may well lead the actor towards an over-emphasis on gestural movements of the peripheral body. It is also an action that combines Direct and Indirect Space: a punch which is executed technically in forms such as boxing and martial arts uses a balled fist and involves a twist of the arm as it hits the target.

The term Thrusting is commonly linked exclusively to movements of the pelvis. Even so, actors tend to find it easier to translate their understanding of Thrusting to other parts of the body than to use the term Punching.

APPENDIX C: FOCUSING THE THEORY FOR THE ACTOR

Notating the Efforts

Laban devised a succinct and elegant way of writing down the Efforts (Effort Notation) using an **Effort Graph**. The four Motion Factors are all represented by different parts of the graph. In order to write a particular Effort, you draw the parts of the graph which represent the Elements that make up the Effort. The actor does not need to be able to write the Efforts like this – it is enough simply to refer to them by name. However, some people may find it useful to visualize the Efforts in this way, and to see how the interrelationship of their component Elements can be pictorially represented.

---

[18] Laban and Lawrence, *Effort*, p. 49.

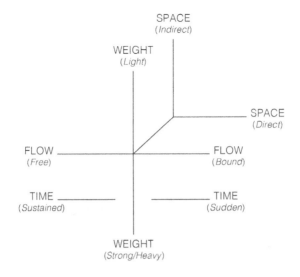

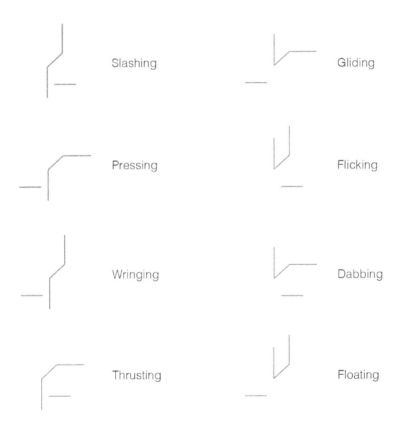

Top: **Figure A.1** The Effort Graph. | Bottom: **Figure A.2** Effort Notation.

The Cube with Efforts

Personal Space can also be envisaged as a **Cube** (see *Figure A.3*). As with the Kinesphere, you imagine that you are standing at the centre of the geometric form. If you reach in any direction, you are able to touch one of its six see-through surfaces, just at the furthest reach of your stretch. Laban placed the Efforts on a diagram of the Cube. The Efforts are placed on certain corners of the Cube because Laban believed that each Effort is easier to express in particular areas of Personal Space.

For some, referring to this diagram can be a helpful way to understand and remember the interrelationships between all the Efforts, and how to move between Efforts. Each corner represents one Effort, and the edges of the cube represent a change in one of its Elements. If you trace a pathway from one corner to another, the relevant shift in Weight, Time or Space will lead you to the new Effort. Efforts which are on two corners at either end of an edge are neighbouring Efforts (i.e. share two Elements). Efforts which are diagonally opposite each other on the Cube are contrasting Efforts (i.e. different in all three Elements).

Referring to this diagram can be particularly helpful when you are exploring Effort Weaves. To move through a Basic Effort Weave (i.e. one which progresses through all eight Efforts one after the other): start at one corner, then travel along each edge of the cube to visit every corner in turn, without ever returning to a corner which you have already visited.

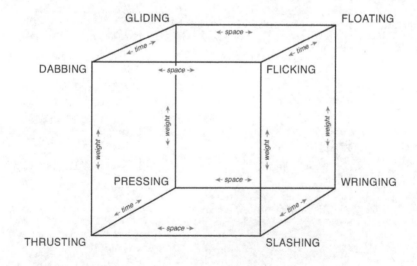

Figure A.3 The Cube with Efforts.

Derivatives

Laban identified subtle variations in the expression of the Efforts, depending on whether one of the Motion Factors of Weight, Time, or Space becomes more stressed than the others. This can occur through a change in its relative importance (rank) or intensity (grade). If an Element is more stressed, 'it becomes the main one, while the others become secondary'.[19] This produces a **Derivative** of the original Effort. Laban identified these as shown in *Table 6*. It can be fun to experiment with the Derivatives, but in general this detailed analysis is more useful for analytical observation of the Efforts than for conscious embodiment of them.[20]

As the actor expresses the Effort through various actions and in different contexts, there is bound to be subtle variation as to whether they stress the Motion Factor of Weight, Time or Space. So, in this process, producing one Derivative or another is not something they need consciously to choose or control. In embodying the Effort, they will naturally move through the Derivatives – i.e. all the Derivatives are subsumed within an actor's embodied understanding of each basic Effort according to its name.

Table 6: Effort Derivatives

EFFORT	DERIVATIVES
Float	strew, stir, stroke
Dab	pat, tap, shake
Wring	pull, pluck, stretch
Thrust	shove, punch, poke
Press	crush, cut, squeeze
Flick	flip, flap, jerk
Slash	beat, throw, whip
Glide	smooth, smear, smudge

Other Drives and the Incomplete Efforts

The Motion Factors of Weight, Time, Space and Flow are always present in every movement. Laban explains that: 'the main characteristics of the Effort attitudes of a living being are, of course, his more complete Effort sequences and not his attitude towards a single Factor of Motion'.[21] However, as you know it is possible to work with the Efforts of

---

[19] Laban, *The Mastery of Movement*, p. 170.
[20] For a clear table identifying how each Derivative is formed, see McCaw, *The Laban Sourcebook*, pp. 200–201.
[21] Laban, *The Mastery of Movement*, p. 12.

Action Drive in which the Motion Factors of Weight, Time and Space combine while Flow remains latent.

Laban also identified the possibility of three other Drives in which three different Motion Factors are perceived to combine while a fourth remains latent. He called these: Spell (combination of Weight, Space, Flow); Vision (combination of Time, Space, Flow); and Passion (combination of Weight, Time, Flow).

Within each Drive it is also possible for one or more of the Elements to become latent (i.e. insignificant compared with the others). When there is no 'definite attitude' towards the Motion Factor, the Element is 'unimportant or, expressed technically, unstressed'.[22] Laban defines movement in which one of a Drive's three Elements is perceived as absent in this way as **Incomplete Efforts or States**. He named them Awake, Dreamlike, Remote, Near, Stable, Mobile.[23]

The other Drives and the Incomplete Efforts are a useful tool for detailed movement observation and analysis. Many actors and theatre practitioners choose to include them as part of their application of Laban's work.[24] However, when applied in a process that includes thinking and feeling as action, the eight Basic Efforts of Action Drive already enable the actor to do their job.[25]

This does not mean that the Incomplete Efforts are neglected entirely. As Laban explains, the Incomplete Efforts are 'very much a part of expressive movement'.[26] So it is inevitable that the actor consciously applying the Basic Efforts will also inadvertently express some Incomplete Efforts. One of the most frequent occasions on which the Incomplete Efforts can be observed is during 'transitions between essential actions'.[27] So, in an Effort Weave, for example, an actor who is consciously choosing to move from one Effort to another will almost certainly move through a few moments in which an Incomplete Effort can be observed. Likewise, moments of Incomplete Efforts can be perceived in an actor working with Effort Duos. This will be particularly true if an actor is working with smaller movements in an internalized mode, as the Incomplete Efforts can be present in any action but are more likely to be perceived in small-scale actions such as 'small movements accompanying speech'.[28]

By concentrating solely on working with the Basic Efforts, a range of Effort expression will still be seen. This means there is a natural nuance which is visible to the observer but which the actor does not need consciously to produce or manage. The actor is able to hand over responsibility for the finer details of Effort expression to their body.

---

[22] Laban, *The Mastery of Movement*, p. 71.
[23] Laban, *The Mastery of Movement*, p. 79.
[24] For an overview of the Incomplete Efforts and the Four Drives in the context of performance practice, see Newlove, *Laban for Actors and Dancers*, pp. 128–142. For a detailed overview of Yat Malmgren's application of Laban's work to acting, see Hayes, *The Knowing Body: Yat Malmgren's Acting Technique*.
[25] Cf. 'Laban for the Actor', p. 12.
[26] Laban, *The Mastery of Movement*, p. 77.
[27] Laban, *The Mastery of Movement*, p. 79.
[28] Laban, *The Mastery of Movement*, p. 70.

APPENDIX D: MUSIC SUGGESTIONS[29]

For Floating

- **A Village Romeo and Juliet / Scene 5: The Walk to Paradise Garden** – Frederick Delius, Orchestra of the Welsh National Opera, Sir Charles Mackerras (from *Delius: Orchestral Works*)
- **Utopia** – Goldfrapp (from *Felt Mountain*)
- **Oedipus: Music for A While, Z583** – Henry Purcell, Andreas Scholl (from *O Solitude*)
- **The Unanswered Question** – Charles Ives, Cincinnati Philharmonia Orchestra, Gerhard Samuel (from *Ives, C: Universe Symphony [Completed by L. Austin] Orchestral Setup No. 2 / The Unanswered Question*)
- **Der Rosenkavelier (2001 Remaster), Act ll: Hat einen starken Geruch wie Rosen (Octavian/Sophie)** – Richard Strauss, Herbert Von Karajan, Philharmonia Orchestra (from Strauss, *Der Rosenkavalier*)
- **A Nightingale Sang in Berkeley Square** – Bob Brookmeyer, Stan Getz (from *The Girl from Ipanema*)
- **Unaccompanied Cello Suite No. 1** in G Major, BWV 1007: Prelude – Bach, Yo Yo Ma (from *Bach: Cello Suites Nos. 1, 5 & 6*)
- **Oblivion** – Astor Piazzolla, Gidon Kremer (from *Hommage A Piazzolla & Peterburschsky*)

For Dabbing

- **Cheap Little Rat** – Thomas Brinkmann (from *Walk with Me*)
- **Popcorn** – Hot Butter
- **Bernie's Tune** – Gerry Mulligan
- **Brejeiro** – Ernesto Nazareth, Iara Behs (from *Nazareth: Tangos, Waltzes and Polkas*)
- **El Flete** – Juan D'Arienzo & Su Orquesta Tipica
- **King Arthur, or The British Worthy (1691) Act 3: What Power art Thou?** – Henry Purcell, Andreas Scholl (from *O Solitude*)
- **Só Danço Samba** – João Gilberto, Stan Getz (from *The Girl from Ipanema*)
- **6 Roumanian Folk Dances, BB 68, Sz. 56:1. Stick Dance** – Béla Bartók, Zoltán Kocsis (from *Bartók: Complete Solo Piano Works*)

---

[29] For further music suggestions and online playlists visit www.labaneffortsinaction.com

For Wringing

- **Spiegel im Spiegel** – Arvo Pärt, Vadim Gluzman, Angela Yoffe (from *Pärt: Speigel Im Spiegel / Fratres / Fur Alina*)
- **Ombra Mai Fu** – George Frideric Händel, Kathleen Ferrier (from *Kathleen Ferrier: What is Life?*)
- **All Cried Out** – Alison Moyet
- **String Quartet No. 3 in F Major, Op. 73: V. Moderato** – Dmitri Shostakovich, Borodin Quartet (from *Shostakovich: String Quartets Nos. 3, 7 & 8*)
- **Fathers** – Anoushka Shankar (from *Traces of You*)
- **Requiem in D Minor, K 626: Vlll. Lacrimosa** – Wolfgang Amadeus Mozart, Nikolaus Harnoncourt (from *Mozart: Requiem [Elatus]*)
- **Someone Like You** – Adele (from *21*)
- **Suzanne** – Leonard Cohen

For Thrusting

- **Mas Que Nada** – Sérgio Mendes, The Black Eyed Peas (from *Celebration: A Musical Journey*)
- **Le Sacre Du Printemps (revised Version for Orchestra – published 1947)** – Igor Stravinsky, Herbert on Karajan, Berliner Philharmoniker (from *Stravinsky The Rite of Spring/Bartok Concerto for Orchestra*)
- **Let's Stick Together** – Bryan Ferry and Roxy Music (from *Let's Stick Together*)
- **Go Down Moses** – Louis Armstrong, Sy Oliver Choir, The Allstars (from *Louis and the Good Book*)
- **Human** – Goldfrapp (from *Felt Mountain*)
- **Infected** – The The (from *Infected*)
- **Sun Set Beyond the River** – Matvey Isaakovich Blanter, The Red Army Choir (from *Red Army Choir: Moscow Nights*)
- **What Keeps Mankind Alive** – Tom Waits (from *Orphans: Brawlers, Bawlers & Bastards* (Disc 3))

For Pressing

- **It's Now or Never** – Elvis Presley
- **Afer Ventus (2009 Remastered Version)** – Enya (from *Shepherd Moons*)
- **Zum** – Osváldo Pugliese & Su Orquesta Tipica (from *Bailando Tango*)

- **String Quartet No. 2: 'Company' – Part 4** – Philip Glass, The Smith Quartet (from *Philip Glass: Complete String Quartets*)

- **Red Dress** – Submotion Orchestra (from *Colour Theory*)

- **Alone and I (2007 Digital Remaster)** – Herbie Hancock (from *Takin' Off [Rudy Van Gelder Edition]*)

- **Vladimir's Blues** – Max Richter (from *The Blue Notebooks*)

- **Bellbottoms** – The Jon Spencer Blues Explosion (from *Dirty Shirt Rock 'N' Roll: The First 10 Years*)

For Flicking

- **Je Ne Sais Pas** – Lionel Hampton Quintet (from *Jazz Masters 26: Lionel Hampton with Oscar Peterson*)

- **Rhapsody on a Theme of Paganini: I. Introduction – Variation l – Theme – Variation ll, lll** – Sergei Rachmaninov, Denis Matsuev, Valery Gergiev (from *Rachmaninov: Piano Concerto No. 3 & Rhapsody on a Theme of Paganini*)

- **Glorianna** – Ipana Troubadours (from *Jazz Age Chronicles Vol. II: The Song Hits of 1928*)

- **Thème varié in A-Flat Major, FP 151: Variation lll. Pastorale (Allegretto)** – Francis Poulenc, Jacques Février (from *Poulenc Intégrale – Edition du 50e anniversaire 1963–2013*)

- **Chega De Saudade (No More Blues)** – Stan Getz (from *The Girl from Ipanema*)

- **6 Romanian Folk Dances, BB 68, Sz. 56:2. Sash dance** – Béla Bartók, Zoltán Kocsis (from *Bartók: Complete Solo Piano Works*)

- **Watermelon Man** – Herbie Hancock (from *Head Hunters*)

- **Symphony No. 6 in B Minor, Op. 74, TH.30:2 Allegro con Grazia** – Pyotr Ilyich Tchaikovsky, Leningrad Philharmonic, Evgeny Mravinsky (from *Tchaikovsky: Symphonies Nos. 4, 5 & 6 'Pathetique'*)

For Slashing

- **Moorea** – Gypsy Kings (from *Gypsy Kings*)

- **String Quartet No. 8 in C Minor, Op. 110: II. Allegro Molto** – Dmitri Shostakovich (from *Shostakovich: String Quartets Nos. 1, 8 & 14*)

- **Black Magic Woman/Gypsy Queen** – Santana (from *Abraxas*)

- **Ace of Spades** – Motorhead (from *Ace of Spades*)

- **Moanin'** – Charles Mingus (from *Blues and Roots*)
- **Watermelon Man** – Herbie Hancock (from *Head Hunters*)
- **Land/Horses/Land of a Thousand Dances** – Patti Smith
- **Filipino Box Spring Hog** – Tom Waits (from *Mule Variations*)

For Gliding

- **Cantus in Memoriam Benjamin Britten** – Arvo Pärt, Antal Eisrich, Hungarian State Opera Orchestra Strings (from *Pärt: Arvo Pärt – A Portrait (Kimberley)*)
- **Angeles** – Elliot Smith (from *Either/Or*)
- **Piano Concerto No. 5 in E Flat Major Op. 73 – 'Emperor': 2. Adagio un poco mosso** – Ludwig van Beethoven, Norman Krieger, Buffalo Philharmonic (from *Beethoven Piano Concertos Nos. 3 & 5*)
- **Fantasia on a Theme by Thomas Tallis** – Ralph Vaughan Williams, Sir John Barbirolli/Sinfonia of London (from *Vaughan Williams: Orchestral Works*)
- **It Must be So** – Leonard Bernstein, Max Adrian (from *Candide*)
- **Miserere Mei** – Gregorio Allegri, Vladimir Ivanoff, Chorus Sine Nomine (from *Allegri: Miserere Mei*)
- **String Quartet No. 8 in C Minor, Op. 110: 4. Largo** – Dmitri Shostakovich, Borodin Quartet (from *Shostakovich: String Quartets Nos. 1, 8 & 14*)
- **Mass in B Minor, BWV 232/Agnus Dei: Agnus Dei** – Johann Sebastian Bach, Kathleen Ferrier, London Philharmonic Orchestra (from *Kathleen Ferrier*)

GLOSSARY

This is not a dictionary. It is not an attempt at a complete and pinpointed explanation of the meaning of these words. Rather, it aims to help the reader by unpacking the applied meaning of these terms as they are used in this work. Each has layers of meaning which feel indefinable. They are an accumulation of all their specific, general and everyday usages and associations. They are then inflected by their use and chosen application in the studio. Many are also words which deliberately provoke bodily experience: they have physical resonances and are used to unlock meaning in the body which bypasses the intellectual articulations of the brain. So the best way to fully understand the words is to use them and work with them. In part, their meaning is defined by you and how the words become an embodied part of your process. This Glossary is simply a guide to prevent wholesale confusion or misunderstanding.

Action The doing of something expressed through movement; can be conscious or unconscious.

The following terms allow the actor to identify, separate and play with different kinds of action. They allow the actor to explore the Efforts as a vehicle for all action. They do not originate from Laban but evolved out of practical work in the studio. (N.B. Unlike in 'Actioning', in this work actions do not have to be transitive.)

   Fundamental Action Universal and ever-present actions, which are often done without even noticing. The actions that are likely to be present in all acting performances.

   Habitual Action The actions someone most regularly chooses to do; and how they choose to do all actions.

   Key Action An action which defines a character; can be related to a character's profession or specialism.

   Passive Action Actions which do not physically negotiate with external stimuli.

   Physical Action Movements of the body that involve interacting physically with something outside of self.

   Responsive Physical Action Physical actions that are carried out in response to, and negotiation with, complex external stimuli.

   Specialist Physical Action (SPA) Physical actions that are distinct and are executed with a high degree of efficiency and skill; actions that require a certain skillset.

Actor Somebody who embodies different ways of being to play characters or roles on stage/screen. Somebody who works with physical expression for transformation. A creative artist who is fascinated by life, and widens our understanding of what it is to be human through their art.

Actor Movement A field of expertise, involving the study, research and development of movement processes used specifically by actors for an embodied understanding of the world and physical expression of the human condition. Sometimes used to refer to the particular process and philosophies as detailed in Ewan and Green, *Actor Movement: Expression of the Physical Being*.

Affinity Inherent connections or attractions between different movement structures leading to natural correlation or pairings of certain ways of moving. Primarily used in this process to refer to someone's natural physical tendencies and learned habits which lead them to an instinctive preference for certain types of movement over others.

Agenda A specified task or point of focus for a practical exploration, set before you begin.

Amoebic One of the stages of the working process for exploring each Effort; an imaginative improvisation in which the actor uses full-body movement to express an Effort as a single-celled organism (amoeba).

Asymmetrical Movement and/or body shapes which are not equal, the same or mirrored in different parts of the body. Often, an outcome of expressing Indirect Space.

Banking Committing something to body memory. Can be helped by consciously registering a physical experience through moments of pausing during practical work and/or brief self-reflection at the end of explorations.

Basic Philosophies Key concepts or beliefs which underpin the whole working process and are returned to repeatedly to inform each step of the work.

Buddy An actor with whom you work through a process who shares in analysis, reflection and feedback; a partner, peer and witness who functions as your Outside Eye.

Centre of Gravity The point where the axes of the Dimensional Cross meet when standing, which is also the centre of the Kinesphere. Shifts location in the body depending on our movement.

Character A created person that an actor embodies on stage or screen; the role an actor takes on during a performance.

Code A set of physical rules which amount to a recognizable behaviour or way of being, e.g. drunk, old, soldier, Effort, etc.

Control The employment of conscious choices to check, regulate, order, guide or limit your movement. Essential for safety.

Core/Core Body The central part of the body, including the pelvis and the torso.

Counter-Tension (Counter-Resistance) A form of internalized resistance which helps us to control our movements and is a key part of maintaining balance. Enables movements in one direction to be simultaneously countered, and therefore controlled, by muscular engagement creating force in the opposite direction. Usually employed instinctively.

Cube A geometrical form defined by having sides of an equal length which join at eight corners, creating six square faces. One of Laban's spatial forms by which Personal Space can be defined.

Dab/Dabbing One of the eight Efforts of Action Drive as identified by Laban.

The Default The immediately accessible and recognizable expression of an Effort; the small selection of movements to which the Effort most easily lends itself, and that nearly all people will naturally use when first encountering any given Effort.

The Demon Any private thoughts, feelings or emotions that are kept at bay – hidden or suppressed – and which the character does not want to be made public.

Direct One of the two Elements of the Motion Factor Space.

Drive The motivating urge, need or desire which provokes action.

Duration The length of time something lasts.

The Efforts A shortened version of 'Efforts of Action Drive'. Refers to the eight Basic Effort Qualities: Dabbing, Wringing, Thrusting, Floating, Pressing, Flicking, Slashing, Gliding.

Effort Archetype A character who expresses everything through one singular Effort and so that one Effort defines them. Human condition (presence of thoughts and feelings) is tied in with the rules of the Effort Code (WTS) to create the Archetype. First encountered as one of the stages of the Discovery Process for embodying each Effort.

Effort Duo A technique for actors involving the expression of two Efforts at the same time. Usually, Thought is expressed on one Effort, Feeling on the other.

Effort Equation A way for the actor to work with an Effort Duo in order to capture the essence of a person/character.

Effort Map The Duo Effort to which someone has the strongest Affinity and so uses most regularly; a simple movement 'DNA' which is recognizably expressive of a particular person's character.

Effort Quality The quality of a movement as dictated by the Effort with which it is motivated/done.

Effort Weave A movement form in which the actor shifts from expressing one Effort to another Effort. Usually, shifts occur by altering just one Element of one of the Motion Factors (WTS) to move through Neighbouring Efforts. An Interrupted Effort Weave involves shifts in which more than one Element is altered.

Elements The polar-opposites at either end of each Motion Factor continuum. The six Elements are: Light, Strong/Heavy, Sudden, Sustained, Direct, Indirect.

Embody To express or experience something in the body. Used to imply a lived, physical experience or understanding that cannot be attained any other way.

The Epic The underlying experience of all humanity revealed through the actor's physical expression.

Exclamations Short vocalizations that tend to emerge unexpectedly as a response to external stimuli and convey our present-tense feelings. They may be words, sounds or a mixture of the two.

Expressive Movement Work which involves discovering ways of allowing or making physical choices that communicate meaning. Used to discover and refine a character and create the world of the play.

Extremities The parts of the body furthest out from the centre. Mainly used to refer to the hands and feet, including fingers and toes, but can also include the limbs.

Facing The spatial orientation of the body in relation to General Space.

Feeling An internal experience of emotion. In this process, feeling is understood as action and differentiated from thinking.

Flick/Flicking One of the eight Efforts of Action Drive as identified by Laban.

Float/Floating One of the eight Efforts of Action Drive as identified by Laban.

Flow One of the four Motion Factors as identified by Laban. Latent in the Efforts of Action Drive. A continuum between Bound and Free.

Force Power, often achieved through increased engagement of the muscles.

Fundamental Movement Work which involves examining and training movement mechanisms to develop the actor's physical capacity to meet the demands of any given job.

Gathering Movement that starts at the periphery and moves in towards the body; the opposite of Scattering.

Gaze The direction in which the eyes are looking. Often also implies the related direction of an actor's focus and attention.

General Space The Space beyond the Kinesphere; the Space that is always outside Personal Space.

Gesture A movement which conveys information, ideas, opinions or emotions to other people; can be done consciously or unconsciously.

Glide/Gliding One of the eight Efforts of Action Drive as identified by Laban.

'Golden' Moments Moments within a practical exploration or improvisation that the actor feels were particularly successful; which taught them something and are worth remembering – moments for the actor to 'bank'.

Human Condition The shared understanding/experience of what it is to be essentially human – a state arising from universally experienced events (e.g. birth, illness, death), emotions (e.g. fear, grief, joy) and situations (e.g. conflict, celebration, ritual). In this work: expressed by the actor through the embodied experience of thoughts and feelings.

Improvisation A process of spontaneous creativity; can be used in rehearsal or performance.

Indirect One of the two Elements of the Motion Factor Space.

Inner Movement which is not outwardly manifested in public space; as opposed to outer.

Glossary

Instinct/The Actor's Instinct An intuitive, often unconscious, response to a given context or circumstance; a trained capacity to respond successfully on impulse to the practical and creative demands of the actor's job.

Intellect Awareness of thoughts and the ability to think and learn.

Internalize/Internalized Placing the powerful movement of thoughts and feelings inside whilst fighting to keep outer expression more measured according to what is felt to be socially appropriate; one of the stages of this working process for exploring each Effort.

Isolations Moving one body part separately to the rest of the body.

Journey One of the stages of this working Process for exploring each Effort; a long-form, guided improvisation, involving an extended passage of exploration and discovery taking the actor through embodied knowledge of the Effort in several forms (Single-celled Amoeba to Archetype to Internalized).

Kinesphere Laban's term to describe the sphere of Personal Space around the body.

Labanotation A system for analysing and recording human movement in written form; includes the notation of Effort. Invented by Laban. Originally known as 'Kinetography Laban'.

Lability Laban's term to describe a state of being off-centre; the opposite of Stability. Used interchangeably with Motility/Mobility in Laban's writings.

Level The height at which the body is located when movement is taking place. Often divided into low, mid and high.

Light One of the two Elements of the Motion Factor Weight.

Location Where in Space someone or something is; a particular, identifiable place or position.

Metaphor Usually, an expressive use of language in which one thing is referred to compared with something else that is considered to have similar characteristics. For the actor, metaphor can be a way of using one action to express the story of something else.

Monologue An extract from a play or a performed scene in which one character speaks at length, often directly to the audience.

Motion Factors Laban's term to describe collectively Weight, Time, Space and Flow: aspects of movement which are present in all motion.

Motivation The impulse, instinct, reason or context that drives an action.

Movement Quality The physical feel or sense of an action as experienced by the person moving and/or the observer.

Neighbouring Efforts Efforts which share two Elements.

Neutral Stance A position of easy readiness from which you can begin many different exercises.

Observation To watch or look at something with embodied attention; to witness.

Obstacle Course A selection of large objects placed in the working space, which you can move amongst and interact with during movement improvisation; a created world.

Orientation The direction in which a person is facing, often described using the words 'front', 'back', 'side', in relation to something else (e.g. the actor is facing the back, towards the door and away from their partner).

Outer Movement which is outwardly manifested in public space; as opposed to inner.

Outside Eye A designated person who is not working practically but observes the work in order to give feedback; normally a director, movement director, tutor or Buddy.

Pathway The route between locations or positions in Space. Often a pre-existing or pre-planned route.

Peripheries/Peripheral Body The outer parts of the body, including the limbs and extremities.

Personal Space The Space around the human body, generally defined as within the distance of one's outstretched reach; defined by Laban through use of different geometrical forms such as a sphere (Kinesphere) and cube.

Personality The distinctive, individual, identifiable self that is visible to the world; often dictated by what the character chooses to show/reveal to the world of their true self.

Physical Score A set sequence of actions that is known and repeatable.

The Planes Laban's term for the two-dimensional forms which help define our sense of Space. Separately referred to as the Door, Wheel and Table Planes.

Press/Pressing One of the eight Efforts of Action Drive as identified by Laban.

Process A series of explorations which lead in gradual stages to a desired end-point (e.g. a rehearsal process which leads to a developed character).

Released A physical state in which the muscles are not holding any unnecessary tension, or over-exerting force.

Scattering Laban's term to describe movement that starts at the centre of the body and moves outwards into Space.

Sensation The felt experience of something; an internal perception of a physical happening formed from the combined impressions of the bodily senses.

Sequential A continuous pathway of movement travelling from body part to body part, each following the last and triggering the next. Used in this process instead of Laban's term 'Successive'.

Simultaneous Laban's term for a movement which happens in at least two separate body parts at the same time.

Slash/Slashing One of the eight Efforts of Action Drive as identified by Laban.

Slow Motion A stylistic effect in which a predetermined movement or sequence of movements is slowed down to last for a significantly longer duration than they had originally. Not to be confused with Sustained movement, which is fundamentally different.

Sounding Vocalization arising from movement of the body which mirrors the quality of the expression; a tool to be able to hear what the body is expressing while moving.

Space One of the four Motion Factors as identified by Laban. Present as one of three Motion Factors in each Effort; a continuum between Direct and Indirect.

Specialist Someone who has acquired a physical skill to the point of expertise. Used in this process to denote someone who is naturally expert at a particular quality of movement because it is the way in which they habitually express themselves in everyday life.

Speed The rate at which someone or something moves; can be objectively measured (e.g. miles per hour) or described in comparative terms (quick, fast, slow, etc.).

Stability A state of being centred, in balance; the opposite of Lability.

Stakes A character's investment in a situation.

Strong/Heavy One of the two Elements of the Motion Factor Weight.

Subtext Meaning contained within written text or spoken words which is not articulated but is implicit; often expressed through the physicality of the actor.

Successive Laban's term for a continuous pathway of movement travelling from body part to body part; replaced by the term 'Sequential' in this process.

Sudden One of the two Elements of the Motion Factor Time.

Sustained One of the two Elements of the Motion Factor Time.

Symmetrical Movement and/or body shapes which are equal, the same or mirrored in different parts of the body. Often an outcome of expressing Direct Space.

Technical/Working Technically Finding out *how* we do certain things; a stage of learning that involves working pragmatically to identify movement challenges and figuring out how to solve them.

Tension Used in this process to mean tightness; physical holding to the point of stasis; lacking Flow.

Thinking An internal experience of using your mind. In this process, thinking is understood as action and differentiated from feeling.

Thoughts-Out-Loud Vocalizing the unspoken thoughts of the character to bring your focus to the movement of your thoughts; an attempt at thinking in the present tense.

Thrust/Thrusting One of the eight Efforts of Action Drive as identified by Laban.

Time One of the four Motion Factors as defined by Laban. Present as one of three Motion Factors in each Effort; a continuum between Sudden and Sustain.

Glossary

Transformation The act of changing your way of being in the world to that of another person, animal, object or thing; involves the ability to see the world through others' eyes, and change your way of being to that of someone/something else.

Transition The time between one identifiable action and the next; should always be regarded as a major part of the story being told. In performances: when something changes; how something changes.

Translation The process by which an actor manifests in their own body the impressions they have gained through observation of others.

Vehicle A physical choice that holds, carries and conveys a particular meaning; movement that allows the actor to embody or express something.

Vocalization The creation of sound using the voice; allowing the sounds of the voice to be a part of the movement of the body; related to Sounding.

Volume Control A tool which involves making active choices to scale your movement up (towards large-scale, full body) or down (towards internalized) during an exploration.

Wafting A colloquial term used in practical Actor Movement work to describe unmotivated movement which does not have precision of expression.

Warm-Up The period of preparation done by an Actor before practical (and other) work. Essential for physical safety.

Wash A colloquial term used in practical Actor Movement work to describe a lack of precision in physical expression; when movement choices are not clearly differentiated from another but blend together into an overall, undefined impression.

Way of Being How somebody/something exists in the world; the way they live; how they interact with life.

Weight One of the four Motion Factors as defined by Laban. Present as one of three Motion Factors in each Effort; a continuum between Light and Strong/Heavy.

Weightlessness Used colloquially as the opposite of 'Weightedness' to imply an experience of lessened or lightened Weight.

Working/Over-Working To pursue a goal so intently that the actor becomes tight and is no longer able to be in the present and allow a process to unfold.

World of the Play The shared reality of any process or performance; discovered when the actor observes the world through the lens of a given story (play/film).

Wring/Wringing One of the eight Efforts of Action Drive as identified by Laban.

WTS A written shorthand way of referring to the Motion Factors of Weight, Time and Space.

BIBLIOGRAPHY

Books by Laban

Rudolf Laban, *A Life For Dance*, trans. Lisa Ullmann (London: Macdonald and Evans Ltd, 1975)

Rudolf Laban, *Modern Educational Dance*, 3rd edition, revised by Lisa Ullmann (London: Macdonald and Evans Ltd, 1975)

Rudolf Laban, *The Mastery of Movement*, 4th edition, ed. Lisa Ullmann (Plymouth: Macdonald and Evans Ltd, 1980)

Rudolf Laban, *A Vision of Dynamic Space*, ed. Lisa Ullmann (London: Routledge Falmer, 1984) (London: Laban Archives in association with Falmer)

Rudolf Laban, *Choreutics*, ed. Lisa Ullmann (Southwold: Dance Books Ltd, 2011)

Rudolf Laban and F.C. Lawrence, *Effort*, 2nd edition (London: Macdonald and Evans Ltd, 1974)

Archives of Laban's work exist around the world, including The John Hodgson Archive at the Brotherton Library, University of Leeds, and the National Resource Centre for Dance, University of Surrey.

Additional Cited Works Related to Laban

Irmgard Bartenieff and Dori Lewis, *Body Movement – Coping with the Environment* (New York: Gordon & Breach, 1980)

Karen Bradley, *Rudolf Laban* (Abingdon: Routledge, 2009)

John Hodgson, *Mastering Movement: The Life and Work of Rudolf Laban* (London: Methuen Drama, 2001)

Warren Lamb, *Posture and Gesture* (London: Gerald Duckworth & Co., 1965)

Dick McCaw (ed.), *The Laban Sourcebook* (Abingdon: Routledge, 2011)

Jean Newlove, *Laban for Actors and Dancers* (London: Nick Hern Books Ltd, 1993)

Jean Newlove and John Dalby, *Laban for All* (London: Nick Hern Books Ltd, 2004)

Additional Cited Works

Marina Caldarone, *Actions: The Actor's Thesaurus* (London: Nick Hern Books, 2004)

Vanessa Ewan and Debbie Green, *Actor Movement: Expression of the Physical Being* (London: Bloomsbury, 2015)

Uta Hagen with Haskel Frankel, *Respect for Acting* (Hoboken, NJ: John Wiley & Sons, 1973)

Janys Hayes, *The Knowing Body: Yat Malmgren's Acting Technique* (Saarbrücken: VDM Verlag Dr Muller, 2010)

Bibliography

Chris Johnston, *The Improvisation Game: Discovering the Secrets of Spontaneous Performance* (London: Nick Hern Books, 2006)

Keith Johnstone, *Impro: Improvisation and the Theatre* (London: Methuen Drama, 1981)

George Lakoff and Mark Johnson, *Philosophy in the Flesh: The Embodied Mind and its Challenge to Western Thought* (New York: Basic Books, 1999)

George Lakoff and Mark Johnson, *Metaphors We Live By* (Chicago, IL: University of Chicago Press, 2003)

Jacques Lecoq, *The Moving Body* (London: Methuen, 2000)

Maurice Merleau-Ponty, *Phenomenology of Perception* (Abingdon: Routledge, 2012)

Maurice Merleau-Ponty, *The World of Perception* (Abingdon: Routledge, 2008)

Katie Mitchell, *The Director's Craft: A Handbook for the Theatre* (Abingdon: Routledge, 2009)

Further Reading: Related to Laban

Barbara Adrian, *Actor Training the Laban Way* (New York: Allworth Press, 2008)

Katya Bloom et al., *The Laban Workbook for Actors* (London: Bloomsbury, 2017)

Eden Davies, *Beyond Dance: Laban's Legacy of Movement Analysis* (Abingdon: Routledge, 2006)

Cecily Dell, *A Primer for Movement Description: Using Effort Shape and Supplementary Concepts* (New York: Dance Notation Bureau Press, 1993)

Ellen Goldman, *The Geometry of Movement: A Study in the Structure of Communication Part 1: The Defense Scale* (New York: Self-published, 1999)

Ellen Goldman, *The Geometry of Movement: A Study in the Structure of Communication Part 2: The Axis Scales* (New York: Self-published, 2005)

Peggy Hackney, *Making Connections: Total Body Integration Through Bartenieff Fundamentals* (Amsterdam: Gordon & Breach, 1998)

Carol-Lynne Moore and Kaoru Yamamoto, *Beyond Words: Movement Observation and Analysis*, 2nd edition (Abingdon: Routledge, 2012)

Valerie Preston-Dunlop, *A Handbook for Modern Educational Dance* (London: Macdonald and Evans Ltd, 1963)

Valerie Preston-Dunlop and Lesley Ann Sayers (eds), *The Dynamic Body in Space: Developing Rudolf Laban's Ideas for the 21st Century* (Southwold: Dance Books Ltd, 2010)

Betty Redfern, *Introducing Laban Art of Movement* (London: Macdonald and Evans Ltd, 1965)

Sam Thornton, *A Movement Perspective of Rudolf Laban* (London: Macdonald and Evans Ltd, 1971)

Further Reading

Stella Adler, *The Art of Acting* (New York: Applause, 2000)

John Berger, *Ways of Seeing* (Harmondsworth: Penguin, 1972)

Antonio Damasio, *The Feeling of What Happens: Body, Emotion and the Making of Consciousness* (London: Vintage, 2000)

Barbara Houseman, *Finding Your Voice* (London: Nick Hern Books, 2002)

Rick Kemp, *Embodied Acting: What Neuroscience Tells Us about Performance* (Abingdon: Routledge, 2012)

Kristin Linklater, *Freeing the Natural Voice*, 2nd revised edition (London: Nick Hern Books, 2006)

Jeannette Nelson, *The Voice Exercise Book: A Guide to Healthy and Effective Voice Use* (London: Nick Hern Books, 2017)

Konstantin Stanislavsky, *An Actor's Work* (Abingdon: Routledge, 2008)

VIDEO AND AUDIO RESOURCES

VIDEO RESOURCES

Understanding Sequential: https://vimeo.com/251493578

Understanding Simultaneous: https://vimeo.com/251493793

Weight: Light and Strong/Heavy: https://vimeo.com/251494021

Time: Sudden and Sustained: https://vimeo.com/251494339

Space: Direct and Indirect: https://vimeo.com/251494730

Floating: https://vimeo.com/251496135

Responsive Physical Action: https://vimeo.com/251505925

Dabbing: https://vimeo.com/251497202

Wringing: https://vimeo.com/251497956

Thrusting: https://vimeo.com/251498690

Pressing: https://vimeo.com/251499214

Flicking: https://vimeo.com/251501834

Slashing: https://vimeo.com/251502316

Gliding: https://vimeo.com/251502819

Effort Archetypes Improvisation: At the Hairdresser's: https://vimeo.com/251508375

Effort Archetypes Improvisation: At the Doctor's: https://vimeo.com/251618326

Effort Archetypes Improvisation: At the Office: https://vimeo.com/251509916

Effort Archetypes Improvisation: Pair Bonds and Relatives: https://vimeo.com/251618485

Effort Archetypes Exploration: Politicians: https://vimeo.com/251618878

Basic Effort Weave: https://vimeo.com/251506266

Effort Duos: https://vimeo.com/251619191

Effort Duos Improvisation: At the Office: https://vimeo.com/251619952

Applying the Efforts: Giving Birth: https://vimeo.com/251631834

Applying the Efforts: Cloning: https://vimeo.com/251632021

Applying the Efforts: Bottling: https://vimeo.com/251632628

Secret Effort Weave: https://vimeo.com/251506763

Using the Efforts to Warm Up: https://vimeo.com/251507200

What are Gestures?: https://vimeo.com/251503673

AUDIO RESOURCES

Frameworks of Instruction

A Floating Journey: https://vimeo.com/251647354

A Dabbing Journey: https://vimeo.com/251647766

A Wringing Journey: https://vimeo.com/251648002

A Thrusting Journey: https://vimeo.com/251650062

A Pressing Journey: https://vimeo.com/251650517

A Flicking Journey: https://vimeo.com/251651300

A Slashing Journey: https://vimeo.com/251652338

A Gliding Journey: https://vimeo.com/251670444

A Journey Using a Story: https://vimeo.com/251652620

Basic Effort Weave: https://vimeo.com/251652803

Speed Weaves: https://vimeo.com/251653121

Secret Effort Weave: https://vimeo.com/251653549

Sounding

Floating Soundtrack: https://vimeo.com/251646519

Dabbing Soundtrack: https://vimeo.com/251647668

Wringing Soundtrack: https://vimeo.com/251647886

Thrusting Soundtrack: https://vimeo.com/251649112

Pressing Soundtrack: https://vimeo.com/251650203

Flicking Soundtrack: https://vimeo.com/251651084

Slashing Soundtrack: https://vimeo.com/251652226

Gliding Soundtrack: https://vimeo.com/251669808

VANESSA EWAN is a Senior Lecturer at The Royal Central School of Speech and Drama. She works to challenge and inspire actors at all different stages of their training through Actor Movement practice. Since her arrival at Central, her work with actors in the studio has formed the backbone for the development and implementation of the three-year movement curriculum for BA Acting (Hons). In addition, she conceived, developed and co-authored the first ever British MA in Movement for actors (the MA/MFA Movement: Directing and Teaching), of which she is joint Course Leader.

Ewan has a unique understanding of an actor's need, having worked as a hands-on practitioner in a multiplicity of settings. Having graduated from the Laban Centre for Movement and Dance, she worked at most of the major UK drama schools including Webber Douglas, Guildhall School of Music & Drama, the Royal Academy of Dramatic Art (RADA), and East 15 where she was Head of Movement. She has used her practical knowledge to inform her work as an external advisor on course curriculum for many institutions.

Ewan is also a movement consultant for film and theatre. The focus of her work with the actor is Movement Expression, and the use of Rudolf Laban's 'Efforts of Action Drive' by actors is an ongoing specialist area of her work. She has lectured on the subject internationally, including at the Laban Centre, Labanarium Launch (keynote), Moscow Arts Theatre School, and for UNAM (Mexico). Her first book, *Actor Movement: Expression of the Physical Being* (Bloomsbury, 2014), was co-written with Debbie Green and offers a practical insight into Actor Movement philosophy and process.

KATE SAGOVSKY is an artist specializing in live performance. She works across theatre, dance and live art as a director, movement director and choreographer; as well as doing extensive work as a teacher and workshop facilitator. She has a background in both writing and movement: after completing a BA in English at Oxford University and an MA in Movement Studies at The Royal Central School of Speech and Drama, she trained in Dance Studies at Laban.

Sagovsky has taught Actor Movement in many contexts. She has worked with students from drama schools and universities across the world both as a Movement Lecturer at Shakespeare's Globe, and as an Associate Practitioner for the Royal Shakespeare Company. As a visiting lecturer, she has taught at drama schools and universities such as The Royal Central School of Speech and Drama, LAMDA, Royal Conservatoire of Scotland, Rose Bruford, AFDA Film School (Cape Town, South Africa).

As a director/choreographer, Sagovsky's work has been performed in theatre and dance festivals around the UK and internationally. She is Artistic Director of MOVING DUST (www.movingdust.com). She has also worked extensively as a movement specialist, including as Resident Movement Practitioner at the Royal Shakespeare Company; movement director for companies such as Paines Plough; and at venues including the National Theatre, The Barbican and the Southbank Centre. For more information visit www.katesagovsky.com

INDEX

Index

CPSIA information can be obtained
at www.ICGtesting.com
Printed in the USA